T0397663

American Mediterraneans

American Mediterraneans

A Study in Geography, History, and Race

SUSAN GILLMAN

The University of Chicago Press
Chicago and London

The University of Chicago Press, Chicago 60637
The University of Chicago Press, Ltd., London
© 2022 by The University of Chicago
Published 2022
Printed in the United States of America

31 30 29 28 27 26 25 24 23 22   1 2 3 4 5

ISBN-13: 978-0-226-81964-8 (cloth)
ISBN-13: 978-0-226-81966-2 (paper)
ISBN-13: 978-0-226-81965-5 (e-book)
DOI: https://doi.org/10.7208/chicago/9780226819655.001.0001

Library of Congress Cataloging-in-Publication Data

Names: Gillman, Susan Kay, author.
Title: American Mediterraneans : a study in geography, history, and race /
    Susan Gillman.
Description: Chicago : The University of Chicago Press, 2022. |
    Includes bibliographical references and index.
Identifiers: LCCN 2021050911 | ISBN 9780226819648 (cloth) |
    ISBN 9780226819662 (paperback) | ISBN 9780226819655 (e-book)
Subjects: LCSH: Caribbean Americans. | American literature—19th century—Themes,
    motives. | American literature—20th century—Themes, motives. | United States—
    Civilization—Caribbean influences. | Caribbean Area—Relations—United States. |
    United States—Relations—Caribbean Area. | Caribbean Area—Race relations. |
    Caribbean Area—Historiography. | Caribbean Area—In literature.
Classification: LCC E184.C27 G55 2022 | DDC 327.729073—dc23/eng/20211025
LC record available at https://lccn.loc.gov/2021050911

for Amy Kaplan
friend, colleague, comrade

Contents

Figures

The Strange Career of the American Mediterraneans

It is not uncommon to find "Mediterranean" names bestowed on far-flung places and things. There are Mediterranean diets, climates, houses, and gardens.[1] "Mediterranean California" is as much of a cliché as the real-estate brand "Mediterranean home." But these locally famous labels don't have the reach or ambition of the "American Mediterranean" that I want to introduce here. Hardly a household word, it might at most evoke a vaguely United States–centric possession, like the Caribbean as an American lake. The tropical aura might echo with the racialization of the "Mediterranean race," associated with American eugenics around 1900. Yet at the turn of the nineteenth century, the celebrated Prussian scientist Alexander von Humboldt gave the name *Méditerranée de l'Amérique* to the Caribbean and, thereby, inaugurated a rich, varied, and variable—though underrecognized—tradition.

My book starts with the question of why, in the Americas, so many bodies of water and land are so frequently compared to the European Mediterranean, both classical and modern. While scholars today find Mediterraneans around the world (including but not limited to the Indian Ocean, an Atlantic Mediterranean, the Caribbean as a transoceanic Mediterranean, and even the Saharan Mediterranean Desert), neither the Humboldt beginnings nor the later literature and art of the American Mediterraneans are at all well known. My book aims to change that by rediscovering this history—a kind of foundational and repeating comparison at the heart of writing the Americas since Humboldt—and speculating on the cultural work it does across space, time, and language, work that is always fundamentally, if not openly, racial.

It may be more apt to call this up front a project not of discovery but of invention. "America" has had to be intellectually invented more than once, both before and after Edmundo O'Gorman's 1958 *The Invention of America, an Inquiry into the Historical Nature of the New World and the Meaning of Its History.* O'Gorman rejected the idea that Columbus "discovered" America in favor of "invented," to underscore the colonial history of domination and unequal power set in motion by Columbus. Like other contemporary explorers and geographers, Columbus had no previous knowledge of and had not been looking for what he found, so as a group these early Europeans created America in their own image, "as a distinct parcel of land—one that could be viewed geographically . . . as equivalent to the other continents," and thus revealed not only the limits of their knowledge but also the impossibility of their understanding what they had found. O'Gorman's conclusion: Europeans could not have discovered America because they were basically incapable of thinking it.[2]

Humboldt, too, is credited, some would say inflated, with the "invention of nature," in his theory of the unity, an ecology before its time, of the physical and human geography of the New World.[3] Just as America had to be invented, the logic would go, so, too, the American Mediterranean—but it is not quite that symmetrical. This whole complex—a physical geography, oceanic heuristic, and intellectual tradition—has to be both discovered and invented, or at least that is how I have approached it. The historians and geographers, scientists and travel writers, climatologists, novelists, and political activists who populate this book are both participants and observers. They use different Mediterraneans in the nineteenth-century Americas as their subject, and they themselves are only later identified with and serve as the object of a "Mediterranean" tradition. The invention of the tradition named "mediterraneanity" didn't coalesce until the late twentieth century, and that modern scholarship, which could be considered footnote material, second order to the primary sources of the nineteenth-century mediterraneanizers, is as much a part of this book as are the practicing Humboldtians. Both following them and taking the lead, I have set for myself a combination of discovering and inventing that is essential to telling the story.[4]

As a term, "American Mediterranean" has an extended shelf life across multiple disciplines and genres: hemispheric tourism and climatology, architecture and agriculture, physical and historical geography, popular history, historical fiction, and journalism. A peripatetic traveler, the American Mediterranean reveals a cast of unusual characters, all those in its current, from the celebrity Humboldt to lesser-known lights, such as the turn-of-the-century American geographer and first woman president of the Association of American Geographers Ellen Churchill Semple and the 1930s Jamaican nationalist W. Adolphe Roberts. Their books, no matter the genre, tend to be lavishly illustrated with engravings, maps, and charts, and beyond the literature, a substantial history of Mediterranean-oriented advertising imagery developed in the travel and fruit industries. Accordingly, my book has a visual dimension, tracing a representative sample of the various images and technologies that are part of the Mediterranean archive. They create another layer in the palimpsest of the Mediterranean comparison itself, which crops up at particular historical moments, and changes across place and time, depending on where and when it emerges.

Perhaps most resonantly, the concept of Mediterraneanism echoes in debates—pro and con—over Americas race slavery, revolt and revolution, freedom, and post-emancipation. Following the term through its travels across disciplines and borders, and time and space, reveals a little-known racialized history, both long-lasting and fleeting, circulating briefly, in visible clusters at specific historical moments, and then just as quickly disappearing from view. Recovering this understudied tradition adds a new element to the stock of race discourses in the Americas, one that can appear paradoxically unraced and appeals to a range of race-neutral ideas and ideals: from the legal fiction of color-blind justice in the US in the 1890s, to the revolutionary banner of raceless nationalism in Cuba from 1895 forward, to the transracial coalitions of the decolonizing 1940s. Indeed, all the American Mediterraneans that I explore turn out to have a racial underbelly—the Mediterranean metaphor is always in part about race, even when it appears not to be.

I call this a strange career in homage to C. Vann Woodward's groundbreaking work, *The Strange Career of Jim Crow* (1955), to link the erratic timeline and uneven racial politics of the Mediterranean discourse with his history, documenting the long and bumpy road following the end of Reconstruction to full, legal segregation in the US South. The local pockets of interracial political alliance and Black power that outlasted even *Plessy v. Ferguson* are, for me, reiterated in the changing historical usage of the American Mediterranean across place and time: used in the mid-twentieth-century extended Caribbean (from Harlem to New Orleans and the West Indies) as an anticolonial appeal to classical slave revolt, and in the mid-nineteenth-century US as a veiled, geo-reference to climatological and racial theories loosely associated with the Mediterranean world. Documenting the strange career of the American Mediterraneans will fill a scholarly and popular gap, the on-again-off-again history of this folk geographical theory.

This short list begins to suggest the extraordinary proteanness of the Mediterranean in the Americas. Its metaphors, maps, and visual icons produce a striking adaptability through time and space and across nations and languages. For each of these historical usages at a specific place and time, there is also a complementary historiography, both primary evidence to be considered among the different scales of observation. Such an archive, defined by different Mediterraneans, ancient, modern, and metaphoric, allows for exploring connections that go beyond business as usual in comparative history. In addition to the transoceanic scale and sweep of the American Mediterraneans, the basic unit of analysis is itself based offshore and thus bears comparison to other oceanically extended regions (Atlantic World, Black Atlantic, circum-Caribbean, Pacific Rim). Put another way, the long-standing split between Mediterranean humanism and colonialism takes on deepened urgency and complexity in the Americas context, where multiple possible positions emerge between those poles.

This model of comparative oceanic study, put forward by so many (novelists, journalists, geographers, travelers, and anticolonial thinkers) throughout the nineteenth and twentieth centuries, manages to both raise and exorcise what Benedict Anderson calls the specters of comparison that subtly haunt colonial (Caribbean and Pacific) imaginings with the shadow of their European counterparts. This is the "incurable doubled vision" Anderson finds in José Rizal's famous nationalist Filipino novel *Noli me tangere* (1887), when the young mestizo hero views the botanical gardens in colonial Manila and sees the shadow of their European sister gardens, as though from the end of an "inverted telescope." The result, from Anderson's perspective as a scholar of Southeast Asia, can be a doubled inversion, a discrepant method of comparison in which the big end of the telescope is placed in the colonial location and Europe is viewed from that standpoint, as though through a doubly inverted telescope. From this perspective, the constitutive parts of the comparison— the here and there, the foreign and native, the first and second order—resist coherence in a symmetrical whole. The resulting uneven comparative perspective could be called an "incomparable" history.[5]

The multiple candidates for what count as an American Mediterranean add up to this kind of discrepant or resistant comparison. Humboldt's different Mediterranean names for the Gulf-Caribbean (Méditerranée des Antilles, Méditerranée mexicaine, and Méditerranée de l'Amérique) demonstrate the oddity of conventional Euro-centered terminology in that the sea between Europe and Africa is known as the singular Mediterranean, rather than one of a number of mediterranean seas in the world. In a very real sense (and as geographers use the term), the Caribbean is a mediterranean, with a small *m*. I use the term in both ways, with the uppercase for the proper names of all Mediterraneans, and, following Humboldt's French, where the lowercase is used for the adjective form—*méditerranée*—not the noun, *Méditerranée*, as well as following English usage of "a mediterranean," to underscore the reference to a geo-region. (One important exception is the French use of lowercase for titles, as in the geographer Jean-Baptiste Arrault's "le concept de *méditerranée*.") Beyond the distinction between an actual sea and a general descriptor (of climate, commodities, culture), this orthographic alternation captures the translational history of Humboldt's sea with many names.

Finally, the plural American Mediterraneans, itself a translated and translational term, pushes toward the limits of the Mediterranean *as* a comparison. Not only does Humboldt question Euro-centered hierarchies of language and civilization, race and nation, as they apply to the Americas, but he also underscores a fundamental counterfactualism in the concept of an American Mediterranean, marked by all the "Black" Spartacuses, Jacobins, and Napoleons that later populate the discourse.[6] The viability, both the limits and possibilities, of such linguistic and cultural translation is fundamental to the Humboldt project and beyond. Starting from his brand of conjectural comparativism, based on hypothesis testing that so often ends inconclusively, captures the speculative dimension of the past and future histories of both basins, those of the Old and New World, that is key to the Humboldtian quest for comparability. It's geography not as (pre)destiny but as prophecy, prefiguring, predicting possible futures.

Rather than simply stringing together a series of more or less arbitrary case studies (raising gatekeeping issues of what's in and what's out), the Americas context on which I focus provides a material archive grounded in the historically specific uses of the term American Mediterranean. It appears occasionally, episodically, reflecting the spatiotemporal-linguistic perspectives of where, when, and in what languages it is adapted. Variants and cognates include "Our Italy," "the Caribbean, our sea of destiny," and "our West Indian neighbors." These possessive names—all those ours—remind us that the Romans commonly called it Mare Nostrum ("Our Sea"), and occasionally *Mare Internum* ("Inner Sea"). They also point to a very different usage, in another register but at the same rough time and place, without an apparent Mediterranean connection, *Nuestra América*. José Martí's famous name for a collective Américas consciousness plays a surprising, understudy role in the translation network of the American Mediterranean.

Including Martí and others, not the usual suspects, in the Humboldt current, I propose to take the history of American Mediterranean nomenclature and thinking as a mode of comparison against the grain. Rather than the usual discrete, nominally parallel units of comparative history, this is "something else," a loose framework attuned to the asymmetrical power relations of putting together uneven, often unequal places, times, and languages. The Mediterranean Humboldt found in the New World produced linguistic and cultural differences as well as geopolitical similarities in the patterns of conquest and colonialism, slavery and emancipation, between the classical Mediterranean and the Mediterraneans in other parts of the world. Humboldt's comparative methodologies work alongside his sense of the importance of large-scale intellectual networks that cross all sorts of borders, linguistic and political as well as disciplinary and spatiotemporal. As such, this oceanic concept, as much historical as geographical, offers a way to rethink comparative study multidimensionally and along various axes. Thinking with the concept of *a* Mediterranean encourages the kind of transnational and translational approach I want to take to the literature and art of *the* Mediterraneans, plural, of the Americas. Beyond the European Mediterranean, this book will reveal ones we don't know but that are everywhere, hidden in plain sight, structuring how we think (or fail to think) about race, imperialism, and revolution.[7]

Beginning with Humboldt

To this day, they have not discovered at the Indies any mediterranian sea as in *Europe, Asia* and *Affrike.*
> JOSÉ DE ACOSTA, *The Naturall and Morall Historie of the East and West Indies* (1604), qtd. in Fernand Braudel, *The Mediterranean and the Mediterranean World in the Age of Philip II*

When the celebrated Prussian naturalist and traveler Alexander von Humboldt wrote his *Relation historique* (*Personal Narrative*), part of his thirty-volume *Voyage aux régions équinoxiales du nouveau continent, fait en 1799, 1800, 1801, 1802, 1803 et 1804*, he set in motion the checkered histories of the "American Mediterranean." Though not at all a household word in the US today, the term, in French, Spanish, and English, circulated widely but erratically, appearing and disappearing across disciplines and genres, spaces and times, from Humboldt's moment to the present. He coined various names, *Méditerranée des Antilles*, *Méditerranée mexicaine*, and *Méditerranée de l'Amérique*, to describe an extended Gulf-Caribbean basin. Shorthand for Humboldt's method of oceanically superimposing the old-world Mediterranean on the new-world Americas, these terms, themselves implicitly comparative like so many place-names he would have encountered (all those Nuevo Léons and New Orleanses), point to his "quest for comparability." His "thirty-volume voyage," the unfinished account of travels during 1799–1804, extending from the "Republic of Colombia" to Cuba (twice) to the "Cordillera of the Andes," and ending briefly in the US, explores whether and how the mountains and seas, flora and fauna, nations and languages—the physical and human geography—of the *nouveau continent* resemble those of *l'ancien monde*.[1]

Humboldt provides the opening point to show how an early nineteenth-century German explorer can model a mode of critique, a method with a particular skeptical and hypothetical take on the comparative that is at the heart of the very idea of comparing the European Mediterranean with various American correlatives. Following his lead allows us to explore the cultural production of this kind of comparative thinking—unsystematic and open-ended. The proper names Humboldt bestowed on the Gulf-Caribbean are themselves essentially counterfactual terms of comparison in the sense that there is no singular, capitalized Mediterranean in the Americas, whether subtitled *des Antilles* or *mexicaine* or *de l'Amérique*. In contrast to the unidirectional westward progression of *translatio imperii*, Humboldt's translational perspective continually looks back and forth between worlds. He pushes back against the grain of classical Mediterraneanism and its assumed continental thinking, to the invention of America that was yet to be identified, still in the future. His hybrid travelogue / scientific and historical narrative brought both space-times of comparison, the New Continent and the Old World, in all their linguistic diversity, into the imperial sphere of Western knowledge— and thereby altered the shapes and ways of knowing both worlds. In the process the singular became plural, the American Mediterraneans.

Put another way, Humboldt's American Mediterraneans rediscovered Europe as much as they invented America. A main stake in Humboldt's comparative Americas project is to gauge the accuracy of old-world theories through new-world applications. In this sense he is as much interested in European ignorance as American knowledge. Traveling to the *nouveau continent*, with all its implied and explicit relations to *l'ancien monde*, gave Humboldt, among many other attractions, the opportunity to test the long-standing hydrogeological hypothesis of an ancient Mediterranean land bridge against the migratory patterns of plants, peoples, and languages in the Caribbean. Gathering data on the botanical and linguistic diversity he found among various native groups within a single region, he pushed back against the taxonomies of the Linnean classification system that dominated natural history of his time. Linguistically, Humboldt demonstrated a complex, often uneven comparability of the Americas not only externally with Europe and Asia but also internally between what he calls Spanish America, Portuguese America, the English possessions in North America, and the United States. In all these spheres, we can start to see a foil against which a Humboldtian method can be distinguished— and why this tradition is an advance over other ways of thinking.

Given the variability Humboldt finds in nature and culture, the *translatio imperii* narrative of westward, imperial continuity fails to fully fit his Americas. Variation emerges in the colonial context within and between racial, national, and linguistically named groups that do not line up in strict Euro-scientific form: from les noirs to les Européens and les Indiens, to the "*blancs créoles* que j'appelle *Espagnols-Américains*" [the white creoles whom I call Spanish-Americans], with an explanatory footnote, "A l'imitation du mot *Anglo-Américain* reçus dans touts les langues de l'Europe. Dans les colonies espagnoles, on nom les blancs, nés en Amérique, des *Espagnols*; et les véritables Espagnols, ce qui sont nés dans la métropole, des *Européens*" [In imitation of the word Anglo-American, adapted in all the languages of Europe. In the Spanish colonies, the whites born in America are called *Spaniards*, and the real Spaniards, those born in the metropole, are called *Europeans*] (*RH*, 4:162; *PN*, 3:435). His own naming practice, Humboldt stresses with characteristic self-consciousness in the footnote, straddles the worlds he inhabits and produces a degree of defamiliarization with all their languages.

Humboldt's special sensitivity to the legacy of European misnaming in the New World, how Spanish colonizers, ignorant of both Indigenous and European languages not their own, mistakenly equated race, place, and identity, leads to his practice of comparing the place-name "errors" in maps across time: "they have been useful to geography, as errors and daring hypotheses are often to the search of truth" (*PN*, 5:819). This hardly qualifies as a speculative philosophy of history, but it does suggest how Humboldt, "a fanatical empiricist" who rejected the Hegelian idealist philosophy of nature, integrated uncertainty and conjecture into his own overarching vision of what he would later call the "cosmos."[2] Yet, still, unlike the "mediterranian sea" in my Acosta epigraph, Humboldt's Mediterraneans do not negate themselves. They risk assuming the originality and primacy of Europe and the imitative second order of the Americas. Whether and how the *translatio imperii* is both implied and questioned, never completely reversed and abandoned in Humboldt's worldview, is a major question that inspired my book.

Because the *translatio imperii*, that alternative model for comparison, is unidirectional, located on a single axis of westward moving time, it represents a more closed and rigid approach to bringing Europe into relation with the Americas, and thus a foil against which we can see what is more dynamic, critical, and speculative about the tradition of Humboldt's American Mediterranean. Humboldt's counterfactual Mediterranean reveals what is embedded in the grain of European thinking about the "Old" and "New" Worlds, those temporal markers themselves indicators of the conventional comparative hierarchy. The older is first, the other always lags behind in relation to the primacy of the original. Humboldt uses the term "*nouveau continent*" in his book title, but his acts of naming liberate these new Mediterraneans from the old, cut the cord to the classic Mediterranean, and leave them free-floating, unmoored, ungrounded in specific or stable knowledges. Vice versa, the classic Mediterranean can be turned on its head under the pressure of the American Mediterraneans, as in the map of W. Adolphe Roberts's "Mediterranean of the West," where the European Mediterranean is miniaturized, relegated to the smaller, inset map in the upper right corner of the primary map of the Caribbean (figure 5).

The Humboldt advantage over *translatio imperii*, his multidirectionalism, is also visible in his "geohistory," Fernand Braudel's term for the connections between history and geographical space. "It might be thought," Braudel admits in the preface to his massive eleven-hundred-page *The Mediterranean and the Mediterranean World in the Age of Phillip II* that these connections "would be better illustrated by a more straightforward example than the Mediterranean."[3] Humboldt, like Braudel, sought to connect geography and history through the even less straightforward American Mediterranean, which set in motion constant comparison to the first, European Mediterranean; and unlike Braudel, Humboldt incorporated into the two disciplinary dimensions of geography and history a third, the linguistic. As an ocean geographer focused on tracing lost migratory patterns that would account for language similarities and differences, Humboldt gathered data for his brother, the celebrated linguist Wilhelm von Humboldt, on Indigenous languages, names and naming practices, based on speculative theories of missing land bridges and ocean-floor histories. Beyond simply sending back language data, raw material comparable to the soil, rock, mineral, plant samples that Humboldt collected and took home, the linguistic research circulated in an import-export, back-and-forth exchange of knowledges, theories, and evidence.

Local data on Indigenous languages of the Americas, Humboldt stressed, hypothetically resolved longstanding old-world conundrums about linguistic similarities in different languages spoken among populations with seemingly little contact. In turn, the migratory patterns of languages that Humboldt investigated pushed back against nation-based geographies in the early Americas. Rather than take as a given the macro geo-units he explores in the Americas, he works with microregional distinctions that force a rethinking of European names and terms for the Americas. Humboldt, like his Spanish-language, Spanish-American sources, is known for writing back to the eighteenth-century French naturalist Buffon and his ilk, who denigrated the New World, human and physical, as degenerate, weaker, less fertile and productive than its old-world counterparts. At the same time Humboldt himself did not consistently cite, translate, or credit his American sources, suggesting the limits of his reverse engineering of the *translatio imperii*.[4]

Thinking in the corrective, multidirectional terms of language circulation and human migration in the new-world Mediterranean concentrates Humboldt's attention on colonialism, its European past and American future. The institution of race slavery produces one of the most systematic through lines in his writings on the Americas, where he repeatedly calculates the costs to the environment, human and natural, of that colonial legacy. In my book, the history of successive empires, with their accompanying conquests and slaveries, in the classical Mediterranean and beyond, provides an avenue to today's field of Mediterranean studies, which regularly takes "the idea of a vast Mediterranean culture" as "a disdainful cultural imperialism" and "in effect a cousin of Orientalism." Braudel, too, admits that his may be an "imperialist history, yes, if one insists."[5] Humboldt likewise describes his own focal point of "the little Caribbean Sea, a sort of mediterranean, on the shores of which almost all of the nations of Europe have founded colonies" ("*la petite mer des Antilles, sorte de Méditerranée, sur les bords de laquelle presque tous les nations de l'Europe ont fondé des colonies*"; *PN*, 3:428; *RH*, 4:153).[6] But Humboldt takes the imperial project in a markedly different direction. What starts as a geographical region, etymologically in French, Spanish, and English the "sea between the lands," leads Humboldt to imagine a shared oceanic past and future as well.

The founding fact of this speculative oceanic history is the arrival of millions of black Africans and white Europeans, linking migratory populations, voluntary and involuntary, with external and internal differences of language, race, and nation. Using statistics from Europe and Asia, Humboldt estimates the relative population growth and topologies of different American nations as indicators of future political and social movements, only to acknowledge after pages of comparative population tables: "These statements of population, considered in their relations with the differences of race, languages, and worship, are composed of very variable elements, and represent approximately the state of American society. . . . There is something serious and prophetic in these inventories of the human race: in them the whole future destiny of the New World seems to be inscribed" (*PN*, 6:845). The results of the mass of population data are at once approximate, serious, and prophetic. Much of Humboldt's *nouveau continent* shares a tropical or subtropical environment as well as a socioeconomic model (the plantation) whose effects, the inequities of colonial rule in the present and the future, are both long-lasting and incalculable. His extended oceanic region, "a sort of Mediterranean," using the French uppercase *M* rather than the translator Helen Maria Williams's lowercase *m*, makes the point that Humboldt is thinking broadly of a new-world Mediterranean rather than a specific hydrogeographical mediterranean.

Humboldt's attention to the language of place-names—Indigenous and colonial sources—as well as his own naming of the Mediterraneans establishes his intellectual stake in translation. In turn, my book makes a link between comparative study and translation, not as a metaphor, but as a material practice. A multivalent translator, Humboldt experimented with inter- and intra-lingual as well as intermedial translation. His illustrations, especially the famous Chimborazo vertical cross-sections, participated in an emerging American textual-visual way of looking at nature. Like the contemporary drawings of Francisco José de Caldas, a celebrated Colombian geographer-cosmographer, one of the *letrados* Humboldt met and knew, the Chimborazo work features dense, explanatory text on the sides of the map of the mountain, comparing the data on plant distribution from top to bottom of the new-world volcano to other major mountains around the world. Instead of the strict, hierarchical taxonomic units of Linnean classification, Humboldt produced a drawing, a "microcosm on one page, he calls it."[7] The Chimborazo illustration, the drawing that incorporates the essay form, rejects the available methods of data presentation (which he uses elsewhere) to present data visually. Humboldt's visual-textual experiment identifies the similarity of plants located in climate zones or bands across different parts of the world as a botanical route to human connectivity as well as the unity he finds in diversity. So, too, the Mediterranean comparison advances this fundamental Humboldtian connectivity.

Humboldt is also known, unlike other contemporary scientific travelers, for acknowledging the power relations implicit in the gathering of knowledge from informants, especially his awareness of how differences of language, and the hierarchy of world languages, operate in translation in the field. "Unacquainted with the language of the people," he confesses in the midst of a chapter in *Personal Narrative* devoted to the different native tribes in New Andalusia, "I do not pretend to have penetrated their character during my short abode in the Missions" (*PN*, 3:230). Nevertheless, he argues for the imperative to compare languages and cultures, asserting, like his brother, Wilhelm, the link between language and ways of viewing the world.

Writing locally on the condition of "the reduced Chaymas, Caribs, and Tamanacs," forced into the homogenized isolation of the mission system, Humboldt argues that they "retain so much the more their natural physiognomy, as they have preserved their languages," and concludes globally: "It is this intimate connection between the languages, the character, and the physical constitution, which maintains and perpetuates the diversity of nations, that unfailing source of light and motion in the intellectual world" (*PN*, 3:219). Humboldt's approach is translational in the broadest sense, what we would now call ecological or environmental, working locally and globally across disciplines and languages, nature and culture, to tap the interrelatedness of the cosmos. "The Mediterranean considered as the starting point for the representation of the relations which have laid the foundation of the gradual extension of the idea of the cosmos" is the way he puts it, somewhat grandiosely, at the headnote of a chapter in *Cosmos*, a scientific best seller, and along with

Personal Narrative, one of his most popular works, subtitled *A Sketch of the Physical Description of the Universe*, which went through numerous editions and translations before his death in 1859.[8]

This statement, made near the end of a lifetime devoted to global research in natural and cultural geography, points back to the beginning, to how the Humboldtian method always required some point from which to advance experimentally and speculatively. The Mediterranean Sea was the baseline for Humboldt's comparison of New and Old Worlds: "the point where [Humboldt] begins his physical history of the world," "the circumscribed space, round which those nations lived who prepared the foundations for our subsequent western civilization."[9] Using "Mediterranean" as a given name thus deepens the connectivity of his worldview. A key passage, naming the Caribbean as a, not the (classical), Mediterranean—capitalized as a proper name—brings together seemingly separate strands, the linguistic, racial, and political dimensions of his work.

Humboldt's linguistic hinge rests on the geography of a middle sea as the starting point. He reminds us that etymologically "mediterranean" refers to the space between (*medi*) two landmasses (*terras*), a sea between the lands. "Considering the sea of the West India islands, of which the Gulf of Mexico makes a part, as an interior sea with several mouths, it is important to fix our attention on the political relations [*les rapports politique*], that result from this singular configuration of the New Continent, between countries placed around the same basin," he notes, linking physical and human geography; "and, [where] as if by instinct a concert is established [*comme par instinct il s'établit un accord*] between men of the same colour, although separated by differences of language, and inhabiting opposite coasts. That American Mediterranean [*Cette Méditerranée de l'Amérique*] formed by the shores [*le littoral*] of Venezuela, New Granada, Mexico, the United States, and the West India islands, may count upon its borders [*compte sur ses bords*][10] near a million and a half of free and enslaved Blacks. . . . This may be said to be the African part of the interior basin [*C'est pour ainsi dire la partie africaine de ce bassin intérieure*]" (*PN*, 3:430–33; *RH*, 4:156). "That American Mediterranean" as it was early on, if not first, named, explored and studied by Humboldt, is the subject of this book.

Beyond Humboldt I: Other Mediterraneans of the Americas

Humboldt was neither the first to speak of the New World in terms of the Old (the West Indies is only one, well-known example, the legacy of Western cartographic misnaming) nor the first to make the classical world a civilizational starting point (*translatio imperii* is a long-standing Western tradition). But the unbroken westward movement assumed in these civilizational discourses, along with the linear timeline on which the spatial axis takes place, is disrupted by the Humboldtian sense of futurity. Humboldt inaugurated a historiographical tradition in which locating the Mediterraneans of the Americas becomes a mode of prophecy, and the oceanic history of the classical Mediterranean past "seems," as he predicts in *Personal Narrative*, to inscribe "the whole future destiny of the New World" (*PN*, 6:845). Following Humboldt's lead, my own speculative history of the American Mediterranean explores why the network of mediterranean texts extends outward from the late eighteenth century to the present but clusters around different historical contexts, flowering especially prominently on the Pacific coast from California northward during the 1890s and in the greater Caribbean during the 1930s and '40s.

The network advantage to creating a Humboldt-headed Mediterranean tradition is precisely that it is neither a fixed Humboldt genealogy nor a static legacy. Rather, starting with Humboldt, what counts as "the American Mediterranean" is itself variable. The most common place referents, whether in Spanish, French or English, are in first place, the Caribbean archipelago; in second place, the California coast, extending upward to the Pacific Northwest, and in distant third place, the ultra-short-lived case of the Long Island Sound as a modern eco-Mediterranean. Similarly, the time referents, the multiple Mediterranean histories that provide a temporal basis of comparison, range from the worlds of classical Greece and Rome (*mare nostrum*) to imperial Spain, modern France, Italy, and North Africa. Transposed to the Americas, these Mediterranean times take into account the histories of contact—empire and revolution, slavery and rebellion-—that differentially defined the basin, its centers and peripheries, from the beginnings to the present. Put another way, the Mediterranean can't be thought apart from its baggage of imperial and civilizational thinking, the colonizing of both histories and knowledges. To recognize these multiple locations and names, I use the plural title "Mediterraneans."[11]

The choice of figures included in these networks also speculatively extends Humboldt's Mediterranean worlds. With their own encyclopedic method and mission, geographers and artists, foreign policy writers and travel writers, as well as anti- and postcolonial thinkers, expand "*cette Méditerranée de l'Amérique*" to posit other Mediterraneans of the Americas. Some mediterraneanizers work in a multivolume form, others through texts divided into multiple, cross-regional chapters, organized geographically and historically, with visual as well as textual representation. The genres also include the travelogue and recruitment brochure, designed to attract settlers, businessmen, and travelers. Many of the texts feature illustrations (drawings, botanical plates, photographs, fold-out maps) that would appeal to a broad audience (late eighteenth- and early nineteenth-century European elites interested in geography and astronomy, late nineteenth- and early twentieth-century middle-class American consumers of Mediterranean revival art and architecture).

The subject matter and form of these visuals fall into four main categories: maps (figures 1–8); house and garden, landscape panoramas and close-ups (figures 9–17); ethnographic portraits (figures 18–20); travel and product advertisements (figures 21–26). Grouping the illustrations together in these four categories shows how very different writers, in very different genres, linked only by a thin Mediterranean thread, relied on common conventions of visual representation. The many maps, for example, used by both the geographer Élisée Reclus and the Caribbean historian W. Adolphe Roberts not only show topographical and physical features but also superimpose on templates of the region both political events and social elements, mapping historical time onto geographical space and place. Reclus's West Indies volume includes 192 maps, showing wind currents and depth temperatures of *la méditerranée américaine* as well as political divisions and "predominant races" ("prépondérance des diverses races") [figures 2–3].[12] So, too, Roberts opens his historical study *The Caribbean* with a map called *The Caribbean Area* and moves across time with sixteen more maps of the region, including *The Caribbean in 1700*, and at the end, *The Caribbean Today* (figures 5–7).[13] The racial underbelly that has such a submerged presence in the American Mediterranean history is also sometimes visible in the illustrations while less spoken in the text, or vice versa. The drawings, often taken from photographs, typically present either a landscape, viewed from a distance (bird's-eye view [*vue génerale*]), with small-scale human subjects in the mid-ground, typically well-dressed, leisured white men and women, or close-ups, sometimes of interiors, always of natives (Indian [Indien]), in tribal or local dress, or nearly naked. Together, the textual-visual elements of the projects, racialized more or less openly and more or less audibly, shape the practice and refract the philosophy of their authors.

Ever since Humboldt coined his various names for the new-world Mediterranean, and the anarchist geographer Élisée Reclus, writing in 1891, referred back to Humboldt, including a map labeled *Méditerranée américaine* (figure 1), and Reclus then appeared in the epigraph to the foreign correspondent and diplomat Stephen Bonsal's 1912 *American Mediterranean*, the term has had an erratic history. In addition to its on-again, off-again contextual circulation, textually the term is used intermittently, often in titles and captions, and then dropped.[14] A short list of representative uses in chronological clusters around the early nineteenth century, the 1890s, and the 1930s and '40s outlines the range of the terms, texts, and contexts included in my book and suggests as well why the Mediterranean, as both a term and a concept, found special purchase in those specific periods, roughly mapping onto their shifting race discourses.

The popular US novelist (and coauthor with Mark Twain of the 1873 satire of post–Civil War political corruption, *The Gilded Age*) Charles Dudley Warner wrote the best-selling *Our Italy* (1891) to celebrate the culture and climate of Southern California as "Our Mediterranean, Our Italy! . . . without marshes and without malaria," a sanitized US version of the modern Mediterranean, supposedly lacking its racial disadvantages. During the same late nineteenth-century period in California, the best-selling romance of Indian reform, *Ramona* (1884), was credited with originating the California "fantasy heritage," bypassing Mexico in favor of Spain, and thus popularizing Mediterranean / mission-revival art and architecture. Written by Warner's East Coast friend and neighbor, Helen Hunt Jackson, the novel was translated into Spanish by the Cuban activist-artist José Martí, with the added subtitle, *Novela americana*.

The "Mediterranean of the West" is the Jamaican nationalist W. Adolphe Roberts's jumping-off point, the title of the introductory chapter of his 1940 *The Caribbean: The Story of Our Sea of Destiny*, his history of the Caribbean and the source of the "startling resemblances in imperial implications" he finds in the comparison. The Cuban novelist Alejo Carpentier's "Mediterráneo Caribe" evokes the classical Mediterranean as a touchstone en route to the revolutionary sensibility and history of Haiti in his *El reino de este mundo* (*The Kingdom of This World*; prologue, 1949) as well as his 1962 novel *El siglo de las luces* (*Explosion in a Cathedral*). And in *Poetics of Relation*, Édouard Glissant takes up but reverses Carpentier's Caribbean Sea as a new-world Mediterranean; in opposition to the Mediterranean, "an inner sea surrounded by lands, a sea that concentrates," "the thought of the One," the Caribbean is "a sea that explodes" and "diffracts," producing a fractal landscape and "a poetics of relation"—of creolization, openness, and instability. Counterpointing the cultural geography of the two seas, Glissant looks to the connection between landscape and aesthetics, the question of how the geography and ecology of the basin inform Caribbean poetics and literature—and, I would add, by extension, the relationship between the nineteenth-century California-Pacific Mediterranean and its literature.[15]

Most important are the terms of the networked widening out from the Humboldt beginnings. Rather than lean into the mediterranean comparison, the artists and activists in this book stand back and assess its fit with the Americas, most often questioning and qualifying, verging on negating it. They force a critical awareness of the asymmetry of the units being compared, both skepticism about imposing one geography on another and more open-ended, historical speculation about the alternative histories that result. This history of nay-saying starts with the Braudel epigraph (which I reuse as my own epigraph for this introduction) on the title page of his massive history of the Mediterranean: "To this day," wrote the sixteenth-century priest José de Acosta in his own massive *Natural and Moral History of the East and West Indies*, "they have not discovered at the Indies any mediterranian sea as in *Europe, Asia* and *Affrike*."[16] The quotation embedded in the epigraph, itself another instance, like the prevalence of "American Mediterranean" titles and captions, of intertextual citation at the edges of the main text, refers to a factual negative ("not discovered at the Indies any mediterranian sea") that depends for its meaning on a positive comparison ("as in *Europe, Asia* and *Affrike*"). Put another way, Braudel's Acosta invokes the presence of mediterranean seas in the Indies only by virtue of their comparative absence.

Braudel himself temporarily takes up negative terms in the preface to the first edition of *The Mediterranean* when contemplating how clearly the Mediterranean has been defined by the geographer. But, he asks, "what of the Mediterranean of the historian? There is no lack of authoritative statements as to what it is not. It is not an autonomous world, nor is it the preserve of any one power" (*MMW*, 17). The *nots* form the strategic starting point for the historian's task of boundary drawing: "To draw a boundary around anything is to define, analyse, and reconstruct it, in this case, select, indeed adopt a philosophy of history" (17). So Braudel follows Acosta in his emphasis on what has not been discovered, other mediterranean seas beyond the ones we know. The concept of plural Mediterraneans emerging here differs in revealing ways from the Humboldtian complex of seas interconnected linguistically through difference, the diverse names for the same Gulf-Caribbean place.

Repeating and further updating this strategic negation, the Cuban activist-intellectual Roberto Fernández Retamar, tracing the derivation in *The Tempest* of the name Caliban as "Shakespeare's anagram for 'cannibal' . . . that comes in turn from the word *carib*," which itself refers to the Carib Indians, whose "name lives on in the name Caribbean Sea," concludes with a wry parenthetical on the Caribbean, "(referred to genially by some as the American Mediterranean, just as if we were to call the Mediterranean the Caribbean of Europe)". The counterfactual comparative, expressed in the conditional, "just as if we were to call the Mediterranean the Caribbean of Europe," makes the imaginative reversal of *translatio imperii* that underlies so much of the mediterraneanism of the Americas.[17] While what might be the most prevalent circulation of the term comes from its foreign-policy roots, in which the American Mediterranean is used as a direct analogy between US power in the Caribbean and Roman supremacy over the Mediterranean Sea in late antiquity, it's unclear how far other, counterdefinitions grounded in the Americas can go in opening up the imperial-racial structure at the heart of this particular oceanic term. The question is whether and how it pushes back against its Euro- or US-centricity. One thing is clear, though: Acosta's Indies, the mistaken location of Fernández Retamar's Caribs, forces an unintended positive consequence in accurately recognizing the Caribbean for what it is not. Together, the network Acosta-Braudel-Retamar goes some distance toward unraveling the imperial history of the Mediterranean even as they are all discovering and inventing it.

Taking off from the moments of greatest concentration in the history of the American Mediterraneans, my book is divided into four parts, starting with an overview of the whole, to highlight the chronological clusters of historical flowering and extend their speculative dimensions. The three periods have corresponding geographical locations, identifying when and where the concept of an American Mediterranean found special purchase. As an ensemble the four parts work forward through a space-timeline that shows the changes in the concept, depending on the place and historical moment when and where it emerges.

To honor the visual culture that plays such a starring role in the American Mediterraneans—the maps, the house and garden design, the art and architecture, and the advertisements—I have included a representative sample that shows both the continuity and the change of the imagery across space and time. The landscape panorama, for example, appears and reappears in slightly different formats in very different contexts, the Caribbean Mediterranean of Élisée Reclus and W. Adolphe Roberts, and the Pacific Mediterranean of Charles Dudley Warner and P. C. Remondino. It is striking that writers as politically different as the anarchist geographer, the Jamaican nationalist, and the two California boosters all rely on the same highly conventionalized forms of historical mapping and landscape panorama. To show simultaneously both this general visual pattern and the local variations, I depend on cross-referencing, first to preview the whole, the umbrella set of images, and then to focus on particular visual clusters, the subsets, as they emerge.

Similarly, the structure of the book repeats the far-off/close-up perspective. Each part opens with a bird's-eye, or panoramic, to use the terms from the illustrations, view of all the Mediterranean references and variants I have found to date in that specific period, no matter how seemingly minimal. Following these distant readings, the subsequent sections become increasingly speculative, narrowing the focus to networks of mediterraneanizers that are not part of the "Humboldt current," neither directly indebted to nor inspired by him, whose presence challenges and complicates the more readily recognizable work of the rest.[18]

Part 1 begins with an overview of the Mediterranean archive. Here I survey the whole space-timeline, roughly from the 1790s to the end of the twentieth century, extending to the primary-source practitioners (Humboldt and others) as well as today's commentators, scholars (Mike Davis, Kevin Starr, and others) who write about the historical use and utility of the Mediterranean. Their collective presence establishes the crossover, popular-scholarly, intermedial, and interdisciplinary outlines of the American Mediterranean as subject matter. Part 1 then zeroes in on how race historically informs these mediterranean networks, most often out at the edges of the texts, only partially visible and audible in their different contexts. Part 1 also offers an extended consideration of method: a way to do comparative work without lapsing into the oft-cited problems of comparison. In part, this must be attributed to the writers engaged in my study and to the Mediterranean concept itself. Thinking *with* as much as about my subjects is critical to the definition of an American Mediterranean method. But ultimately I am the one pulling the strings, showing how the method works, how the disparate materials come together in networks of texts and contexts—in short, inventing as much as discovering. So the subjects of my book are approached simultaneously as preexisting objects, brought into view through vantage points that are alternately synoptic (bird's-eye) and close-up, and as networks I construct to show meanings in and across discrete texts and contexts. Methodologically, the book necessarily alternates between following the mediterraneanizers and taking the lead, between discovery and invention.

Part 2 covers the nineteenth-century geographers, broadly defined, starting with Humboldt and Jedidiah Morse, moving to Élisée Reclus and the popular journalist-foreign correspondent Stephen Bonsal, and concluding with Ellen Churchill Semple and Frederick Jackson Turner. These odd couples, joining famous names with the little-known, mark an outer limit of the networks. They are, as a group, perhaps the most challenging of my sources, in part because of their disciplinary locations. Readers who are familiar with nineteenth-century geography won't be likely to know about Bonsal, and Reclus may be little more than a celebrated but otherwise neglected figurehead. The same holds true for other clusters in other parts of the book—and my task is to give for each of the fairly obscure texts a sense of its content and aims, and why it is or isn't considered significant for a given discipline (geography, literary studies, history, Black studies). The nineteenth-century geographers work with different degrees of acknowledged reference to Humboldt but always in his shadow, and with different relations to the "American Mediterranean" concept (as we know, not everyone even uses the phrase), but always invested in some form of Mediterranean thinking. Whether the Pacific Ocean is proposed as a new American Mediterranean or whether a Mediterranean analogy is anxiously elided, the racial baggage that comes with Humboldt always hovers at the edges of these geographies. One of the payoffs will be to show how the choices—aesthetic, political, intellectual—of different geographers resulted in particular racial conundrums.

Parts 3 and 4 are by far the most speculative case studies of the book. Part 3 turns to the Pacific Mediterranean in the 1890s, with the explosion of California travel and tourism writing, and specifically to the afterlives of Helen Hunt Jackson's 1884 novel *Ramona*, which spawned a Spanish colonial revival in art and architecture that might also be called a Mediterranean revival. Here too race is the absent center of the story, for a mediterraneanizing lens in this case is about not seeing Indigenous Mexico in turn-of-the-century California. This part of the book models the text-network comparative method, culminating in a reading of Martí's translation of Jackson's *Ramona* as a novel of Our America, which returns us to the shores of a key American Mediterranean: the Caribbean.

Part 4 proposes mediterranean thinking as a form of anticolonial theory in the mid-twentieth-century Gulf-Caribbean. Opening with "America's Caribbean" as a contested touristic and policy arena in the decolonizing 1930s and '40s, part 4 then looks back through that lens to the 1890s US, 1790s Haiti, and 1870s Reconstruction, and closes with a sketch of what I call the American Spartacus. The classical figure of the slave gladiator-rebel as he is adapted in sculpture and on stage, page, and screen is a backbone of Black and Caribbean classicisms as well as a broad-ranging history that reiterates and extends the whole American Mediterranean in miniature. C. L. R. James's figure of Toussaint L'Ouverture, whom he calls a black Spartacus, is at the center of this final network. The aim is twofold: to show how the history and literature of ancient slave revolt translates to American Mediterranean traditions of revolutionary, anticolonial thinking, and to make a specific case for the Gulf-Caribbean cluster as a text network of forgotten pasts, unfinished revolutions, and speculative futures, adapted to fit the political needs of the 1940s.

An epilogue closes the book, following on the various counterfactual black Spartacuses and Jacobins, George Washingtons and Napoleons, that raise fundamental questions about the nature and status of the comparative thinking under the mediterranean umbrella. The epilogue takes their cue and will open out to a provisional endpoint, on the as-yet uncompleted history of ocean studies. Here Fernand Braudel is both the kingpin and the elephant in the room. Indebted to his Greater Mediterranean as well as his concept of the *longue durée*, Mediterranean studies itself comprises a comparative set of fields, counterposing not only the Atlantic and Pacific Worlds but also their subsets (Black, Spanish, Amerindian, and other Atlantics, Pacifics, and Indian Oceans). Braudel once set the stage for revisionist thinking about oceanic space and time, and now, from a perspective informed by translation studies, for potentially bringing language into the center of the inquiry. The whole project is thus bookended by Humboldt and Braudel: the epilogue both goes back to fill in the latter's occasional presence here at the opening, otherwise dedicated to Humboldt, and looks forward to a new, not-yet actualized Braudel for the Mediterraneans of the Americas.

My book assembles the many Mediterraneans that have been imagined in the Americas since Humboldt, to trace their history—spatial, temporal, and linguistic—of appearance and disappearance, and to consider the changing cultural work they do. In charting the correlations between the term and its times, the scholar needs the same kind of speculative comparativism as the American Mediterranean itself produces. The language of "race" underlying Humboldt's *Méditerranée de l'Amérique* correlates to the relative historical presence and absence of racial thinking that defines the mediterranean discourse at large. The continuum ranges from full-blown racism to nominal racelessness, with a space in-between left, as in the Humboldt passage on *la Méditerranée de l'Amérique*, for possible, provisional, "as if" race-based alliances: "comme par instinct il s'établit un accord entre des hommes d'une même couleur séparés par la différence du langage et habitant des côtes opposés" ("where as if by instinct a concert is established between men of the same colour, although separated by differences of language, and inhabiting opposite coasts"; *PN*, 3:430–33; *RH*, 4:156). The speculative dimension of those as-yet unrealized racial coalitions formed around the basin of the interior sea is critical to my work in *American Mediterraneans*. Taking Humboldt's Mediterranean as far as I can, it becomes, for others later, especially during the decolonizing 1930s and '40s, more than a region or concept, a strategy for thinking coalitionally, re-mining differently raced, oceanic histories for uncompleted or untimely revolutions and using them to imagine alternative futures.

Beyond Humboldt II: Mediterraneanity, or the Mediterranean Concept

My starting points in this checkered history are both the term Mediterranean and the concept of what scholars later call variously mediterraneanity, the mediterranean metaphor or analogy, and Mediterraneanism. Thinking in conceptual as well as geographical terms demonstrates how the concept has its own history, not well known, an ecologically driven oceanic analysis with the potential for helping us rethink the parameters of space/time/language in comparative studies. The historian of the classical Mediterranean David Abulafia warns against a homogenizing "Mediterraneanism" that would reduce the region to a predetermined set of unified characteristics and instead advocates for "diversity" in writing the history not just of the Mediterranean but of "Mediterranean-like spaces"—seas such as the Baltic, larger ocean units such as the Atlantic—and of course the Caribbean.[19] It's worth noting that one of Abulafia's Mediterranean-like spaces, the Sahara desert, echoes the extension of oceanic thinking that Humboldt had already made, writing of "cette Méditerranée de sables mouvans [that Mediterranean of moving sands]" in book 3, *Relacion historique* (*RH*, 3:32; *PN*, 6:64). Braudel, too, has a Sahara in *The Mediterranean*, but his is the desert as the geographical space of Islam, far removed from the metaphoric Mediterranean of moving sands imagined by Humboldt.

The advantage of thinking this way, through an extended mediterranean heuristic rather than with a mediterranean sea or region, whether the classical Mediterranean or others, is, first, when the term isn't used at all, the concept steps in to fill the breach. A wide range of secondary sources, historians and theorists, become primary evidence for identifying the history as a whole. Second, the concept supplies a more expansive definition than the geography alone, one that takes in a wider range of case studies; some, like James's *The Black Jacobins*, challenge the fundamentals of the orthodox mediterranean *translatio imperii*, while others, such as the many figures of a Black Spartacus, bring in related areas of study, Black classicism, for example, that haven't yet been explicitly read through a mediterranean lens. When James calls Toussaint L'Ouverture a "black Spartacus," the *translatio imperii* is turned on its head with his Toussaint, who brings classical slave revolt counterdirectionally forward into the American Mediterranean to produce a revolutionary countergeography, along with a reverse timeline where the liberated African future originates in the prediction of the uncompleted Caribbean past. Third, mediterraneanity, Mediterraneanism and its cognates, the Mediterranean metaphor or analogy, raise the underlying issue, the extent to which the concept of the Mediterranean can travel elsewhere, whether and how to use the term *mediterranean* to describe areas other than *the* Mediterranean. This remains an open interpretive question in Mediterranean studies despite the proliferation of candidates for other Mediterraneans across the world.

The Mediterranean concept has been separately historicized in California studies with a more explicit focus on US Americanity. The California historian and state librarian Kevin Starr sees the site-specific "dream of California as a mediterranean littoral" through the broad lens of the "mediterraneanizing mind" that thinks in terms of metaphor and analogy. For Starr the analogy, "arising from similarities of landscape and clime . . . developed into a metaphor for all California offered as a regional civilization," in the nineteenth century creating a fantasy Spanish heritage that skipped over the racialized people and past of Mexican California. "Deep Mediterraneaneity" is the cultural critic Mike Davis's term in *Ecology of Fear: Los Angeles and the Imagination of Disaster* (1998) for the underlying climate conditions that are misunderstood by Angelinos. The disconnect between the Mediterranean environment of Southern California, its characteristic cycles of drought and rain, which was readily recognized by the early Spanish padres, themselves "Mediterranean men," and the "Anglo-American conquistadores" who saw the ecologies of the New World as a schizophrenic alternation between garden and desert, produces the apocalyptic imagination of disaster.

Davis's *Ecology of Fear* focuses specifically on the language questions that are critical to my study. "In the most fundamental sense," Davis concludes on a Humboldtian note, "language and cultural inheritance failed the newcomers. English terminology, specific to a humid climate, proved incapable of accurately capturing the dialectic of water and drought that shapes Mediterranean environments." As a result, and central to one of my more speculative case studies, the *Ramona* texts of Southern California, the "more befitting" Spanish terms have been preserved in place-names all over California, some enshrining *Ramona*'s main characters, but their meanings forgotten, erased because the Anglo settlers could not grasp their environmental context. For both Davis and Starr, the Mediterranean climate and culture account for the historically specific invention of California as an exercise in fantasy, the product of promotion and imagination. For me the takeaway is the potentially broad application of their focus on the invention of a Mediterranean tradition through language and metaphor as twin indices of a translingual and translational oceanic history.[20]

American Mediterraneans draws on this work, tapping how scholars across the disciplines from Fernand Braudel to Paul Gilroy have conceived of the geopolitics of waterways through new frameworks and units of analysis. Ranging from the many Atlantic worlds and worldviews in different languages and colors (Black, Spanish, Amerindian, and other Atlantics) to the newer Pacificist perspectives (Bruce Cumings), some of these go beyond but do not jettison conventional categories of the nation-state or area studies. The history of Mediterranean studies, indebted to and under the shadow of Braudel's Greater Mediterranean as well as his concept of the *longue durée*, is most

proximate to my book. The maritime spaces of connection known as Middle
Seas, the other Mediterraneans, designated by Abulafia, Michael Herzfeld,
and others as areas of both connectivity and intense geopolitical conflict, with
colonial and orientalist imprintings, set out the oceanic offspring that test the
bounds of the Mediterranean as a unit of study.[21]

For my study, the French geographer Jean-Baptiste Arrault's mediterranean concept ("le concept de *méditerranée*") helps particularly to historicize
the circulation of my texts in relation to their contexts and to establish the op-
erational conditions for the networks that mediterraneanity characteristically
produces. Network thinking promotes connectivities between and among discrete texts that might otherwise seem to have nothing in common, no demon-
strable intertextual conversation. Arrault argues that the Mediterranean "analogy" used between the mid-nineteenth and mid-twentieth centuries by many
authors, geographers in particular, registers a growing awareness of globalization; however, the debates among French geographers about the "invention" of this broad concept or analogy are insufficiently historicized, with a
few figureheads, "geographers of exception," Humboldt and Reclus, credited
as founders of the American Mediterranean.[22] Humboldt's role in my book
is similarly double-edged. For such a famous and fertile founding figure, he
himself uses the Mediterranean comparison quite unsystematically, in a pattern of isolated moments scattered throughout his *Personal Narrative*. Yet it
and he serve as major touchstones for the geographers and historians interested in reimagining Mediterranean and ocean studies beyond the classical or
modern Euro-centered Mediterranean.

Moreover, Humboldt himself, biographically, is a contradictory figure, especially in the United States, where he has been forgotten and recovered several
times over. He has been variously judged, either celebrated as an environmen-
talist, eco-critic before the fact (Andrea Wulf), assimilated as another imperial eye (Mary Louise Pratt), excoriated as an imitator of Spanish-American
letrados without acknowledgment of his sources (Jorge Cañizares-Esguerra),
dismissed as a colonial mouthpiece readily appropriated by later nineteenth-
century advocates of American racial science (Aaron Sachs), or distanced by
the lack of accessible English translations. During his own lifetime, he was
a celebrity, sometimes known as "Baron Humbug," the mocking name bestowed for his overly "rosy picture" in popular writings on Latin America
of opportunities for enterprising Europeans, especially in mining around
Potosí.[23] My approach is to take Humboldt as an exemplary mediterranean
thinker precisely because of the shifting sands of his presence, absence, and
authority in the networks that follow him. The unstable foundation of the
Mediterranean concept defines its advantage as a comparative approach

that is notably disjunctive, skeptical, questioning its own terms of use. As a thinker whose writings expressly opened the humanism of Europe to the geographies, environments, and peoples of the Americas, Humboldt inaugurates a practice of connectivity that is contingent, self-critical, and finally capable of something like secular prophecy—able to imagine racial histories and counterhistories, and potential futures in the Americas.

For all the pretense (Humboldt's own and that of his critics) to a totalizing descriptive project, shaped by his own brand of planetary consciousness, Humboldt's writings are constitutionally incomplete: recycled, reassembled, ever unfinished.[24] So, too, his Mediterranean is not just a geographical marker but also a mode of critique, of witnessing and watching for the in-between in terms of historical eras and periodizing, climatological data and feelings, national traditions, linguistic registers, and racial identifications. The very idea of the Mediterranean as a folk geographical concept must begin with Humboldt as the first to extensively postulate an American Mediterranean beyond a merely geographical one. His work (and not just the phrase he coins) represents a certain kind of lens, one that can be connected with what other writers have used to think about the subjects of environmental determinism and the geohistory of race in the Americas. These Humboldtian networks show why and how a transoceanic perspective serves as a fulcrum for articulating memories of unfinished emancipations together with unrealized possibilities for the future. The cultural work achieved by these writers is varied; but all grapple in one way or another with the American legacies of European imperialism and slavery, as those histories give shape to different racial struggles, coalitions, and possibilities.

Scholars of the classical Mediterranean are now working to define the kind of racial thinking, before the modern "race concept" (W. E. B. Du Bois), that shaped relations in the basin.[25] Extending this work forward, the chronological clusters of mediterraneanisms in the early nineteenth century, the 1890s, and the 1940s propose their own possible historical confluences between racial terms and their times, how and why these clusters of texts/contexts emerged at particular historical conjunctures. The racialization of Italians, Greeks, and Spaniards as a "Mediterranean race" coalesced in a variety of eugenics writers in the turn-of-the-century US—Madison Grant, William Z. Ripley, Carleton Coon, Thomas Huxley—just when the branding of California as a Pacific Mediterranean, a temperate mecca for tourists and invalids alike, was at its height.[26] Appearing and disappearing across time and space, that pattern defines the strange career of the American Mediterraneans: long-lasting and short-lived, raced and color-blind, oceanic and landed, imperial and revolutionary, material and imaginary.

The advantages of thinking comparatively though the mediterranean concept start with its being by definition oceanic as well as by design transnational and translingual, breaking out, as so many scholars in Black Atlantic, circum-Caribbean, and Pacific studies advocate, of the artifice of the nation-state along with the one nation–one language equation. The multiple Mediterranean names reflect the places referred to and the languages of those places, both colonial and Indigenous. It's their term, not ours, with a long historical lineage, an invention with a material history, an imagined cartography with a definable genealogy of circulation. As both a material space and an imaginary, the Mediterranean brings with it an imperial-colonial complex, histories of conquest and slavery in the Old and New Worlds, differentially raced, and a particular skeptical and speculative take on the comparative. This combined scholarly and folk geographical concept, striking both for its longevity and instability, is a model for comparative historical thinking *otherwise* about the Americas.[27]

1

American Mediterraneans:
A Space-Timeline

Jumping off from the Humboldtian beginnings at the turn of the nineteenth century, we've already been introduced to a few representative figures working across the range of languages, genres, places, and times that define the American Mediterranean history. They include major players, those who actually use the phrase American Mediterranean or one of its cognates, as well as minor, more distantly related to the Mediterranean concept, whom I bring speculatively into the mix. Of the main lights, we've seen the nineteenth-century French anarchist geographer Élisée Reclus and the popular US author Charles Dudley Warner, the twentieth-century Jamaican nationalist W. Adolphe Roberts, the Cuban novelist and musicologist Alejo Carpentier, and the Caribbean poet-theorist Édouard Glissant. The satellites, who, against the grain, become increasing central to my book, include Helen Hunt Jackson and her translator José Martí as well as C. L. R. James, none of whom recognize the Mediterranean as relevant to their work but for whom mediterraneanity turns out to be a revealing lens.

The next step is to place these key figures and their historical contexts in relation to all the mediterraneanizers I've found from the Humboldtian 1790s through the 1990s, when a secondary, critical historiography about the American Mediterranean emerged. Those later writings form key primary evidence for the space-timeline of the American Mediterranean. The invention of the plural Mediterranean space-times by Humboldt and others is coextensive with the study of the tradition across the disciplines. The long fetch helps to establish the historical trajectories of the Mediterranean usages in different languages and media, at specific times and places, as well as the networks, both textual and contextual, that cluster in the early nineteenth century, the turn of the century, and the 1930s and '40s. This tradition of comparative oceanic thinking is critically recognized, named by the later scholars clustered in the 1990s and thereafter.

We've glimpsed how sparingly even the main players tend to use the terminology of the American Mediterranean. Their cross-citations, almost always confined to titles, epigraphs, captions, and illustrations, demonstrate, in turn, how wide but shallow the networks of connectivity are. The degree and kind of connection varies by discipline and genre. The nineteenth-century geographers, explicitly aligned with Humboldt in their attention to the Mediterranean comparison, are all linked by the debate over the stakes, political and ethical, of the environmental determinism that dominated the international field. The issue they confronted was whether and how, the degree to which environmental conditions cause or shape the identity and destiny of different human groups, "peoples" racially defined. At roughly the same period, in the long 1890s, California and Caribbean travel writers and regional boosters, whom we might expect to embrace the civilizational drumbeat, assuming the mantle of the singular old-world Mediterranean as producer of later new-world versions of classical knowledge and culture, treat the comparison with considerable skepticism. For them the racial valence of thinking through the Mediterranean analogy runs the gamut from coded and half-spoken to invisible. The twentieth-century mediterraneanizers, for the most part cultural critics, historians, and international politics scholars, some broadly postcolonial and antiracist, others US-focused critics, are the most widely dispersed and politically conscious, generally connected by their varying commitments to coalition politics, grounded in transoceanic histories of African-descended people across linguistic and national lines.

From this long Mediterranean perspective, a series of problematic postrace valences at the three key periods comes into view: first, in the sustained questioning by geographers throughout the nineteenth century about the nature and extent of geo-environmental influence on race and ethnicity; second, in late nineteenth-century debates around race and the law in the Jim Crow US and race and the nation in Cuba and elsewhere in the Spanish Caribbean; third, in the mid-twentieth century emergence of new transracial intercolonial alliances and global decolonization movements. Put another way, the racial underbelly of this combined Mediterranean metaphor and ecology tracks often unrecognized connections between different historical moments, difficult to discern, where race goes underground, alternates between partial visibility and unspeakability, coded presence and apparent absence.

Tracing these historical moments through the networks of interrelations they produce reveals the "connectivity" (Peregrine Horden and Nicolas Percell's term for the linkages of the Mediterranean's diverse peoples) that defines the circulation of the American Mediterraneans.[1] Some of these networks self-identify through cross-citation; others I extrapolate from their common patterns of mediterranean thinking that correlate with their locations in space, time, and language. Humboldt's own pattern of appearing and disappearing from textual view sets the standard. Hence even writers who never expressly mention the term American Mediterranean still count as extending Humboldtian connectivity. To model a way of moving dynamically along all three of these scales—space, time, and language—a network (as opposed to a singular "work") of texts, radiating out from Humboldt, foregrounds the material conditions of how they circulate. The texts themselves move through multiple translations, adaptations, and significant editions and republications, each instantiation punctuated along the scales of time and space, tracking when, where, and how the original Mediterranean references are retained or omitted.

Both the Mediterranean name and the mediterranean concept are defined by their erratic, ephemeral—fundamentally fugitive—circulation. The pattern of references, never at the center, always around the edges, whether of text or context, points to the instability of "American Mediterranean" as a foundational hermeneutic. That instability has been, oddly, an interpretive advantage from the Humboldtian beginnings. One of the few thesis statements Humboldt made about the Mediterranean comparison centers on "the Mediterranean considered as the starting point for the representation of the relations which have laid the foundation of the gradual extension of the idea of the cosmos," an enigmatic headnote to a chapter in his last work, *Cosmos* (1:119). The uncertainty, even the grandiosity of this late claim, contrasts with his earlier work in *Personal Narrative*, where we know he stresses the uncertainty of generalizing about the inhabitants of the Americas, "their relations with the differences of race, languages, and worship, . . . composed of very variable elements, . . . [that] . . . represent approximately the state of American society" (*PN*, 6:845). Linguistically, "the Mediterranean considered as the starting point" produces comparative analysis with a transnational complement that allows different scales of observation, variable and approximate in Humboldt's terms, to operate simultaneously. Language thus both anchors and destabilizes Mediterranean studies as Humboldt set the standard and others practiced it.

The multiple names for the Mediterraneans in the Americas tap different linguistic patterns that include a variegated and multiple set of registers, dialects, and socially significant lexical and grammatical usage, all scalable by social influence, access, and power. The degrees and scales of proficiency in languages—native and foreign, dialect and register, creole and patois—are expressed and thematized in some of the texts I consider, in particular those of California in the 1890s and the extended Caribbean of the 1940s. Finally, the shifting languages of the American Mediterraneans complement the counterfactual histories of old-world empires, conquest and revolution, slavery and emancipation, transposed to new-world contexts in which they specialize. Questioning their own mediterranean terms of use and mining the uncompleted past, the not-yet of a Black Spartacus, these works imagine alternative futures. Humboldt's summary line that I have repeated several times, concluding with an indeterminate futurity at the end of the passage on race, language, and religious differences, says it all: "There is something serious and prophetic in these inventories of the human race: in them the whole future destiny of the New World seems to be inscribed" (*PN*, 6:845).

These possibilities and limits make it a challenge to read the loose archive of works I've assembled under the rubric of Humboldt's variable American Mediterraneans. The best approach I've found is a three-dimensional spatiotemporal-linguistic mapping that adapts different kinds of distant and close reading, incorporating book history with the concept of a literary geography centering the six degrees of connectivity—social, political, literary—between people and places. In concert with traditional close reading that takes the text as primary evidence, this macro-micro mapping can follow the erratic circulation patterns of the American Mediterraneans. Tracking the textual appearance and disappearance of the various terms for the region used in titles, captions, and cover matter across different editions and translations is especially critical to understanding the fugitivity of the mediterranean concept in the Americas context.[2]

Accordingly, part 1 tacks back and forth between bird's-eye and close-up views. The alternating scales, shifting between macro and micro, provide an overview of known mediterraneans and mediterraneanisms as well as a close reading of specific clusters as they explicitly or implicitly cite or otherwise refer to one another. The following section charts a long list of all the American Mediterraneans from the Humboldt beginnings through the 1990s and then moves in for a close look at the nature of the networks thus generated. The intertextual networks are linked by a mediterraneanism that is loosely, largely paratextually connected to Humboldt, yet, I will show, initiated and sustained by extending him.[3] The long Humboldtian shadow becomes a measure of their distance from the source of their Mediterranean thinking, as each network takes off from and goes beyond his skeptical view, privileging uncertainty, on the possible futures encoded in the region's geographical conditions. The overall effect is to dislodge a text from any singular comparative relation with another text, or from any one literary genealogy or tradition, by placing it instead within a text network—attending to translation, adaptation, and other forms of relation across language, place, and time. By multiplying the times and places of any given text, Mediterranean scholars, both practitioners and observers, are confronted with overlapping frames of analysis— a sometimes dizzying effect that unsettles the many foregone conclusions of traditional comparison and linear historical thinking, and thereby tends to honor the hypothetical and produce speculative forms of knowledge.

Bird's-eye View: American Mediterraneans, 1790s–1990s

Starting with the geographers in the late eighteenth century and continuing throughout the nineteenth century, a network history reveals clusters of mediterraneanizers, who differ dramatically in their own language for and positions on race, difference, and the possibility for sociopolitical change, driven in part by their different disciplinary identifications and generic locations. In the US early national period, when geography played a major role in educational and cultural spheres at home and abroad, geographers saw the subject, with its international reach, as a boost to nascent nationalism. A network of prominent geographers came together at this period of American fascination with geography and cartography, as the American Geographic Society became an official institution, oceanography as an academic discipline found its first iterations, and the publication of geography books spiked as its study became central to national citizenship. Formally, the geographers aspired to a Humboldtian global reach; generically they wrote in the nineteenth-century multiformat, dividing the world into subregions by chapters or volumes, illustrated with maps and engravings; and politically they differed in how they mobilized the Mediterranean. Race as a contested measure of progress and civilizational thinking dominated the discipline of historical geography through the discourses of climatology, both of supporters and critics. Geographers from the late eighteenth to the early nineteenth century, such as William Robertson and Jedidiah Morse, who both predate and continue into the Humboldt period, to turn-of-the-nineteenth-century geographers, such as Élisée Reclus and Ellen Churchill Semple, used the classical Mediterranean speculatively to conjecture on patterns of migration that could account for linguistic and racial differences among contemporary populations within a single region. At stake for them is the fundamental desirability and possibility of making systematic comparisons between human geographies, patterns of migration, and oceanic and land-mass changes over time.

This heterogeneous group of geographers, all of whom work explicitly with the geo-region of the American Mediterranean, anchors a wider context of other, loosely related nineteenth-century figures in their orbit, who touch only briefly on the Mediterranean concept. This subset includes Daniel Webster, the naval oceanographer Matthew Fontaine Maury, and, surely most surprisingly, the historian best known for his frontier thesis, Frederick Jackson Turner. Webster is said (by several historians and book blurbs) without a specified source to have described the Long Island Sound as an American Mediterranean, a claim for which I have been unable to find any evidence. But his repeated mention, despite the lack of documentation, is itself evidence of the fugitive Mediterranean that I've repeatedly found, the on-again, off-again history of its presence and absence as a reference, especially its racialized resonance.[4]

Maury, a Confederate naval officer and oceanographer, perhaps the most renowned geographer of nineteenth-century America, planned before the Civil War to export slaves to Brazil and afterward viewed the Gulf of Mexico as an experimental location for post-slavery unfree labor. He once described the Gulf by drawing "a line from the Delta of the Orinoco to the east end of Cuba . . . but a thousand miles long; and yet, to the west of it lies this magnificent basin of water, locked in by a continent that has on its shores the most fertile valleys of the earth. All and more, too, that the Mediterranean is to Europe, Africa, and Asia, this sea is to America and the world."[5] The broad analogy was typical of Southern intellectuals who conceived of the Gulf of Mexico as the South's Mediterranean, destined to be the center of both slavery and world commerce. Maury's Humboldt connections extend to his *Physical Geography of the Sea* (1855)—the title suggested by Humboldt—which proved immensely popular, went through eight US editions, and was translated into French, Dutch, Italian, Swedish, and Spanish. Maury, who had joined the US Navy in 1825 and studied Spanish aboard the frigate USS *Brandywine*, using an old Spanish work on navigation, had interests in southward Americas expansion. He championed a ship canal and railroad across the Isthmus, by way of Panama or Nicaragua rather than the alternative Tehuantepec, and he advocated the colonization of the "surplus" black population of the South in the valley of the Amazon.[6]

The best-known spokesman for westward expansion as a completed project, Frederick Jackson Turner made a Mediterranean comparison in his signature 1893 closing-of-the-frontier essay: "What the Mediterranean Sea was to the Greeks, breaking the bond of custom, offering new experiences, calling out new institutions and activities, that and more, the ever-retreating frontier has been to the United States." This is the penultimate line of the essay, an upbeat note of renewable newness and openness to the final, semi-elegiac last line on the closing of the frontier and the end of "the first period of American history."[7] Turner, for whom the Mediterranean reference is a onetime comparison (highlighting the "and more" of the relation), uses it here in the Humboldtian spirit of "that Mediterranean of moving sands," his extension of oceanic spaces to the Sahara. In this case, it's the newness of the Mediterranean to the Greeks that translates to the "ever-retreating frontier "of the US. Turner's own trajectory shifted after the 1893 speech from analysis of the influence of the frontier to an explicit focus on the study of American sectionalism. His presence speaks to the shifting tectonics around the question of the degree of environmental influence, control, or determinism, as well as to the emerging interdisciplinary dialogue of geography and history. He will reappear in part 2 as cofounder, with Ellen Churchill Semple, of the modern subdiscipline of American historical geography.

While all the nineteenth-century geography texts take the Gulf-Caribbean as their Mediterranean in the Americas, in the 1890s California provided a different Mediterranean focal point for a cluster of US travel writers, tourist promoters, and reformers. An extended Caribbean that diverged from the geographers' region also emerged in works of popular history and policy. The different genres produce a cornucopia of different possible Mediterranean comparisons. Travel writers specialized in representations of late nineteenth-century California as a temperate Mediterranean climate and history, healthful because lacking the extremes of the Old World. The novelist Charles Dudley Warner wrote the best-selling *Our Italy* (1891), a guide book illustrated with drawings and photographs of places (and occasionally people) from the Mojave Desert and Mojave Indians to the places illustrated in *Scenes in Montecito and Los Angeles* (figure 9) and the *Pueblo of Laguna* (figure 12), to celebrate the culture and climate of Southern California as "Our Mediterranean, Our Italy!"[8] One of Warner's footnotes thanks Dr. P. C. Remondino, whose 1892 *The Mediterranean Shores of America: Southern California; Its Climatic, Physical, and Meteorological Conditions* draws on his authority as a physician to make an argument about the health advantages, physical and psychological, of the region. Remondino favors the conventional illustration of landscape scenes from a distance, inset with a circular iris for close-up detail (figures 13–14). Northward up the coast, W. C. Riley produced a small illustrated pamphlet of drawings, from a handsome two-page spread of a San Francisco panorama (figure 15) to the interior of a Chinese restaurant in Portland, and even farther north, the compiler O. M. Moore produced a map titled *Puget Sound: The "American Mediterranean"* (1910; figure 4).[9] Steamship lines advertised the Caribbean as an American Mediterranean (*Porto Rico Cruise, Good Bye to Winter*), and the railroads did the same for *Puget Sound, The Mediterranean of America* (figures 22–24).

Beyond this cluster of tourism writings, other late nineteenth-century California mediterraneanisms took shape in the built environment, where Mediterranean revival architecture could be neoclassical Greco-Roman, Spanish colonial, or Moorish—or an Orientalizing fantasy combination of all of the above. Architectural examples range from the red-roofed Spanish mission-revival architecture popular in California (and also in Florida) to the 1905 Kinney's "Folly," the Los Angeles project of developer Abbott Kinney to create Venice of America (figures 8 and 21). A different Mediterranean adaptation was produced by Helen Hunt Jackson's *Ramona* (1884), a novel intended to influence federal Indian reform. Jackson and Kinney had coauthored the 1883 *Report on the Conditions and Needs of the Mission Indians, Made by Special Agents Helen Jackson and Abbot Kinney to the Commissioner of Indians Affairs*, published as an appendix to later editions of the novel, but the novel was touted for its romance rather than reform. Jackson was said, with *Ramona*, to have single-handedly produced the revival of both Spanish colonial culture and the Spanish language that characterizes California Mediterraneanism. The many *Ramona*-derived brand names for local fruit, California streets and places named after the novel, as well as its better-known adaptations, the novel's spin-off, *The Ramona Pageant*, staged annually in Hemet since 1923, and several stage and movie versions, form one node of the speculative Mediterranean network in the California of the 1890s. It extends to José Martí's Spanish translation of *Ramona*, one of his favorite novels, grafting Jackson's reformist vision onto his own anticolonial project and providing a possible link between the Pacific and Caribbean Mediterraneans.

During the same turn-of-the-century period, the Caribbean also reemerged through new popular history, travel, and policy writings. The hybrid history-travelogue, organized by chapters on the geography, politics, art, and architecture of individual Caribbean islands, was the preferred genre. *Our West Indian Neighbors: The Islands of the Caribbean Sea, "America's Mediterranean": Their Picturesque Features, Fascinating History, and Attractions for the Traveller, Nature-Lover, Settler and Pleasure Seeker* (1904), by the travel writer, lecturer, and special commissioner to the Chicago Columbian Exposition Frederick Albion Ober, promotes the trade and political possibilities of expanding the US sphere of influence to "our" West Indies, while also decrying the effects of colonization, since Columbus, on the Indigenous population of the Caribbean. The US foreign correspondent Stephen Bonsal's *The American Mediterranean* (1912) interweaves his views of the racial composition of the populations in each island he covers, plus features an appendix called "The Race Question." In *La Méditerranée américaine: L'Expansion des États-Unis dans la mer des Antilles* (1927), the Belgian diplomat Jacques Crokaert uses the Mediterranean comparison for a critical account of American expansion and designs in the Caribbean.[10]

The political dimension of the US Caribbean presence introduced by both Bonsal (pro) and Crokaert (anti) points to the foreign policy roots of what may be the best-known usage of the American Mediterranean in relation to the Caribbean. Some would say that in the twentieth-century Caribbean context, the term has lost America as a geographical reference and simply means the "US Mediterranean." Yet a third group of texts, clustered around the concept of a Caribbean Mediterranean during the decolonizing decades of the 1930s and '40s, produced a striking flowering of experimental literary and historical writing that circulated from New York to Cuba, Jamaica, and Trinidad. A variety of Mediterraneanities linked the work of these Hispanophone, Francophone, and Anglophone writers in the Caribbean and the US. The "Mediterranean of the West," as we've already seen, is the Jamaican nationalist W. Adolphe Roberts's name for the region—the title of the introductory chapter, visualized in the opening map (figure 5), in his 1940 *The Caribbean: The Story of Our Sea of Destiny.* This pioneering history of the Caribbean written from the Caribbean is in Peter Hulme's words, "the first historical expression of a pan-Caribbean historical consciousness." During the same decade, the Cuban novelist Alejo Carpentier's "Mediterráneo Caribe" uses the classical Mediterranean as a shorthand for the revolutionary history of Haiti in the famous preface to *El reino de este mundo* (*The Kingdom of this World;* 1949) as well as his 1962 novel *El siglo de las luces* (*Explosion in a Cathedral*). Carpentier's Haiti and Roberts's Caribbean are nodes in a broader network of contemporaneous mediterraneanizing works that together assemble an unfamiliar comparative history of decolonization.[11]

C. L. R. James's *The Black Jacobins* (1938) comes into the picture here in part through Roberts, one of the "West Indian visionaries . . . , who took note of the topographical analogy between the American archipelago of the Caribbean and the Mediterranean archipelago of the Greek islands and on that basis projected a cultural analogy."[12] James famously calls Toussaint L'Ouverture a "black Spartacus" in the spirit of the black Jacobins of the title, and like the other comparatively named "black" George Washingtons and Napoleons that populate American Mediterranean writing.[13] In turn James's *The Black Jacobins* brings in W. E. B. Du Bois's *Black Reconstruction in America* (1935), published three years earlier, as a textual pair working in the tradition of radical black history that represents perhaps the most unexpected development of American Mediterranean thinking. (Neither James nor Du Bois capitalizes *black* except when it is used in a title, so I follow suit when I am referring to them and their usage.) Putting these two figures together brings out the internationalism of Du Bois's intensely localized work on Reconstruction (which follows the local politics of individual Southern states and concludes with a worldwide view of conflict over colonialism and the "second slavery") and the crisscrossing of revolutionary histories, old- and new-world, Atlantic and circum-Caribbean, in James. Both writers reveal the potential of the mediterraneanizing mind for thinking historically and transnationally in the context of asymmetrical comparisons (the US South and the world, the Haitian and French Revolutions) about decolonization and civil rights from the 1930s through the 1960s.[14]

Tracing the literatures of these often-uneven histories leads to two more mediterraneanizers, working locally toward deimperialization in unlikely regional and interregional networks, from Laurel, Mississippi, to Oriente, Cuba, and Pensacola, Florida, to the hills of Jamaica. Together they shed new light on the making of race and anti-imperial politics during this period in locations across the Americas: Roberts, who followed his Caribbean book with a trilogy of historical novels on the history of slavery, the Civil War, Reconstruction, and their aftermath, set in New Orleans in the 1840s, 1860s, and 1880s, as well as a separate fourth novel, set in Cuba in the 1890s; and James Street, Baptist preacher, journalist, and author of his own series of historical novels written, like Roberts's, in New York City during the wartime decade of the 1940s, and set between 1794 and 1896 in Lebanon, Mississippi, the center of what became known as the Free State of Jones, a dissident county that rebelled against the Confederacy during the Civil War. Both Roberts and Street end up in Cuba, their historical novels concluding with Roberts's *The Single Star: A Novel of Cuba in the '90s* (1949), which centers on the role of expatriate Southerners who became Jamaican planters and fighters in the Cuban War of Independence— framed with an epigraph by José Martí, Cuban patriot-poet killed in the war— and Street's *Mingo Dabney* (1950), which puts his American hero in Cuba in 1895, crossing paths with none other than the revolutionary martyr Martí. These two unsung novels are paradigms of the mediterraneanizing that puts Du Bois and James in the same broad context as Roberts and Street.

Beyond this third and final period of Mediterranean flowering, a group of sources by historians, geographers, and cultural critics that emerged in the 1970s–1990s and beyond, continuing to the present, completes the overview of American Mediterraneans. In contrast to all the earlier historical usages, which approach the Mediterranean comparison as an analytical tool, a method of interpretation in its own right, these largely secondary sources take a historiographical perspective, commenting on and complementing rather than contributing directly to that history. Braudel's terms are "participants" and "observers" of the "historical undertaking," in my terms, perhaps, those who are "mediterraneanizers" and those who study "mediterraneanity" (*MMW*, 16). Yet I consider those late twentieth-century historians as more than footnotes to the story I want to tell. They form part of the generically wide-ranging, cross-disciplinary practice of Mediterranean writing on the Americas, they confirm my identification of key figures in the networks, while also working with different timelines, and they exhibit some of the same erratic use of the Mediterranean terminology that characterizes the whole tradition. Late twentieth-century policy experts point critically to earlier uses of the term Mediterranean as forms of US interventionism (Lester Langley, Jorge I. Dominguez), the enviro-critics warn about past and future environmental degradation in the various American Mediterraneans (Robert H. Gore on the Gulf of Mexico, Tom Andersen and Marilyn Weigold on the Long Island Sound), and the California critics (Davis, Starr, Carey McWilliams) ground their local histories of the region in a Mediterranean hermeneutic. Individual case studies focus on the micro-history of particular uses of the term, such as Matthew Guterl's study of Southern slaveholders and the Caribbean as "a kind of dream world for the South" in the "age of emancipation" (*American Mediterranean*, 21).[15]

The 1976 case study of American policy in the Gulf-Caribbean, Lester Langley's *Struggle for the American Mediterranean*, looks back to "the journalist Stephen Bonsal, father of the last American ambassador to Cuba, [who] employed the term in the title of a popular historical account." The timeline of the term is Langley's focus in the preface: "The phrase *American Mediterranean* refers to turn-of-the-century usage after the Spanish-American War, when many Americans came to think of the Gulf-Caribbean as their 'Mediterranean.' The term was popularized in the protectorate era of the early twentieth century, when Americans looked naturally upon themselves as the carriers of civilization to backward peoples" (n.p.). This is perhaps the most prevalent and dominant circulation of the term from its foreign-policy roots, in which the American Mediterranean, as a direct analogy of Roman supremacy over the actual Mediterranean Sea in late antiquity, assumed US control over the greater Caribbean, and Langley centers the originary meaning of the term in Bonsal's usage to critique the hegemon.

Among contemporary eco-historians, Marilyn Weigold's *The American Mediterranean: An Environmental, Economic and Social History of Long Island Sound* is a model example of how the secondary sources themselves take on key aspects of the Mediterranean concept along with the keywords. Originally published in 1974 by a small Port Washington, New York, publisher, Kennikat Press, Weigold's book was brought out by New York University Press in a new edition in 2004, now titled *The Long Island Sound: A History of*

Its People, Places, and Environment. Only a few references to the omitted term from the original title remain, notably in the back-cover matter, which starts with Daniel Webster's nineteenth-century "christening" of the Long Island Sound as "the 'American Mediterranean'" and ends with the environmental hope that in the twenty-first century, the Sound will become a model urban sea, a protected "our Mediterranean"—making Weigold's book, which might otherwise appear only in a footnote, a paradigmatic example of the history, the strange career of the term itself.[16]

Finally, Kevin Starr speaks for the California mediterraneanizers as a group that self-consciously uses the "mediterranean metaphor" as both evidence and narrative method for the histories they tell. He approaches this Mediterranean-ism as "an interaction of fact and imagination," encapsulated in "the dream of California as a Mediterranean littoral," and then goes on to stress primarily the figurative ("arising from similarities of landscape and clime, this analogy developed into a metaphor for all California offered as a regional civilization") (*ACD*, 408, 370). He applies the metaphor with critical restraint, noting of one of his case studies, Warner's *Our Italy*, "Although it figures in the title, Warner does not overuse the Italian metaphor" (*ACD*, 378). From my perspective Starr thus not only confirms Warner's role as a key California "mediterraneanizing mind" (to which I will return in part 3) but also points to the title as a key textual feature, always subject to modification, including being disappeared. Starr himself, best known for his multivolume series on the history of California, *Americans and the California Dream*, titles one chapter "An American Mediterranean" in his earliest 1973 volume on the state from 1850 to 1915 but drops it in the later 1985 companion volume, which covers Southern California during the same period, while both editions include his key Mediterranean descriptors ("the dream of California as a Mediterranean littoral," the "Mediterranean metaphor" or "analogy").[17] As a late twentieth-century historian, Starr, like Langley and Weigold, who work in different subfields, demonstrates a similar combination of writing in and on the Mediterranean as the earlier mediterraneanizers and their later critics do. In all these ways, Starr and the others provide an apt concluding point for this overview, the history of a volatile hermeneutic, both a term and a concept, shorthand for a protean geo-cultural complex, a real-world metaphor and a counterfactual, defined by its constitutional ephemerality as well as its material elasticity.

Close-up: Mediterranean Networks, Race, and the Paratexts

This bird's-eye view of the networks of mediterraneanizers of the Americas outlines the circulation of their work, set in motion by Humboldt, across genres and media, languages, space, and time. We've already seen how often the Mediterranean references tend to cluster in book titles, forewords, epigraphs, and jacket copy, while scattered throughout the body of the texts. They are thus often relegated to the textual edges, the places where readers read for documentation, sources, and commentary. Even these references, we know, can appear, disappear, and reappear in different editions and translations. To trace such a seemingly elusive, intractable history means reading, as I have said, paratextually. Paying attention to the text-network also necessitates attending to the different genres, the shifting paratexts that often accompany translations but also histories, geographical works, fiction, and nonfiction more broadly. It makes sense in this way that paratextuality turns out to be a key formal element of writing about the American Mediterranean.

"Paratext" is Gérard Genette's term for the accompanying materials in and around a work, including prefaces, illustrations, citations, front and back matter, notes, prepublication advertisements, and author interviews. The literary work rarely appears in a "naked" or "raw" state but rather is presented with these "accompaniments" that, for Genette, are located on the "threshold," " 'an undecided zone' between the inside and the outside."[18] Spatially at the edges of the text, paratexts are also temporally open-ended, if we adopt as point of reference the date of appearance of the text, coming both before ("prenatal") and after ("posthumous") the first or original edition (264). The "duration of the paratext is frequently subject to eclipse" (265), just as "the ways and means of the paratext" are not "uniformly constant" but instead "modified unceasingly, according to periods, cultures, genres, authors, works, editions of the same work" (262). It is an open question whether to consider that they belong to the text or not. Genette thus makes the paratext a centerpiece not despite but because of its anomalous status.[19]

The connectivity that links the Mediterranean networks paratextually identifies what belongs in them but also reveals things that we wouldn't see if the texts were analyzed individually. Recent critical work has taken Genette's bottom line in unexpected directions, going beyond his Euro-canonical frame of reference to consider black American writers and writing, starting with the slave narrative. The vexed role of the paratext in those narratives, so often authorized by white-authored introductions and afterwords, is notorious. Reading paratextually, the critic Brent Edwards historically reorients the framing devices that authenticate the slave narrative through a focus on the prefaces in the black anthologies that were popular during the 1920s. Looking back to Du Bois's experimental anthology of his own writings, *The Souls of Black Folk* (1903) and forward to James Weldon Johnson's 1922 anthology *The Book of American Negro Poetry*, Edwards shows how the preface, "on the textual border," "speaks double," frames blackness through a fundamental instability: it eludes the frame of the nation while framing the unique cultural contribution of the black subject and articulating "an epistemology of blackness." The broad linkage of race and the "paratextual condition" thus extends Genette's undecided zone to accommodate new degrees of uncertainty, the particular way the preface can be an unstable frame of blackness.[20]

The American Mediterranean texts go still further, making use of many of Genette's paratexts, both to repress and to reveal racial content and positions: to tell a story of the racially disappeared, what's subordinated, subtracted, negated, defined by fleeting presence and absence of dominant race discourses. In this the Mediterranean paratexts constitute "a zone not just of transition but of *transaction*: the privileged site of a pragmatics and a strategy, of an action on the public" (Genette and MacLean, "Introduction to the Paratext," 261). In turn, Genette's theory of how paratexts generate meaning through transactions across different sites provides a model for how and why Humboldtian networked connectivity is an advantage when it comes to the connectivity of figures that don't belong to the Humboldt current, by either self-identification or proximity. Stephen Bonsal's appendix G, note 3, "The Race Question," in his 1912 *American Mediterranean* is one example where the question of race and the paratext presents even more of a complication. There Bonsal quotes an excerpt from a work called "White Capital and Colored Labour" by the British governor of Jamaica that functions as commentary, bordering on a manifesto, on the many, often contradictory, references that could be construed as racial scattered through Bonsal's multi-island history. Ventriloquizing the West Indian governor's voice, the appendix advocates against "negrophobists in the United States" and for "the possibilities of racial interaction" in "mixed" or "blended" communities, here the "colored intermediate class" in Jamaica (450, 453, 455). Caribbean race distinctions are maintained while European class divisions do not polarize colonial working conditions into capitalist and proletariat—and with this race-class, periphery-core, foreign-domestic frame, the appendix works transactionally to make the Bonsal text more "pertinent" for the US reader.[21]

Another example of racial transaction is the paratextual network of cross-citation that starts with Humboldt, implicitly referenced in Reclus's map of the Gulf-Caribbean labeled *Méditerranée américaine*, and then moves to Reclus, directly quoted in Bonsal's epigraph to *American Mediterranean*: "The American Mediterranean lands, although lying almost entirely within the tropics, are perfectly accessible to man for all purposes of permanent settlement. In this respect they present an absolute contrast with the vast regions of Africa situated under the same latitude."[22] That Bonsal cites not Humboldt but Reclus, and Reclus only paratextually in the epigraph, is the perfect starting point for this strategic chain. Ending with the assertion of the lack of fit, the "absolute contrast" between the American tropics and those elsewhere, specifically in (black) Africa, this network of citations establishes the reflexive questioning that characterizes the paratextual use of the mediterranean concept. The racial substratum, most visible at historical margins and peripheries rather than as the main event, reflects in a literary register, at the textual level, the historical contexts of several nominally post-race moments in Americas history, past and future.

The paratextual location of the American Mediterranean references, deepens, and complicates the racialization of both the name and the concept. As nodes of a fugitive network that forms most often out at the edges of the texts and their contexts, they branch out to other Mediterranean networks of even looser connectivity. The turn-of-the-century umbrella set of Humboldt-Reclus-Bonsal points forward to the little-known contemporaneous subset of the oceanic geographer Ellen Churchill Semple and the frontier historian Frederick Jackson Turner, as well as backward to the early national geographer Jedidiah Morse; later in the World War decades of the 1930s and '40s, the Caribbean mediterraneanizers Alejo Carpentier and W. Adolphe Roberts provide a pathway to the more speculative mediterraneanizing work of C. L. R. James and W. E. B. Du Bois. Reading paratextually allows us to include texts that might otherwise appear to have nothing in common with the overall network.

To make sense of this unruly archive, crossing time and space, genre and discipline, language and media, the best approach is to follow alternate scales, shifting between macro and micro, from a distanced overview of known mediterraneans and mediterraneanisms to close reading of specific clusters as they explicitly or implicitly self-identify. Accordingly, the next section, part 2, follows that alternating structure, starting with the macro-history of the Mediterranean in nineteenth-century geography and then moving to a close-in look at one early Humboldt current, the intertextual network of Morse-Reclus-Bonsal-Semple. As a typical set of thinkers who only briefly name or indirectly acknowledge him through others in the network, their mediterraneanism is loosely connected to Humboldt, always located at the paratextual edges. This cluster will demonstrate anew the potential in distance from Humboldt, how what doesn't belong to or fit fully in the American Mediterranean orbit is as instrumental in maintaining the historical tradition as the direct descendants.

2

Nineteenth-Century Geographers
and Their Mediterraneans

Humboldt may be the gold standard for the Mediterranean comparison in the Americas, yet, as with his overall reputation in the US, where he has had to be continually rerembered, he is most often honored in the breach. He has the dubious honor of the obligatory naming as founder at the headwaters of the comparative Mediterraneans tradition, who is then summarily dropped. Likewise, Humboldt's equivocal role in the nineteenth-century US geography texts makes him a classic absent presence. He enters in scattered references focused on geographical measurement and oceanic and migration questions, and is most consistently used, ironically, as a source to authenticate questionable data or uncertain metrics. However, Humboldt is never credited as "author" of the term American Mediterranean, which appears instead in the literature fully formed and free-floating, a term circulated as a citation without attribution, origin, or source. It is used as though ready-made, a found object that paradoxically appears to be newly made with each iteration.

Like a term that shifts with rather than fits the times, as Gérard Genette would say, appearing at any moment, an element of the paratext can equally disappear, "definitively or not" ("Introduction to the Paratext," 264). This frequent suppression or eclipse produces the "intermittent character" (264) of the mediterranean paratextual elements that attach themselves to different, sometimes distantly related bodies of mediterranean knowledge. These include the varying geography and history, art and architecture, of the classical Mediterranean, subdivided into the spaces, times, and languages of Greece and Rome, themselves differentially associated with slavery and empire, rebellion and revolution. Extended outward to all the other mediterraneans of the Americas, the network takes off, operates like a chain of translations without an original, sourceless and authorless.

The elusive Humboldt provides a way into reading the nineteenth-century geographers close-up, by following whether and how they invoke his legacy as a mediterraneanizer. Like him, each of the three geographers considered here has been differentially forgotten. Tracking Humboldt's presence-absence reveals their different, sometimes overlapping networks of circulation, and reading paratextually drills down further on the particular ways their mediterraneanity is raced. Samuel Morse, Humboldt's contemporary working during the period of the German scientist's greatest celebrity in the US, relies frequently on Humboldt as a source for multiple measurements in *The American Universal Geography* (1812); Reclus refers famously in *La nouvelle géographie universelle: La terre et les hommes* (1876–94) to Humboldt's 1803–4 journey as a "second discovery of Mexico," along with a map that features the Caribbean labeled as a Humboldtian "Méditerranée américaine" in a chapter titled "Méditerranée Américaine: Golfe du Mexique et Mer des Antilles" (figure 1); and Semple's *American History and Its Geographic Conditions* (1903) includes a long chapter titled "The United States in Relation to the American Mediterranean," but no direct references to Humboldt." For each of these three geographers, the Mediterranean works comparatively, as it does for Humboldt, to connect the particular ("Special," Bernhardus Varenius's term in his 1650 geography, widely read in the US through the early 1800s) and the general (Morse's "Universal," Reclus's "*Universelle*"), by highlighting similarities and differences between analogous entities in different regional locations.[1] As a text-network they display the long space-timeline, beginning even before Humboldt, while they reveal some of the even more unexpected figures at the edges of the texts.

My focus, however, is on how the three variously disrupt the Mediterranean comparison, to different degrees using the Humboldtian frame while questioning its terms. Like that chain of references from Reclus to Bonsal, which stresses the lack of fit between the racial tropics and the Americas, each of the geographers forges a very thin line to Humboldt. Their Humboldtian references correlate suggestively with their own reputations in the field. Morse unsurprisingly, given Humboldt's heyday following the 1804 US visit, uses him the most but never invokes his signature American Mediterranean, and perhaps symptomatically, Morse himself remains the most forgotten node of the network. At the other end of the spectrum, Semple gives Humboldt implicit pride of place, alluding to him in her "American Mediterranean" chapter title but making no other mention, and, for her association with the German geographer Friedrich Ratzel and his environmental determinism, she has been reviled or at least sidelined, then and now. (The Ratzel stain is so ineradicable that Braudel spends time in *The Mediterranean* refuting his own association with that unapologetic brand of geographical determinism.) In the middle, Reclus, by far the most politically progressive, has both the Humboldt cites and the map titled *Méditerranée américaine*, yet is burdened, up to the present moment, with the overdetermined racial terminology that comes as excess baggage with Humboldt. Both Humboldt and Reclus, repeatedly and fleetingly credited at the American Mediterranean headwaters, are celebrated equivocally for their antislavery and anticolonial but not thoroughly antiracist views. All three show the tensions in the dominant geographical paradigms of the nineteenth and early twentieth centuries, the geographical determinism of Morse and Semple responsible for their checkered reputations, then and since, while Reclus's radical break with political forms of authority has overshadowed his geographical work.

Geo-Network 1: Morse and Humboldt

The best-selling early American popular geography textbook *Geography Made Easy* (1784), by Jedidiah Morse, and Morse's magnum opus, *The American Geography* (1789), were part of the wave of geography texts developed by and for the new nation during an era when nationalism and geography went hand in hand. While recognized for contributing to the emerging sense of nationalism in the US, *The American Geography* went into multiple editions that devoted nearly equal time and space to comparative data on the rest of the world.[2] The titles, characteristically the locus of this change, are long and descriptive in the style of the period, from the (modest) 1792 edition, *The American Geography, or A View of the Present Situation of the United States of America*, to the (more grandiose) 1793 edition, *The American Universal Geography, or A View of the Present State of All the Empires, Kingdoms, States, and Republics in the Known World, and of the United States of America in Particular, Vol. 1 of 2: Being a New Edition of the American Geography, Corrected and Greatly Enlarged*. In *The American Universal Geography,* the Mediterranean is accordingly included but not foregrounded, just one among the world hydrogeographical comparators along with other seas, oceans, and rivers.

Much the same goes for Humboldt, who doesn't show up in Morse's works until after 1808, when his writings on the Americas voyage started to become available in English in the US. Their reputations, too, are approximate mirror images: Morse's textbooks dominated the US geography scene through midcentury, the period of Humboldt's greatest celebrity, in the wake of his triumphal 1804 visit to Philadelphia and Washington. But while Morse has since been thoroughly buried, Humboldt, lionized in the US as elsewhere when he died in 1859, has been forgotten and periodically remembered anew, as Morse has not.

Humboldt is known to have admired Morse, whose *The American Universal Geography* (1793) he highly praised.[3] And reciprocally, Morse cites Humboldt as an exceptional European authority in the 1812 *The American Universal Geography*. A new copyright had to be obtained for this edition, because, according to the preface, it had been "so greatly altered . . . in consequence of the great changes, which have taken place in the world, and the flood of information which has been poured upon us."[4] Morse's main object in 1812 is corrective, to remove from "the minds of *his own* countrymen" the "false impressions respecting this country" purveyed by some foreign travelers and philosophers, "Europeans inflated by a conceit of *continental superiority*," naming the Comte de Volney and Buffon among them (preface, iv–v). Alluding here to the debates, especially heated between Buffon and Jefferson, over whether new-world flora, fauna, and peoples were inferior to those of the Old World, Morse turns to Humboldt, but not to the anti-Buffon Humboldt, who argued for the natural productivity of the Americas, nor to the Humboldt of the American Mediterranean. Instead Humboldt is Morse's authority on Mexico; indeed, "Humboldt's interesting description of *Mexico* is the source from which the whole of that article has been derived" (preface, v).

For key measurements about Mexico, Morse cites Humboldt in multiple footnotes, but when the name Humboldt appears in the text proper, it is most often to establish the baseline for data that are notably uncertain and remain inconclusive. So Humboldt is paradoxically Morse's authority on uncertainty. In the Mexico section, on the city of Durango, "Humboldt has given us but few data to determine its breadth" (625), whereas on the Cordillera mountain range: "Humboldt has given us in his travels three perpendicular sections of the table land of Mexico. These are undoubtedly drawn with great accuracy, being the result of barometrical observations in 208 different places" (624). Ultrascrupulous in assessing the accuracy of all his sources, not just Humboldt, Morse not only bemoans the incomplete maps in current geographies, the imperfect state of geographical knowledge, but also pays regular attention to the missing pieces, the "known omissions" and what exists only "in imagination." On the 1793 census of the population of Mexico: "Like similar enumerations . . . it fell far short of the truth: Humboldt says at least one-sixth. The following table contains the result of the census of 1793; also Humboldt's estimate of the population in 1803, founded on that census, on the known omissions . . . and on the natural increase" (619). On possible "points of communication between the Oceans," addressing the long-standing question, attracting "the attention of merchants and statesmen," of the optimal location for an interoceanic canal, Morse reports that "Baron Humboldt" mentions "no less than nine of these"; "he arranges them according to their geographic position. . . . The ninth exists in imagination" (129). Morse's Humboldt, a guardian of what we might call measured uncertainty, goes well beyond the references to the Mediterranean (never preceded by "American"), used only eight times in *The American Universal Geography*. So, too, do their Mediterraneans differ. Morse uses the Mediterranean as a stable reference point, a reliable comparative index (consistently warmer than the Atlantic, for example), whereas Humboldt's *Méditerranée de l'Amérique* is stewarded through a heterogeneous mass of shifting data, hypotheses, and conjectures, not to mention names.

In contrast, Humboldt himself has a more extensive, embedded presence in *The American Universal Geography* as a key source of the Mexico section. Most typical are Morse's repeated qualifying phrases—"Humboldt estimates," "Humboldt supposes," "called by Humboldt," "according to Humboldt"—used both to frame data chains as evidence and to assess their accuracy. In the "Soil and Agriculture" section on Mexico (625–26), the several "Humboldt estimates" culminate in Morse's comment that "the banana of Mexico, called the *plantano-arton*, probably yields more nutriment on a given spot of ground, than any other vegetable" (626). This evocative statement of probability refers back to Humboldt's own extravagant but ultimately equivocal conclusions in *Political Essay on the Kingdom of New Spain* on the counterproductive productivity of bananas in tropical America.[5] "I doubt there is another plant on the globe that can produce such a sizeable amount of food on a small expanse of land," Humboldt writes in a widely circulated paean of praise to the "Torrid Zone" of the New World (*Political Essay*, 515, 518). "What a difference between this product and the cereal graminacea in the most fertile parts of Europe!" (*Political Essay*, 515). Yet the contrast in agricultural output between Old and New Continents ends up reversing itself when Humboldt concludes, in *Personal Narrative*, that "the richness of the [tropical] soil and the vigor of organic life . . . retard the progress of nations in the paths of civilization."[6]

The association of bananas and barbarism has produced a long Humboldtian legacy of popular-academic "banana cultures," intertwining ideas about race, nation, and civilization. Humboldt's bananas circulated widely, his observations about bananas in tropical America requoted in speeches (for example, by the Eliot Professor of Greek Literature at Harvard, Edward Everett, in 1824) and geographies. Morse was one of the earliest geographers to purvey this "bio-geographical and social stratigraphy," a human geography based on Humboldt's homology in the "Geography of Plants," where social characteristics and cultural distinctions are derived from geo-location in the highlands or lowlands. Morse does so, notably, by seizing on Humboldt's *estimate* of the productivity of the banana and its sociopolitical consequences.[7]

Despite these gestures toward incorporating uncertainty into his geography, Morse ultimately lacks the Humboldtian speculative spirit. A key indicator: Morse never uses the fundamentally counterfactual term American Mediterranean, with all its built-in conjecture, in any of the many editions of his *American Universal Geography*. Morse's Humboldt is the source of authority on conjectures and suppositions, but they are no more than that, inconclusive data awaiting confirmation or refutation, with no further opening, meaning, or possibility, no Humboldtian futurity. In contrast, even Edward Everett's 1824 *Oration Delivered at Plymouth* comments briefly, in relation to Humboldt's interest in the migrations of plants and the languages that name them, on their "age that speculates, and speculates to important purpose, on the races of fossil animals . . . and which compares the dialects of languages, . . . which ceased to be spoken a thousand years ago importantly." Similarly, the Scottish Enlightenment historian William Robertson offers a brief mention of a Mediterranean comparison that "may" obtain in his *History of America* (1778): "In all of these respects America may bear a comparison with the other quarters of the globe. The gulf of Mexico, which flows in between North and South America, may be considered as a Mediterranean sea, which opens a maritime commerce with all the fertile countries by which it is encircled." Robertson, associated with the genre of conjectural history, was one of the contemporary writers from whom Morse is thought to have borrowed liberally during this period before international copyright and in that context makes a suggestive figure at the edges of this early geo-network, bringing in the possible cross-citation between his work and Morse's.[8]

When Morse says, echoing both Everett and Robertson, "it may be conjectured" (10) and "it is not improbable" (11), there's no follow-up comparable to theirs, Everett's examples of fossils and dialects, Robertson's of commerce. Seemingly incurious, Morse approaches the Mediterranean simply as a hydro-geographical location, with no special status, just one among many of the world's comparator bodies of water. When he first mentions it in the introduction in the context of the Roman historian Herodotus, he says, rather dismissively, "It seems rational to conclude that by the *sea* was meant no more than the Mediterranean" (12). The term American Mediterranean is thus tellingly absent, a sign of the missing Humboldtian conjectural comparative thinking. Possibly, we might speculate, Morse has been forgotten not only because of his racial/environmental positions but also because he doesn't fit or travel readily with the Humboldt current.

Geo-Network 2: Reclus and Bonsal

In contrast, Reclus's nineteen-volume *La nouvelle géographie universelle: La terre et les hommes* (1876–94) includes in volume 17, *Indes occidentales: Mexique, Isthmes Américains, Antilles*, the chapter "Méditerranée américaine" and a map of the Gulf of Mexico–Caribbean Sea with the same title. In the English edition, *The Earth and Its Inhabitants: The Universal Geography*, which reverses the order of the French title, the "American Mediterranean" appears in volume 2, *Mexico, Central America, the West Indies*.[9] Humboldt appears in scattered comments throughout this volume, but in the opening reference in chapter 2, "Mexico," to his 1803–4 journey as a "second discovery of Mexico" (*EI*, 17)—celebratory words freighted with overtones of the conquest—Reclus sets up the double-edged comparisons that shape his Mediterranean.

Reclus is, characteristically for the Mediterranean context, recirculating an earlier line, footnoting (in the French edition only) two sources for his comment that "Humboldt's journey has been described as [*à été qualifié de*] a 'second discovery of Mexico'" (*EI*, 17; *NG*, 25). On one hand he complicates the timeline of new-world second-ness when he praises "Humboldt's labours as a sort of revelation": "after the long sleep imposed upon Mexico by the system of absolute monopoly . . . he showed what the Spanish colony was capable of at the very time when its emancipation was already at hand" ("*il montra ce que pourrait devenir la colonie espagnole au jour de l'émancipation déjà prochaine*"; *EI*, 18; *NG*, 26). The multiple temporalities embedded in both the French and the English terms for time, "*déjà prochaine*," capture the fluid possibilities of a mediterraneanizing history. Prophecy and the future are "already at hand," and the conditional "*pourrait devenir*" is the futurist tense, the "would be able to become," of the unfinished project of emancipation for which conditions would be required. There is still hope in this phrase, making clear the ideological reason for the disjunctive temporality.

On the other hand, Reclus sets out the limits of the Mediterranean comparison at the very outset of the volume: chapter 1, "General Survey" (*Vue d'Ensemble*), opens with "*Les régions, insulaires and péninsulaires, qui baigne la double méditerranée américaine . . . constituent une partie bien distincte*" ("The insular and peninsular regions that are bathed by the double American Mediterranean . . . form a perfectly distinct section"; *NG*, 1; *EI*, 1), a geographical assertion that is undercut by what soon follows. The 1897 Augustus Keane translation reads, "The so-called 'Mediterranean' of the New World, which like the Mediterranean of the eastern hemisphere, is divided into secondary basins, but which in other respects presents little resemblance to that great inland sea" ("*La grande méditerranée du Nouveau Monde, d'ailleurs peu semblable de forme à celle de l'Ancien Monde*"; *EI*, 1; *NG*, 2). The English "so-called" adds a further layer to the skeptical language of the comparison, which asserts the lack of resemblance between the two seas supposedly being compared.

Following a few paragraphs after this discrepant comparison, the passage that Bonsal cites as his epigraph reiterates the lack of fit, the "absolute contrast" ("*contraste d'une manière absolue*"; *EI*, 2; *NG*, 3) between the tropics of the Mediterranean latitudes in the Old and New Worlds. Reclus's Americas do not align with the conventional European mirror image of themselves, even when it comes to their racial views of the tropics. Not only is the climate of "tropical America" more moderate, the vegetation more abundant than that of Saharan Africa, but also the "white race . . . itself" ("le blanc lui-même," *EI*, 2; *NG*, 4) "has adapted" ("*s'accommoder*," *EI*, 2; *NG*, 4) to the climate, notably in Cuba and Puerto Rico. In the highlands of Mexico, "offering a climate analogous to that of temperate Europe" ("offrant un climat analogue à celui de l'Europe tempérée"; *EI*, 3; *NG*, 4), "flourishing European colonies have been founded" ("des colonies prospères de Européens se sont fondées"; *EI*, 3; *NG* 4), giving "their usages, language and culture" ("*moeurs, langue et civilisation*"; *EI* 3; *NG*, 4) to the aboriginal populations. At the same time that Reclus disavows some of the key assumptions in the dominant discourse of environmental determinism—the inferiority of new-world nature, for example—this passage, as elsewhere, resubscribes to its basic thinking. So, too, does he cite, along with Humboldt, the German apostle of geo-determinism, Friedrich Ratzel, who plays a role in one of the later American Mediterranean networks we'll see in the next section, "Geo-Network 3" (see *NG*, 220n1, on *Aus Mexico*).

Reclus (1830–1905) wrote and published his multivolume geography in mid-to-late life (1876–94) with the authority of both the revolutionary and the academic credentials he ultimately earned. Both voices, that of the decorated geographer and that of the political outsider, are audible, conflicting at times, inside the text if not outside. Exiled from France following the 1871 Paris Commune, Reclus was nonetheless honored with the gold medal of the Paris Geographical Society in 1892 for *La nouvelle géographie universelle*. The English edition appeared almost simultaneously with the French, edited and translated in part by the British anthropologist Augustus Henry Keane, who reported that "advance proofs were regularly supplied to [him] by Messrs. Hachette, the Paris publishers." Keane's prominent role as editor-translator (he shared the editing with the cartographer Ernest George Ravenstein) reflects the growing importance of the field of geography to anthropological "students of man" interested in human origins (and divided over the issue of whether there is one or more human species).[10] Influenced by the noted geographer Carl Ritter (credited with Humboldt as one of the founders of modern geography), whose lectures Reclus attended in Berlin between 1849 and 1850, Reclus is said to have single-handedly completed the project Ritter left unfinished, a world regional geography. Reclus retrofits Ritter's religious teleology to his own anarchist vision of organic regions joined in decentralized harmony, producing a radical new adaptation of the large-scale work of global regional synthesis.

Today, almost reversing his divided nineteenth-century reputation, Reclus is remembered primarily as an anarchist thinker while his geographical work gains less consistent attention, undergoing periodic revival. One of those revivals just happens to be happening right now, in the first two decades of the twenty-first century. With Humboldt, Reclus remains among the few "geographers of exception," named and honored by the French geographer Jean-Baptiste Arrault in 2006 with American Mediterranean founding credentials. The historical geographer Kent Mathewson reads Reclus in a 2016 article as a Latin Americanist geographer and zeroes in specifically on the chapter titled "American Mediterranean" in *Nouvelle géographie universelle*. "It is uncertain," notes Mathewson, "if Reclus was the first to use this apt characterization, but after the Spanish-American War the concept was evident in the emerging North American geo-political discourse."[11] Yet Reclus, so famous for his radical, anticolonial politics, may be semi-sabotaged by his association with Humboldt's Mediterranean concept. Reclus's adaptation of it as an umbrella term for mapping nature and culture, the human and nonhuman elements of a geographical space-time, creates unacknowledged tensions between the differing views of race underlying its physical and historical geographies.

Reclus's American Mediterranean operates primarily as a putatively neutral hydro-geographical analytic, measuring depth, tides and currents, temperature, salinity, and the frequency of hurricanes. Each chapter of the volume, dedicated to a different location in the region, from Mexico, Guatemala, and Panama to Cuba, Jamaica, and Haiti, opens with the physical features of mountains, rivers, volcanoes (if there are any), winds and rains, and then moves to the human inhabitants: their language, race, and political, economic, and cultural history. The maps, too, register this movement by superimposing separate geo- and human histories onto various sectional views of the Gulf-Caribbean. Some maps display physical features, ocean depths and currents, while others isolate historical features, but all use a template of the same basic area map, usually with the coordinates "West of Greenwich" and "West of Paris," on the two horizontal axes, top and bottom. The map labeled *American Mediterranean* at the beginning of the chapter of that title displays watersheds draining to the ocean and at the end of the chapter is twinned with one of several maps throughout the volume showing the "preponderance of races" (figures 1–3).

The maps, together with other paratextual elements, the appendices and running headnotes, provide a stripped-down and simplified visual translation of or index to the complexities of the text. In an account of hurricanes in the physical geography of the American Mediterranean chapter, for example, Reclus addresses the linguistic origin of the term, without the extended analysis he regularly provides in the human history sections. "The American Mediterranean is also exposed to hurricanes, whose very Carib name (*hurakan, huiranvucan*) shows that the European navigators regarded these atmospheric disturbances as peculiar to the West Indian waters" (*EI*, 345). In contrast to this single statement, lacking commentary or reflection, when he invokes the Caribs in the context of human geography, under the heading "*Population des Antilles*" in the French edition (*NG*, 643–49), "Inhabitants of West Indies" in the English edition (*EI*, 350–53), the language question is foregrounded, extended in the text. Analyzing the speech "of all the local jargons," Reclus compares "the Negro English patois" to "the French creole" ("less harmonious but . . . equally lively and terse" and notes retentions of "a few Carib and Goajir terms" (*EI*, 353). The split between the two approaches, physical and human geography, is even more starkly visible in the maps, which display either natural phenomena like ocean currents, depths, and temperature, or cultural elements, such as the predominant races around the Gulf of Mexico and the Caribbean Sea. The maps rely on available terminology to label their measurements—"*Indiens purs*," on a map of the races of Central America, for example, that mirror the often contradictory intersections between and among language and race, geography and history, in the text—along with a few telling differences between the French original and Keane's English translation.

Reclus summarizes, and where necessary hypothesizes about, the tumultuous history, known and unknown, before and after the conquest, in the region, "physically distinct from the continental masses of north and south" ("*bien distincte des masses continentals, du Nord et du Sud, l'Amérique méditerranéenne . . . elle-même*"; *EI*, 3; *NG*, 4). The name, with the feminine gender, of course appears only in the French and points the attentive English-speaking reader to Reclus's own systematic attention to language as an index of sociopolitical identity: "The great diversity of languages formerly spoken in the Antilles and still current in Mexico and the isthmuses is sufficient evidence of long isolation and dispersion in the fragmentary world lying between the northern and southern continents. . . . Communications were rare and difficult, and no ethnical cohesion had been developed amongst these isolated elements" (*EI*, 3). Only with the discovery and conquest as temporal reference points, Reclus argues, does "a certain unity, at least in a political sense" ("*au moins unité politique*"; *EI*, 4; *NG*, 7) become possible. But political unity comes up against racial divisions produced by the different environmental and historical conditions of national independence for the "Hispano-American race" in Spanish America and "Anglo-Saxon America" (*EI*, 10). Those differences, Reclus concludes repeatedly in this volume defined by the *Méditerranée américaine*, come down to the Indigenous population, exterminated in the United States and "assimilated" (*EI*, 10) in all the Spanish-speaking regions under the Mediterranean umbrella. His mediterraneanizing method, attentive to the unstable languages for race that combine ethnicity with place, allows for the cultural and the geographical determinants shaping history to diverge rather than reinforce one another.

The environmental influence assumed in Reclus's geo-narrative of physical fragmentation of terrain and climate on land and sea crosses here with the human geography of tribes and nations. The crossing produces an explicit racial component in the language of the French original that is missing in the translation. The precontact Indians, who, according to Bernal Diaz del Castillo (the source footnoted in the French but not in the English version), traveled in canoes big enough for fifty, over time forgot their "common descent" ("*ceux qui étaient frères de race*"; *EI*, 4; *NG*, 7). This is one of several places in the texts, the original and the translation, where the language of race in French contrasts with the more abstract, generalized terms, seemingly raceless, used by the English translator. Elsewhere as well the available terms in each language for racial mixing further complicate the picture through the derogatory meaning associated with terms in English as opposed to French and Spanish. We can hear that difference reflected in Reclus's "*métisses*," "*une sous-race nouvelle, . . . ce type nouveau, . . . cette race mêlée*" (*NG*, 643, 645) and the translator's "half-breeds," "mongrel race" (*EI*, 351, 352). The raceless and the racist overtones alternate in the Keane translation, in marked contrast to Reclus's own consistent linguistic embrace, in French, of biological and cultural blending of races and ethnic groups.

Biographically, Reclus is said to have solidified his antislavery views during a brief period of self-exile in Louisiana, from 1853 to 1855, following the 1851 coup d'état of Louis-Napoléon. In the bilingual city of New Orleans, he worked as a tutor to the children of Septime Fortier on their upriver sugar plantation, Félicité. The experience of witnessing firsthand a slave auction and the punishment regime of the plantation made Reclus into a vocal advocate of radical abolitionism at the time and a lifelong proponent of *métissage*—not the whitening of *mestizaje*—as a solution to the long history of race conflict in the Americas. He published several short pieces, framed as travel narratives, an extended critique of the plantation system that intersected with his own anticlericalism, anticolonialism, and anticapitalism. The 1855 "Fragment d'un voyage à la Nouvelle Orléans," published in the popular French journal *Le tour du monde*, includes a searing account of a slave market.

At the same time, Reclus further developed his environmental understanding of the Mississippi geography and the river-based economy of New Orleans, which he compared to "an enormous raft on the river's water" in "Le Mississippi, Études et souvenirs" (1859). Finally, most relevant to the tradition of engaged geography in *La nouvelle géographie universelle*, Reclus's writings after he returned to France in 1857 confirmed his endorsement of what the historical geographer Federico Ferretti calls "generalized miscegenation" to counter the intertwined problems of race and class in the "disguised slavery" following formal emancipation and juridical equality. In his final book, published posthumously in 1908, *L'homme et la terre*, Reclus concludes: "Despite what is being said, the population of the United States, red, white and black, is ready for this despised evolution called miscegenation. . . . Finally, among Americans, misery often associates the wretched of the two races. In the big army of revindications, Blacks and Whites march side by side, and the shared sufferings made the colour diversity disappear."[12]

Much the same focus on the possibilities of *métissage* forms a through-thread linking the chapters and locations of the West Indies volume. Under the heading "*La Méditerranée américaine*" in chapters 1 and 6, Reclus writes with special attention to the different histories of interracial sexuality in the Americas. The predominant legacy of Indigenous assimilation in the south of "*les Néo-Latins*" versus extermination in the north of "*les Néo-Saxons*," together with the "preponderance of the Negro race in the Antilles" corresponding to that of "the Indians in Mexico and Central America," produces different conditions for racial intermixture (*NG*,14; *EI*, 9). In Central America, the Spaniards, once "abominable" masters of the aborigines, "are now merged with them under the name of *ladinos*" ("*se confondent maintenant avec eux sous le nom de 'ladinos'*"; *EI*, 9; *NG*, 13); and a bit later, "the very term *ladino*, has become synonymous with 'enlightened' or 'civilised' throughout Central America" (*EI*, 11). Similarly, throughout "*L'Amérique dite 'latine', qui est en même temps l'Amérique polygénique*" (*NG*, 15), the names in Reclus's French, translated literally as America called or known as "Latin," which is at the same time polygenic or heterogeneous (the word used in Keane's translation, *EI*, 10) America, convey his conclusion, in English, that "crossings and common usages have effected a reconciliation between various races which were formerly hostile, and even totally alien, to each other" (*EI*, 10). Notably, these positive conclusions rest on the evidence of language itself, what racial categories are called, their names and terms.

The explicitly racial brotherhood that links the Latinness of the Americas with the Indigenous via the name *ladino* accords with the ultimate outcome of the history sketched in the last third of the General Survey at the opening of Reclus's West Indies volume. It is a history produced by forces intertwining both language and race. Reclus traces the enslavement and "extermination" of one "race" and its replacement by "another race" (*EI* 8), "the negro race" ("*la race africaine*"; *EI*, 9; *NG*, 12); the "endless crossings" ("*les croisements à l'infini*"; *EI*, 9; *NG*, 13) of blood and language through which "the native dialects of the slaves disappeared [*les dialects africains des esclaves se perdirent*] . . . and the slaves rapidly adopted the languages of their Spanish, French, or English owners" to become "the numerically dominant race" (*EI*, 9; *NG*, 13). The intertwined roles of racial, national, and linguistic affiliations point for Reclus even further into future, when he predicts that English would not become the mother tongue of all the Americas, as some asserted— but that the "growing influence" of the United States, "the powerful northern confederacy," is already emerging as the new threat to the "Latinised peoples of America" (*EI*, 12, 10).

The factors contributing to these changing power relations between masters and slaves, African and Indigenous, reflect the forces of both the physical and social environment. But the terms of Reclus's environmentalism differ a little in the original text, which includes "*langage*" as the first cultural factor, and the translation, which omits it entirely. In English: "But if in this respect, as well as in the usages and outward forms of civilization, they were brought under European influences, their physical constitution was better suited for the environment of the West Indies" (*EI*, 9); in French: "*mais si, par le langage, aussi bien que par le genre de vie et les dehors de la civilization, ils subirent l'ascendant des Européens, ils ont su mieux que ceux-ci s'accommoder aux milieu des Antilles, et finalement ils sont devenus la race prépondérante*" (*NG*, 13). The French prioritizes the role of "*langage*" in the European civilizational mix, while the English prioritizes "physical constitution" in acclimatization, and the two versions similarly, equivocally, stress environmental adaptation as both a natural and a cultural phenomenon.

Reclus follows up on this equivocal environmentalism with an unequivocal endorsement of political unity achieved through human agency. Here in the New World, which has become "an ethnological dependency of the African Continent" ("*au point de vue ethnologique, la dépendance du continent africaine*"; *EI*, 9; *NG*, 13), "by a sort of retributive justice, the negro race has even acquired political autonomy in the large island of Haiti" ("*par un juste retour de choses l'une des communautés politiques des Antilles est composée d'Africains indépendantes*"; *EI*, 9; *NG*, 13). The French counterpoints the two opposed forces, environmental and human, "*la dépendance du continent africaine*" and "*d'Africains indépendantes*," while the English injects "the negro race" as a third term, a substitute for "*Africains indépendantes*," privileging nature over culture.

The echoes of environmental determinism that can thus be heard especially loudly through the translation of Reclus's geohistory of race and language in the West Indies are countered here by the complex politics of national revolution, specifically the event of world-historic importance in 1799. The accompanying illustrations both reduce and amplify the complexities— ambiguities and contradictions—of Reclus's account of race in *La Méditerranée américaine*. The maps simplify by separating out and isolating competing elements ("race" as a single metric in figures 2–3), whereas the engravings, from unpeopled landscape panoramas, viewed from a distance, to small-scale human figures grouped in middle-ground images of urban and rural scenes, to close-up ethnographic portraits, enshrine and deepen the racial contradictions (figures 16–20). While the racially unidentified figures pictured working in the countryside are too far-off for us to see the details of their generic period costume, the Black, Indigenous, and Creole subjects are often shown in full native regalia, and only "*les Indiens*" are half-naked. (figures 18–20) The portraits, especially, draw on crude, visual stereotypes that conflict with the nuance of Reclus's text and remind us that he, unlike Humboldt, did not have the means to reproduce his own drawings (and even Humboldt nearly bankrupted himself in so doing) and therefore relied on the available work of others, photographers and commercial artists, with all the well-known problems in those representations.

Revealingly, the text may even push back against the racial hierarchies and visual stereotypes of the illustrations. Immediately following the drawing *The Snake-Catcher and Charcoal Girl, Martinique* (figure 18), the chapter titled the "American Mediterranean" concludes with a broad paean to the world-historical event of the Haitian Revolution. Reclus, who had earlier, in the opening chapter, championed its outcome (the "retributive justice [by which] the negro race has even acquired political autonomy in the large island of Haiti" [*EI*, 9]), creates an extended timeline of the slave revolt that became a national revolution. It started when, "notwithstanding the measures taken to prevent combinations and conspiracies," the slaves of Saint-Domingue, forced to abandon their original languages and affiliations, united "to exercise their political rights in 1790" and declare their own emancipation from slavery and independence from France. "This was the beginning of the new era for the Antilles," and "the work of social transformation was completed in 1886, when the last slave was liberated in Cuba" (*EI*, 352). Human agency triumphs politically in the anticolonial context, but Reclus's race history of the West Indies ends on an equivocal note, erasing difference and producing "*les 'créoles' des Antilles*" ("the Antillean 'Creoles'"), "*blancs ou gens de couleur*" ("whether white or coloured"), "*malgré les différences d'origine*" ("despite differences of origin"), "*offrant certaines ressemblances dues au milier*" ("present certain outward resemblances, due to their common environment"; *NG*, 646; *EI*, 352).

From this perspective, Reclus's place of honor in the epigraph at the head of Bonsal's *American Mediterranean* counts as yet another dubious distinction. Bonsal played a major role as a vocal advocate of US interests, economic and political, in "our Mediterranean" (*AM*, 3–4, 6–7), as he repeatedly refers to the American Mediterranean. This is surely not Reclus's Méditerranée américaine. Bookended by opening and closing meditations on the term that provides the title, Bonsal's history-travelogue of the "Caribbean world," with chapters on each island nation, boils down to an argument, as the Panama Canal was being completed, for a controlling American influence in the region. An introductory note celebrates "his many voyages in the American Mediterranean, where "the genius of the American people" has produced "the possibilities of the new world that borders the great South Sea to which the shipping and the industries of two hemispheres will soon penetrate through the water-gates of Panama" (*AM*, xiii); by the final chapter he asserts, "a new era is dawning in that part of the world which lies just outside our gates and which is called, with increasing frequency, the American Indies and the American Mediterranean" (*AM*, 399). For such a US booster as Bonsal to make Reclus the source of his epigraph may be unlikely but not unheard of, given other proximate instances of misappropriation via translation. Humboldt was, to his own and others' chagrin, reincarnated as a pro-slavery advocate in one notorious translation, by a rabid Southerner, of his Cuba volume.[13]

Reclus is thus, on all of these fronts, a bellwether for the protean legacy of Humboldt's mediterraneanism. Constrained by the sanitized appeal to the American Mediterranean concept as a physical geography, even Reclus's relatively restrained use of the term brings out the bio-determinism that he rejects in accounting for the human history of the Mediterranean. While not a perfect correlation, this demonstrates the limited historicizing of the geographical discourse and the Mediterranean analogy itself. The plot thickens in the English translation, which reduces the more frequent appearance of "la Méditerranée américaine" in the French version; the missing references may also dispense with, or at a minimum blunt, the pointed historical association, embedded in the French usage, of region with the extermination of the native population.[14] Reclus dramatizes the challenges of navigating the American Mediterranean as a historical geography, very much the same vexed interdisciplinary zone that, as we'll see, in a different professional and institutional context, Semple and Turner found so difficult to occupy.

Geo-Network 3: Semple and Turner

Ellen Churchill Semple's first book, *American History and Its Geographic Conditions* (1903), a landmark in American historical geography, the subfield linking human history to physical geography, features a chapter called "The United States in Relation to the American Mediterranean"—key to the Semple node in the Humboldt network of mediterraneanizers.[15] She is one of those acolytes who references Humboldt only indirectly through the term he coined. Following Humboldtian logic, Semple saw ocean basins as coherent frames for historical investigation. Chapter 18 advances her view of the differing "civilizations" in "the two Mediterraneans"—"the Old World Mediterranean . . . marked above everything else by the constant recurrence of Asiatic influences emanating from the Phoenicians, Syrians, Persians, Saracens, and Turks; in the New World sea . . . the youngest, freshest, most progressive civilization of the Anglo-Saxon race" (*AH*, 400). The point of this comparative geohistory is its future "promise that . . . the geographical location of the United States in the American Mediterranean will be exploited to the full limits of its possibilities" (*AH*, 419). Placed near the end of the book, this penultimate chapter, paired with the final one, "The United States as a Pacific Ocean Power" (*AH*, 420–35), endorses the bottom line for Semple: to promote the Pacific Ocean as a future American Mediterranean. With this surprising move, Semple swims against the dominant current among her contemporaries, most of whom looked to the Caribbean as their one and only American Mediterranean. Instead Semple posits this other, still-unknown oceanic future in US expansion across the Pacific as a counterpart to the Gulf-Caribbean basin. She touts the proposed interoceanic canal and "the outlook of piercing the Isthmus" for extending the Gulf coast, south-facing advantage to "the whole Pacific coast of the two continents." The connector between the two creates "the promise of a new historical era for the American Mediterranean" (*AH*, 398).

The book opens as well as closes with that prediction, based on the recurrent historical rise and decline of both Mediterraneans. They "regained their importance when they became avenues to the Pacific, and it is this world ocean which is to determine the final significance of the Caribbean Sea and Gulf of Mexico" (*AH*, 399). Semple, who had a lifelong passion for linking history and geography, having earned both her BA and her MA in history at Vassar and studied at the University of Leipzig under the German anthropogeographer Friedrich Ratzel, sought to make good on that connection throughout her first book. A sweeping narrative of "American history" through its "geographic conditions," the 1903 book describes how the natural environment of the US had conditioned the course of American history. Nineteen chapters, thirteen of which feature a variant of the word *geography* in their titles, trace in chronological order the nation's major historical events, figures, and epochs, from the "discoverers and colonizers" (*AH*, 1), to the Louisiana Purchase, the War of 1812, and the Civil War, to westward expansion, immigration, and urbanization. Semple wanted the connection between history and geography to temper the determinism of physical geography with the agency of human history, and to inject geography into historiography. But instead she became embroiled in, consumed by, and ultimately compromised by debates over the environmental determinism of Ratzel in his best-known work, *Anthropogeographie* (1882, 1891). Asked by Ratzel to translate it, Semple produced her own best-known and most controversial work, *Influences of Geographic Environment on the Basis of Ratzel's System of Anthropo-geography* (1911). As a result, her acknowledged source and mentor left her vulnerable to charges of geographical and racial determinism.[16]

Semple's influence is debated, then and now, around the nature and extent of her own environmentalism. Her reputation has fluctuated in parallel, never fully escaping the taint of the Ratzel tar brush. None of her considerable accomplishments—her influential early articles, especially her most personal work, reflecting her Kentucky birthplace, "The Anglo-Saxons of the Kentucky Mountains" (1901), her 1911 *Influences of Geographic Environment* introducing Ratzel's work to an English-speaking intellectual community, or her late work, *The Geography of the Mediterranean Region* (1931)—ultimately mitigated the critique. In fact, *Influences*, which Semple calls "an adapted restatement" rather than a literal translation (*IG*, v), initially garnered a positive reception for its perceived scientific qualities and nomothetic approach. Oddly enough, this is the one work where Semple openly references Humboldt, in a list in the preface of forerunners who, like Ratzel, she says, put his subject on "a secure scientific basis" (*IG*, v). Despite this effort to distance herself from Ratzel the scientific outlier and instead to burnish his reputation as a Humboldtian, the book later earned Semple the label "the modern apostle of determinism."[17] Even her notoriety contributes to the ongoing process of tearing down and then re-enshrining the icon.

Semple's professional career was full of such public displays of disaffection. "Miss" Semple, elected in 1921 the first female president of the Association of American Geographers, never received a doctorate from Leipzig, where she studied under Ratzel from 1891 to 1892 and again in 1895 (women were not permitted to matriculate). Although she lectured at the University of Chicago, teaching every other year from 1906 to 1920, she did not have a permanent academic appointment until 1922, when she was hired at Clark University, where she was paid significantly less than her male peers.[18] Even a promising partnership with the renowned historian Frederick Jackson Turner, who organized a session of historians and geographers, including Semple, at the 1907 annual meeting of the American Historical Association (AHA) in Madison, Wisconsin, failed to produce the interdisciplinary recognition that both he and Semple hoped for. Returning to the circumstances of that failed collaboration and what it says about the shifting sands of Semple's always qualified reputation, as well about her mediterraneanism, will help me to close this section.

Given the career-long pressure on Semple to navigate the fallout of Ratzelean determinism, it's not unreasonable to read the primacy of history in her 1903 *American History and Its Geographic Conditions* as a cover for the book's foundation in geography—and the American Mediterranean as the locus of the cover-up. Typical of Semple's twin use of history to distance herself from full-scale geographical determinism and of geography to naturalize the history of conquest and empire, she portrays the Mediterranean as a palimpsest of historical inevitabilities. Her American Mediterranean justifies imperial expansion in the present by appealing to historical precedent in the past and to predict the future—risking charges of determinism, whether by history or geography. A close reading of Semple's language in chapter 18, "The United States in Relation to the American Mediterranean," reveals the gyrations she goes through to make good on the opening line of the book: "The most important geographical fact in the past history of the United States has been their location on the Atlantic opposite Europe; and the most important geographical fact in lending a distinctive character to their future history will probably be their location on the Pacific opposite Asia" (*AH*, 1).

Heralded by that "probably," Semple's American Mediterranean is a region of geographical possibility and historical promise, yet one simultaneously regulated by "what we may call the politico-geographical law of gravity" (*AH*, 403). The text of the American Mediterranean chapter is filled with variations on that formula, alternately the "law" or "principle" of "geo-location," "of being" (*AH*, 404). The language is designed to parse the degree of determinism, how close to total it is, and thereby to soften the equation between geography and destiny. This means mobilizing a variety of linguistic qualifiers. The basins of both Mediterraneans follow "different lines of development, *resulting largely from* differences of geographical location" (*AH*, 399–400, my emphasis). Both Mediterraneans "therefore *seem destined* by nature as great transit basins" (*AH*, 401, my emphasis). Although all oceanic land-masses, islands, and continents obey the laws or principles of their geographical being, Semple, using another strategy, stresses the *historical* variation across time and space in these Mediterranean "operations." She identifies a worldwide range of islands whose comparative isolation makes them "detached physically and detachable politically," from the Pacific Ocean geo-location of the American annexation of Hawaii to Corsica, Cyprus, and Sicily, to the "island fragments of broken empires" in the Caribbean Sea (*AH*, 403, 404).

The most extended politico-geographical account in the chapter follows the "natural expansion of the American people" in the Caribbean. The focus is on the island of Cuba, its role in the nineteenth-century conflict over slavery and, most important, in relation to the future endpoint of an interoceanic canal to connect the Atlantic and Pacific shores of the US. This timeline turns on the 1898 Cuban-Spanish-American war that "raised our geographical status in the American Mediterranean, magnified our interest in the canal and at the same time increased our power to control it" (*AH*, 405, 409). What's most striking here is, first, how history overtakes and eclipses geography as the dominant force and, second, how their collective determinism is muted, along with the racial component for which Semple became so controversial. She aims for a nominally raceless historical geography, and indeed the only notable racial reference in the American Mediterranean chapter is to the "Anglo-Saxon republic and the steadily developed aptitude of its citizens for vast enterprises" (*AH*, 412).

If we judge from a positive review of the book, in *the American Historical Review*, by the historian Albert Bushnell Hart, Semple succeeded. Reviewing her book in 1904 along with Albert Perry Brigham's *Geographic Influences in American History*, Hart praises both books for the relationships they propose between geography and history—a connection too little noticed by experts in either subject. Himself a leading American historian, one of the first professionally trained generation, Hart recognized, albeit in patronizing terms, how "Miss Semple" worked to subordinate geography as the "handmaid" of history, whereas "Professor Brigham," a geologist, has it the other way around. "Miss Semple's book is larger, more ambitious and more distinctly historical"; "Miss Semple concerns herself with the human element, with man upon the land . . . [and] . . . has constantly in mind not so much the face of the country as the movement of people across it."[19] Semple has succeeded not only in centering human history but also in foregrounding the nation rather than race and ethnicity. Most striking for my focus, Hart zeroes in on Semple's oceanic vision, where "America is part of the earth surface, connected rather than divided by great oceans," and further singles out as "a fair example of her conception, the term 'American Mediterranean', which she applies to the Gulf of Mexico" (572). The racial substratum of the term is subsumed by the more immediate academic debate at this moment in 1904 over the relations between history and geography, and so Hart elevates Semple for her geographical description that follows the "historical advance of the frontier rather than by a pre-determined geological system" (572).

Eight years later in 1911, Semple's Ratzel book, which came close to inverting this strategy, made race impossible to ignore. The preface to *Influences of Geographic Environment*, as we have already seen, declares the book an adapted restatement rather than literal translation of Ratzel's *Anthropogeographie* and asserts that "the writer" (as she refers to herself in the third person throughout) does not subscribe to Ratzel's account of the reciprocal relations of environment and society, a now-outdated appropriation of Herbert Spencer's organic theory (*IG*, vi–viii): "The writer speaks of geographic factors and influences, shuns the word geographic determinant, and speaks with extreme caution of geographic control" (*IG*, viii). Semple's own method is instead "to compare typical peoples of all races and all stages of cultural development, living under similar geographic conditions" (*IG*, vii). Inferring that such similarities are "due to environment and not to race," Semple concludes that "the race factor" is "eliminated for certain large classes of social and historical phenomena" (*IG*, vii). For all that, the preface, which regularly uses an incompatible language of determinism, is at odds with the text itself, as several commentators have noted.

Because of its notoriety, these contradictions underwrite this most controversial of Semple's books, the one that continued to appear on undergraduate reading lists in England through the 1960s, as some speculate.[20] In contrast, her Mediterranean work, including the 1931 *The Geography of the Mediterranean Region: Its Relation to Ancient History* and the 1933 *Manual to Accompany American History and Its Geographic Conditions* (in collaboration with Clarence Fielden Jones), spanned her lifetime but has been less career defining. In this sense Semple's reputation as an internationally renowned geographer and pioneer in the study of human-environment interaction may best be traced as a series of failures or forgetteries, through the ups and downs of how she has been differentially remembered as a racial theorist.

The failure of the Semple-Turner collaboration in the 1907 AHA panel on geography is thus a telling moment. Semple and Turner are frequently paired as cofounders of the modern subdiscipline of American historical geography, and they unknowingly crossed intellectual paths in 1893, the year of Turner's frontier thesis, when Semple returned from two years of study in Leipzig under Ratzel. Both were drawn to exploring the reciprocity between history and geography in providing the "master key" to American history (Turner's term, from an 1897 unpublished paper, "Influence of Geography upon the Settlement of the United States," read to the Geographic Society of Chicago). In 1905 Turner published his own review of Semple's and Brigham's books together, as Hart had, but in the *Journal of Geography* (Turner's first publication in a geographical journal). There he praised Semple's analysis of "the geographic forces which determined the growth of the United States to a continental power" and concluded that with more such work in historical geography, "we shall come nearer to an understanding of the meaning of our nation's history."[21] The AHA session, organized as a further exchange of ideas between historians and geographers, including not only Semple but also Brigham among the invitees (he did not attend), in hopes of finding common ground, instead produced dissension, blowback, altogether a failure to communicate. Semple was defensive, the other panelists were skeptical, Turner was disappointed, and the whole debacle was later put down to the race problem in her thinking.[22]

Semple and Turner exchanged letters when he invited her to the conference, and she immediately cautioned him: "My experience is that historians as a rule do not know geography. They may know the natural features of the areas in all corners of the world which they have taken for their field, but they are unable to interpret these in their effect, because they are ignorant of the rest of the world" (Semple to Turner, October 4, 1907, qtd. in Block, "Frederick Jackson Turner," 38). She also requested extra time for her paper, alluding to race as her reason: "Anthropogeographical perspectives have to be abundantly illustrated . . . to show that they operate regardless of race or . . . cultural status. . . . To do this takes time. . . . [A short paper] would misrepresent my subject" (Semple to Turner, October 18, 1907, qtd. in Koelsch, "Miss Semple Meets the Historians," 52). Reactions to her paper, "Geographical Location as a Factor in History," summarized in Turner's AHA "Report of the Conference on the Relations of Geography and History," from both the other panelists and the audience confirmed her own skepticism. They challenged her single-factor interpretation (despite the title, she argued that a country's location is the "supreme geographical fact in its history") and distanced themselves from her argument, some taking positions diametrically opposed, others intermediate between the role of geography in history as a condition and causative factor.[23]

Turner's disappointment with the historians at the AHA led him to turn to the geographers' forum, where he had greater success, perhaps in sync with his own intellectual shift from the frontier to the study of American sectionalism. Semple, later, echoing her own reluctance even before the Madison AHA meeting, wrote to Brigham that her experience at Madison, "where I had the chief paper, leads me to think that the historians represent a big field for propaganda. They are not an open-minded set of men, with the exception of a few progressives. . . . Merely mention geographic factors in the Historical Association, and the fur flies" (Semple to Brigham, November 28, 1910, qtd. in Block, "Frederick Jackson Turner," 38–39). Semple's letters may have, unbeknownst to her or Turner, anticipated the more deep-seated problem, linking "propaganda" to "race," which looms larger in the long term than the history-geography alignment, soon to be resolved in the emergence of historical geography as a subfield.

The race question comes up both so frequently and so indirectly in assessments of Semple's work that it's hard not to notice. Tracking what the historian of geography Innes Keighren calls the "geography" of her books reveals a trend line that can only be called highly irregular. Semple was continually, though nonlinearly, reassessed almost from the start, enshrined as a formative figure in the discipline yet dismissed early on because of her racial determinism, and now re-reconsidered from that very vantage point. There's no straight line to rehabilitation in the Semple case.

In the 1920s and '30s, when she was subject to critique by Franz Boas, Carl Sauer, Lucien Febvre, and others, Semple's books, both the 1903 *American History* and the 1911 *Influences*, were still on geography department reading lists in the US and the UK. Keighren shows that Semple's work was encountered more positively where racial geography and anthropology formed part of the curriculum (the University of Liverpool) and more negatively elsewhere. Keighren documents marginalia accusing "RACISM!" in copies of *Influences* held by the University of Birmingham, for example, and accounts of Semple's "racialist" work in later memoirs of geography students at the University of Sheffield. Keighren's point in charting the geography of her reception is that Semple's varying reputation reflects the disciplinary contexts of her readers, their different engagements "across space and through time"; together, Keighren says, they constitute "nodes in an intellectual topography" that, I want to stress, included racial thinking, often subsumed in the coded language of determinism.[24] Other historians of geography point to the contradictions in the reputation of "the luckless Ellen Semple," "the alleged arch-determinist herself," which outlasted her own moderation of her views during the 1920s and '30s. Her third and final book on the ancient Mediterranean, published in 1931, is read as further evidence of her revised focus on human agency and folk experience over the natural environment.[25]

Scholars in the 1980s and '90s have re-revised the critique of Semple's environmental determinism as itself overly simplistic and have recognized her as a pioneer in the modern study of human-environment interaction. Semple's brand of environmental determinism is now undergoing something of a revisionist reclamation. Wilford A. Bladen and Pradyumna P. Karan go so far as to suggest Semple as the first "location theorist." Even for such an on-the-fence historian of the discipline as the human geographer Tim Cresswell, who pushes back against Semple's full rehabilitation, the range of environmental influences in her work is "enormous, not simply a matter of climate producing racial characteristics"; he concludes, "Semple is clearly sensitive about the difficulties involved in thinking and writing about 'race.'"[26] Semple's successive makeovers as a racial geo-determinist, point for Cresswell, writing in 2013 and citing James Blaut in 1999, to the larger arc of the discipline, in which "many geographers and geography textbooks assume that environmental determinism has been safely relegated to a rather unsavory past" (*Geographic Thought*, 51). Especially for many geographers in the modern environmental movement, Semple is a hero, responsible for the revised versions of her beliefs that are very much alive today. Cresswell's example of Semple's long shadow is the best-selling geographer Jared Diamond's *Guns, Germs, and Steel* (1997), which advances a version of the determinist argument about how broadly European societies were destined to dominate because of a combination of environmental factors; part of Diamond's point here, Cresswell says, is to dismiss arguments that this has been due to any notion of "racial superiority," but he simply replaces "one argument rooted in nature (race) with another (environment)" (*Geographic Thought*, 52). My point is to underscore how "race" again and again enters the Semple story, but only parenthetically.

The critics' half-spoken barometer of race therefore does not so much measure the racial degree of Semple's work as it charts the ups and downs of her checkered reputation. As such, her 1903 *American History and Its Geographic Conditions,* which foregrounds the American Mediterranean, dramatizes the limits of the approach. Offered as a kinder, gentler form of geo-historical determinism, her oceanic thinking uses "the scene of history," from the heyday of the "Mediterranean period in history" to the "Atlantic period" that followed, in order to predict a Pacific future (*AH*, 3). Semple's ocean-based periods naturalize the history of conquest, empire, and commercial expansion, just as nature functioned as a proxy for race throughout her writing. We know, though, that Semple largely failed in both her book project, to study the US as facing the Atlantic and Pacific, and her disciplinary project, to introduce her field, in her mission as a geographer, to the historians. As parallel projects they ultimately collided, at odds, at cross-purposes with one another. Semple wanted to make the historical past a, if not the, predictor of the present as well as a future indicator, and to inject geography into history, but neither one panned out. Her clarion call for "our American Pacific" (*AH*, 422) went unanswered.[27] Yet apparently entirely unbeknownst to her, the vision of a Pacific future that would recapitulate the Mediterranean past was alive and well in contemporaneous California writing. Her lack of awareness, we might say, is a measure of the separate spheres that she fought futilely against. This was the California of 1890s boosters and reformers—"Our Mediterranean! Our Italy!"—to which we'll turn in part 3.

3

1890s California-Pacific Mediterraneans

Part 3 follows the shift—not seismic, but one that still moves the needle in region and genre—to the 1890s invention of a Pacific Mediterranean in travel and touristic literature. In then-popular works by now-forgotten Charles Dudley Warner, P. C. Remondino, MD, and W. C. Riley, "Our Mediterranean! Our Italy!"—Warner's phrase—was rediscovered on the West Coast of the US. The region went all the way from Southern California to Puget Sound, extending the Caribbean Mediterranean from the Atlantic to the Pacific Ocean. "Profusely illustrated," as the subtitle of *Our Italy* read, mostly with black-and-white photographs and a few maps, these works of folk geography, in the form of books and throwaway pamphlets, were intended for a broad reading public, designed to attract attention to the Mediterranean character of the climate, commerce, and culture of the Pacific coast.[1] In contrast to the geographers' transtemporal, multidimensional, broadly comparative world-view, the Pacific Mediterraneanizers use a more static and circumscribed, two-dimensional analogy limited to two regions. Writing at roughly the same period as the geographers Élisée Reclus and Ellen Churchill Semple, the travel writers and regional boosters, whom we might expect to embrace the civilizational drumbeat, assuming the mantle of the singular old-world Mediterranean as producer of later new-world versions of classical knowledge and culture, treat the metaphor with considerable skepticism.

The centerpiece of this part of the book will sound odd in that context of the California 1890s, a speculative case study of Helen Hunt Jackson and her popular novel of Indian reform, *Ramona* (1884), which she called a second *Uncle Tom's Cabin*. My focus is less on the novel itself, which has virtually no explicit Mediterranean connection to speak of, than on its afterlives in the California Spanish colonial revival Jackson is said to have initiated.

Both Jackson and the author of *Uncle Tom's Cabin*, Harriet Beecher Stowe, are known for their blockbusters with extraordinary abilities to translate and be translated. Among *Ramona*'s Mediterranean legacies, the invention of California's "fantasy heritage," as Carey McWilliams famously called it, a white-washed colonial history that bypassed Mexico, with its racial baggage, in favor of Spain, took place in a variety of venues. The most notable go beyond even the usual adaptation histories on page, stage, and screen to embrace the Mediterranean or mission revival in art and architecture, the built environment, and the place-names in both Northern and Southern California.[2]

Jackson's novel, with its later presence in California state toponymic history, grounded in Spanish-language usage and translation, points in unexpected directions to José Martí and his translation of her novel for a Spanish audience in the US and abroad, *Ramona: Novela americana* (1888). With the addition of the subtitle *Novela americana*, Martí reclaims Jackson's North American work as, his preface announces, "*nuestra novela*." Including Martí's *Ramona* in the mix with all these late nineteenth-century California writers points further to the occluded linguistic legacy of Spanish, in the original and in translation, as the language of the place—alternately named Our Italy, America's Mediterranean, the Mediterranean Shores of America—they invented. The shifting history of languages that are both destroyed and adapted under the pressure of conquest, colonialism, and slavery is squarely part of the Humboldtian tradition of speculative comparison. We know that Reclus, following Humboldt, incorporated language change, the study of historical linguistics as a systematic metric of human geography, throughout *The Earth and Its Inhabitants* (*La nouvelle géographie universelle*), especially as evidence for or against conjectures about group origins and future political affinities. Part 3 tells another story of the politics of American literature in languages other than English.

"Island on the land": Travel, Tourism, and Race in "Our Italy!"

The Mediterranean network of the California 1890s has nodes that go beyond the boundaries of the decade and the Pacific region. Jackson's 1884 *Ramona* looks forward to Warner's 1891 *Our Italy* and later still to the 1970s and '80s cultural critics who see California through a mediterraneanizing lens. Kevin Starr, we know, refers in his 1973 omnibus history, *Americans and the California Dream, 1850–1915*, to "California as America's Mediterranean littoral" and to "the dream of California as a Mediterranean littoral" (414, 408), and his examples include both Warner's and Jackson's books. Starr complicates the timeline of American attempts to identify with a Mediterranean California, locating its beginnings pre-statehood, in the 1840s, with the explorer John Charles Frémont and his wife, Jesse Benton Frémont, would-be political grandees of the Bear Flag Republic, and fans out to Robert Louis Stevenson, Bayard Taylor, Mary Austin, and Isadora Duncan, among many others. Starr's list of mediterraneanizers—writers, artists, and performers who celebrated Italian, French, and Spanish cultures and histories—may seem like a formless grab bag, but the multidisciplinary reach and generous timeline are key to the proteanness of his Mediterranean "Californianism" (*ACD*, 310).

Starr even brings into the mix the first Stanford University president, David Starr Jordan, through his design for the landscaping and architecture of the campus. Working with Frederick Law Olmsted, Jordan imbibed what Starr sees as the architect's Mediterraneanism; Olmsted advised that "a great University in California ideals" should look to Syria, Greece, Italy, Spain for models, "an architecture of open, sun-drenched plains, like that of the Santa Clara Valley" (*ACD*, 316). Jordan, a eugenicist, "more biological elitist than bigot," "ideologue of an Anglo-Saxonism" (*ACD*, 310, 311), whose name has now, in 2021, been removed from the Stanford Psychology Department building, nevertheless followed a vision of the campus as a reflection of Spanish California, not only in the built environment but also in the language. He named campus streets after figures from the Spanish and Mexican past, and speaking about California's Spanish place-names, he told a Monterey audience in 1893, "We feel everywhere the charm of the Spanish language—Latin cut loose from scholastic bonds, with a dash of firmness from the Visigoth and a touch of warmth from the sun-loving Moor" (*ACD*, 318). The romantic racialism undergirding Jordan's embrace of Spanish, it turns out, is part and parcel of the linguistic dimension of "California-as-Mediterranean" (*ACD*, 370). His selective association of the Spanish language with preferred racialized traits is one of those partly visible elements that make up the occluded linguistic legacy of Spanish in California. The language-race nexus will be key to my unfolding of the limits and possibilities of what Starr calls variously the Mediterranean metaphor and analogy.

Mike Davis's term in *Ecology of Fear: Los Angeles and the Imagination of Disaster* is the "deep Mediterraneaneity" (title of chapter 1, section 2) of Southern California, which he uses to bring into view the environmental and linguistic lack of fit between Anglo settlers and the mediterranean climate of California. While the early Spanish padres, "Mediterranean men (mainly from Majorca)" appreciated the "*cienagas*" (springs) as part of the region's waterscape and recognized its dramatic pattern of alternating drought and flood, three-quarters of a century later, "Anglo-American conquistadors" were flummoxed by the unfamiliar new-world ecology (*EF*, 10–11). The new settlers in the 1850s to '70s, used to the more predictable climate of the Northeast, veered between perceptions of garden and desert. Davis, fascinatingly, puts this ecological incomprehension down to a specifically linguistic failure: "English terminology, specific to a humid climate, proved incapable of accurately capturing the dialectic of water and drought that shapes Mediterranean environments. By no stretch of the imagination, for example, is an arroyo merely a 'glen' or 'hollow'—they are the results of radically different hydrological processes. The Anglos often had little choice but to preserve the more befitting Spanish terms although they failed to grasp their larger environmental context" (*EF*, 11). The links Davis makes between geography and language, specifying how much they are at odds with one another, will be important to the special role Spanish terminology plays, more or less visibly, for better or worse, in the history of the California Mediterranean.

The Spanish topographical (as well as historical and literary) names that now locate so much of the California urbanscape (La Cienega Boulevard in Los Angeles, Arroyo Seco in Pasadena, El Camino Real statewide) mark a long-standing historical gap between Spanish and English that continues to this day. The Spanish-language legacy baked into the place-names (according to Starr, "surviving mellifluously in a thousand Spanish place-names which dotted the landscape" [*ACD*, 47]) conflicts with periodic national "English-only" revivals in a state where the second-most-often-spoken language is Spanish, and Latinos are projected to compose more than 50 percent of the population when the 2020 census data are released. Add to the early "fundamental failure of language and cultural inheritance" the later discovery of the California aquifer that enabled the agricultural industry and made possible the selling of the region as a definitive Eden—and the result for Davis is the pseudo-Spanish "Mediterranean California" repackaged by railroad publicists and chamber of commerce promoters as "Our Mediterranean! Our Italy!" (*EF*, 12). Warner, named in a Davis footnote, is thus credited with, better blamed for, "this Mediterranean metaphor," the "'Mediterranean' facade," that has been "sprinkled like a cheap perfume over hundreds of instant subdivisions, creating a faux landscape celebrating a fictional history from which original Indian and Mexican ancestors have been expunged" (*EF*, 12). In the early 1920s, Frank Lloyd Wright was "sickened" by the same neo-Mediterranean architecture on display at the Panama-California Exposition in San Diego (1915–17): "Another fair, in San Diego this time, had set up Mexico-Spanish for another run for another cycle of thirty years" (qtd. in *ACD*, 410–11). From my perspective, the fundamental failure of language itself becomes in this case an unlikely form of communication, the Spanish place-names used but misunderstood, misspoken as they were often mispronounced and Anglicized, to produce a whole cultural phenomenon based in or defined by mis- or un-translation. "Mediterranean California" is its name.

In the context of Mediterranean misnomers, Carey McWilliams also plays an outsize role. The California writer-activist, longtime editor of *The Nation*, and cult hero is known for the subtitle of his iconic 1946 book, *Southern California: An Island on the Land*. He adapts the line from something Helen Hunt Jackson "once said, and it is the best description of the region yet coined, 'It is a sort of island on the land.'"[3] She gets the credit, but he provides no provenance, reflecting how the Jackson line was cut off from its source and thrown without identification into circulation. Similarly, we'll see, another of the lesser-known California mediterraneanizers, P. C. Remondino, also quotes the Jackson line in his 1892 book touting the benefits of Southern California, *The Mediterranean Shores of America*. I put this source-less citation in the same class as the term American Mediterranean itself, which we know circulated without a stable source, as I've said, like a translation without an original. Both demonstrate the strategic communication of incomplete or mistranslation.

Jackson's line taps into the now-famous early European cartographic misrepresentation of California as an island. Maps in Latin, Spanish, French, and Dutch, dating from the early sixteenth through the eighteenth centuries, depict California as a carrot-shaped island floating off the mainland coast. That cartographic error, the mistaken idea of California as an island, has itself captured the public and scholarly imagination, outlasted all correctives, and morphed from physical fact to cultural metaphor. More than that, the erroneous maps continued to be produced long after geographical knowledge had superseded them, one (Japanese) even dating to 1865, and today a collection of surviving examples is archived at Stanford University, valued, not despite their error, but because of it.[4]

Compounding his use of Jackson's line for his subtitle, McWilliams also mockingly credits, or blames, her for the original invention of the *Ramona*-based Spanish-mission past. The "little, plump, fair-skinned, blue-eyed Helen Hunt Jackson, 'H.H.' as she was known to every resident of Southern California," he says with characteristic McWilliams satiric wit, was almost solely responsible for the evocation of its Mission past" (*SC*, 71). This is what McWilliams calls, in his 1948 *North from Mexico: The Spanish-Speaking People of the United States*, the California "fantasy heritage" that honors an invented Spanish past of saintly Catholic padres and their willing Indian converts while bypassing the living, and more threatening, Mexican presence/present. The McWilliams subtitle makes the crucial link to language, "the Spanish-speaking people of the United States," as the marker of that group threat. Like

H.H. herself, the fantasy heritage is another of the false leads that turn out to be so fruitful in the circulation of the Mediterranean California.

The faux Spanish heritage points first to the real language of the Spanish speakers and second to the complicated, multidimensional incorporation of Spanish in the Mediterranean-California literature and built-environment. Even the word "Mediterranean" itself is "misleading," McWilliams says, when applied by geographers to Southern California (*SC*, 7). But it is a fertile false lead that needs only to be modified by McWilliams with a few nos to be meaningful. "Unlike the Mediterranean coast, Southern California has no sultry summer air, no mosquito-ridden malarial marshes, no mistral winds" (*SC*, 7). All his negated comparisons point to an understated American exceptionalism, Southern California–style. "This is not a desert light nor is it tropical. . . . It is Southern California light, and it has no counterpart in the world" (*SC*, 7). Put another way, the comparisons that produce California Mediterraneanism, whether made by writers then or historians now, boil down to the region's *incomparability*.

Likewise, Charles Dudley Warner's *Our Italy*, which we know Starr once described as "not overusing the Italian metaphor" (*ACD*, 378), also waxes eloquent with negatives, the nots and withouts. They cluster in the passage that Davis cites with such scorn, the place where Warner introduces the star of the book. "Here is our Mediterranean! Here is our Italy! It is a Mediterranean without marshes and without malaria, and it does not at all resemble the Mexican Gulf, which we have sometimes tried to fancy was like the classic sea that laves Africa and Europe. Nor is this region Italian in appearance" (*OI*, 18). The Mediterranean comparison is most often invoked only to be almost instantaneously questioned, qualified, or outright negated. Warner's repeated comparisons to other mediterranean regions always end in the "unparalleled" (*OI*, 5), the "incomparable" (*OI*, 17, 190), the "anomaly" (*OI*, 8, 39) of our Italy. The California exceptionalism applies to both physical and human geography. On the Hotel del Coronado in San Diego, for example, Warner says, "Taking it and its situation together, I know nothing else in the world with which to compare it" (*OI*, 82). The wonder of Yosemite, too, is "without parallel or comparison" (*OI*, 148).

As a nay-saying mediterraneanizer, Warner anchors a rich node in the network that centers around Southern California. His book, marketed as a travelogue, with illustrations of scenes from the Mexico border to Yosemite, is more a booster's brief for regional development, written by a California convert. The illustrations *Scenes in Montecito and Los Angeles* and *Midwinter, Pasadena* (figures 9–10) by and large take that view. They are both typical of the highly conventionalized representation of a picturesque landscape, depicted from a distance or enclosed in ornate frames. Human inhabitants are either absent or dwarfed by the landscape, and when depicted, they resemble the travelers and tourists of Warner's audience. He wrote from their perspective as an East Coast native from the Hartford, Connecticut, literary neighborhood of Nook Farm, Mark Twain's coauthor of *The Gilded Age* (1873), and an editor of the *Hartford Courant* and *Harper's Weekly*. From Warner's own perspective as a frequent winter traveler to the warm climates of the Southwest and Mexico, *Our Italy* touts the agricultural potential and health advantages of Southern California.

Warner himself identifies another node in the California Mediterranean network, first paratextually citing in a footnote, then discussing in a lengthy chapter called "Health and Longevity," his main medical authority, one P. C. Remondino, MD. Born in Torino, Italy, Dr. Peter Charles Remondino served as a physician in both the Civil War and the Franco-Prussian War, ultimately moving to San Diego, where he became, Kevin Starr comments in *The Dream Endures: California Enters the 1940s*, "a tireless propagandist for San Diego as a health resort," "the Naples-sanitarium of the Pacific" (98). He produced a series of articles on the advantages of the California climate, and the year after Warner's book came out, Remondino gathered the articles together in *The Mediterranean Shores of America: Southern California; Its Climatic, Physical, and Meteorological Conditions* (1892).[5] Like Warner's, his book sells itself on the title page as "fully illustrated," with several full-page plates of similar stylized landscape scenes, with inset close-ups of both places and people in framed squares and rounds (see *In and around Los Angeles, Cal.* and *Scenes at and near Yuma*, figures 13–14). Both mediterraneanizers, Warner and Remondino, defer to each other, specifically in relation to thinking about climate. Remondino quotes Warner for his seal of popular approval, his having pronounced this region of "unique climatic conditions" (*MS*, 129) " 'Our Italy,' or the 'Riviera' of the United States" (*MS*, 116), "the 'Italy of America' " (*MS*, iv), ("I should advise all prospective visitors to read 'Our Italy' " [*MS*, 118]); and Warner quotes Dr. Remondino as his medical expert on climate as a factor of longevity. Both see climate as a key component of Mediterranean California—and in this both venture onto the territory of race through the back door of the science of climatology.

In Warner's case the results are visible in his *fort-da*, repeatedly making the object appear and disappear; almost as often as he invokes the mediterranean metaphor, he rejects it. From the very start, his first ecstatic announcement of "Here is Our Italy!" (*OI*, 18, chapter 2, "Our Climatic and Commercial Mediterranean"), is immediately followed with multiple qualifiers ("Nor is this region Italian in appearance, though now and then" it reminds the traveler of Southern Italy and Sicily, "a Mediterranean with a more equable climate" [*OI*, 18]). "Nature here has the knack of being genial without being enervating" (*OI*, 11), "a climate never enervating" (*OI*, 9). The effect is to implicitly raise while nominally denying the specific specter of enervation associated with natural fecundity, especially in the tropics. The taint of tropical disease is enough to warrant repeating the negative in tandem with the positive: "It lies there, our Mediterranean region, on a blue ocean, . . . ; our New Italy without malaria and with every sort of fruit which we desire (except the tropical)" (*OI*, 87). Next the broad umbrella set of the Mediterranean comes under scrutiny. "I have insisted so much upon the Mediterranean character of this region," Warner writes in chapter 3, "that it is necessary to emphasize the contrasts also. . . . The contrast with the Mediterranean region—I refer to the western basin—is in climate. There is hardly any point along the French and Italian coast that is not subject to great and sudden changes. . . . There are few points that are not reached by malaria. . . . The Southern California climate is an anomaly. . . . A land without high winds or thunder-storms may fairly be said to have a unique climate" (*OI*, 34–38). The exceptionalism, the insistence again on the anomaly, the uniqueness of Mediterranean California, here connected to climate, suggests the reason for the repeated move away from the very comparison that gives the book its title.

Warner's imperative is to distance our Italy from the tropical taint of malaria, along with the tropical threat of "enervation"—and from the racial taint of both. Both he and Remondino, who also touches on the pressure point of enervation in the Warner passages he cites, regularly insist on the "semi-tropical" Mediterranean California. In turn, Warner prefers climate as a cleaner alternative to genetics, environment over heredity. He invokes an unpublished paper by "Dr. Remondino" on the "extraordinary endurance" of men, descendants of Indians and Spanish settlers, and animals, particularly their horses, in the California climate. "It was long supposed that this was racial," Warner comments, but the importation and breeding of Eastern thoroughbreds has shown that "the desirable qualities of the California horse were not racial but climatic" (*OI*, 55). The impossible logic gives itself away. We know that the same argument, the attempt to move away from bio-inheritance to environment didn't work for Elizabeth Semple, that climate was no place of refuge for her either. And, indeed, what McWilliams calls "the folklore of climatology" brings re-racialization in through the back door of climate (*SC*, 96).

To fend off the threat of enervation associated with tropical fecundity, Warner questions whether Southern California will be an exception to "those lands of equable climate and extraordinary fertility where every effort is postponed till 'to-morrow'" (*OI*, 88)—and in so doing he falls back on long-standing Herderian romantic racialism, the association of different cultural characteristics with cold/hot, northern/southern zones. This is the racialized geography that the journalist Charles Nordhoff had explicitly identified in his 1873 tourist and immigrant guide, *California: For Health, Pleasure, and Residence*. Like Warner, Nordhoff uses the negative to make "California . . . our own": "the delights of the tropics, without their penalties; a mild climate, not enervating, but healthful and health-restoring; a wonderfully and variously productive soil, without tropical malaria." But unlike Warner's Mediterranean California, the race connection is the point for Nordhoff: his California "is the first tropical land which our race has thoroughly mastered and made itself at home in."[6] In contrast, Warner goes through multiple gyrations, his own repetition compulsion, to raise and put to rest the racialization of nature and culture: "It has been said that this land of the sun and of the equable climate will have the effect that other lands of a Southern aspect have upon temperament and habits." His counterargument, though, simply reverses the usual value judgments of folk climatology: "This may be a region where the restless American will lose something of his hurry and petty, feverish ambition. He will take . . . something of the tone of the climate and of the old Spanish occupation. But the race instinct of thrift and of 'getting on' will not wear out in many generations" (*OI*, 87–88). Belonging to both nature and culture, the Spanish tone of the climate, like the American restlessness, is not biological, but it is racial. The condition of living in Southern California, the necessity of irrigation, demands "industry," just as "Egypt, with all its *dolce far niente*, was never an idle land for the laborer" (*OI*, 88).

Warner's language is the giveaway here, the slippage in that common Italian code phrase for the sweetness of doing nothing. He stresses the word "to-morrow" by putting it in quotes ("those lands of equable climate and extraordinary fertility where every effort is postponed till 'to-morrow,'" [*OI*, 88]). Notably, however, he doesn't use the Spanish *mañana*, the analogous popular code word for Latin leisure culture in contrast to Anglo-Saxon industry—and one of the relatively few Spanish phrases that were so liberally sprinkled in late nineteenth-century US travel writing as foreignizers to exoticize the Spanish fantasy heritage. Yet it's the Spanish, here masked by Warner's Italian, that carries the racial content, both the promise of the foreign and the problem of its otherness. Spanishness as both language and culture permeates *Our Italy*. Scattered throughout the text are a few untranslated but, from the context, transparent Spanish words ("*patio*," "a Spanish *rebozo*" [*OI*, 166], "the *barrancanas*" [165]). Spanish names ("*cañon*," as in Grand or Colorado, "Santa Fé," "Zuñi") are not anglicized but instead have all the correct diacritical marks.

Even more revealingly, the Spanish architecture is "picturesque" but "the Americans have not the art of making houses or a land picturesque" (*OI*, 67). Warner's California Mediterraneanism becomes the means to meditate on the "foreign" and how well it fits "the American temperament" (*OI*, 69). "There is little left of the old Spanish occupation, but the remains of it make the romance of the country," in contrast to "our modern nondescript architecture," "brought here by "the new American comers . . . from the East," that neither "suits the climate" nor appeals to "such historical associations." Instead of the "prosaic look" of their buildings, the Americans might have taken "hints from the natives" and adapted the dwellings "that the climate suggests," built around "an inner court, or *patio*." No matter, Warner concludes with some irony, "the American likes it, and he would not like the picturesqueness of the Spanish or Latin races" (*OI*, 68–69). There it is, the racial allusion creeps in, seemingly attached to, part and parcel of, the Spanishness. The language, especially the use of a proper name, appears to be a carrier. The Zuñis are "a gentle, amiable race . . . such a race as one would expect to find in the land of the sun and the cactus" (*OI*, 165). Warner has perfected the use of a racialized language, both fluently spoken and unspoken, in which he can have it both ways, California as Euro-Italian and Native American, Indigenous, like the pottery designs he sees at a Laguna pueblo, with "little Spanish influence" (*OI*, 169).

Our Italy's illustrations reinforce the complexities of race in Warner's Mediterraneanism. In addition to the conventional landscape panoramas that are so common in the geography and travel books, sometimes peopled by a few representative, well-heeled inhabitants at work or play, Warner includes two images of a native pueblo in Laguna (figures 11–12). Neither ethnographic portraits nor picturesque scenes, these engravings are crude stereotypes of the hardscrabble life of the Zuñis at the desert pueblo in Laguna. The viewer's focus is on the desert setting and terraced houses rather than the human figures, themselves stereotypes, including the seated child and the women carrying pottery jars on their heads in the foreground of the illustrations. In contrast, Warner's text is more nuanced and self-reflective, his ambivalence more pronounced. He comes close-up to his subjects, recounts the "friendly terms" of conversations with several "young maidens" who had been at the Carlisle boarding school and spoke English ("very prettily"), but glosses over "the idle drudgery of their semi-savage condition," the village, "without water or street commissioners," "swarming" with "litters of children," in part by comparing the place with various Mediterranean analogues (*OI*, 168–69). "Its appearance is exactly that of a Syrian village," and "the resemblance was completed by the figures of the women . . . , carrying on the head a water jar, and holding together by one hand the mantle worn like a Spanish *rebozo*" (*OI*, 165–66). Even the jars, the ones described as having Indigenous designs that betray little Spanish influence, "recall ancient Cypriote ware" (*OI*, 169). The dizzying contradictions, in turning away from the familiar US racial stereotypes of the uncivilized, unwashed Indians by comparing them with the equally but differently racialized Mediterranean south and Middle East, may be hard to absorb.

But the contemporary discourse, defining southern Europeans, Italians, and Greeks, among others, as part of a "Mediterranean race" has much the same contradictory charge. This is a kind of strategic racialization that associates southern European otherness with a Mediterranean heritage, loosely located in space and time, combining cultural exoticism with white ethnicity and managing the threat of blackness. Mediterraneanity produced a hierarchy of whiteness, defined differently as ethnical and racial. Thomas Huxley was an early proponent, who rejected the category "Caucasian" in favor of differentiating between two white "types," "Xanthochroic" or fair, associated with northern Europe, and "Melanochroi" or dark, associated with the whole Mediterranean basin—Spain, southern Italy, Greece, the Middle East, and North Africa—but also with the Irish, Welsh, and Bretons. The concept of a Mediterranean race traveled genetically, linked in part to migratory patterns, reaching regions far from the Mediterranean itself and distinguishing between the ancient and modern Mediterranean as well. While Madison Grant's *The Passing of the Great Race* (1916), the eugenicist bible, later popularized the equation of the Nordic type with racial superiority and the others, including the Mediterranean race, with varying degrees of inferiority, even he held up the civilizational contributions of the ancient Mediterranean race (questioning, though, whether Greco-Roman civilization might not be attributed to Nordic rather than Mediterranean origins). Compounding these ambiguities, racial science in the US, where a black-white binary dominated, traceable to slavery's one-drop rule, has a specific history of blackening both the Italians and the Irish during this long period of European immigration. But the contemporary racialization of the Italians and Spanish on whom Warner drew for his Mediterranean-California analogies turns out to be as much a worlded as a national phenomenon—and as unstable and protean a source as most, if not all, of the stock racial discourses of mediterraneanity.[7]

Thus does Warner work both sides of the race debate, using climate as stand-in to circumvent, trump, or otherwise efface biological race, only to bring it back in through the back door of folk climatology. His aim: a sanitized American version of the modern Mediterranean, supposedly without its racial disadvantages. According to an unidentified California writer, who sounds a lot like Warner: "[Here is] . . . the climate of the tropics without its perils; here is the fertility of Egypt without its fellaheen; here are the fruits and flowers of Sicily without its lazzaroni; . . . the sunshine of Persia without its oppressions." The familiar formula of the "withouts" interrupts the Mediterranean comparison but the metaphors are cryptic, their racial implications submerged, half-spoken. Historians have commented that the booster language of the 1890s, came primarily from the " 'Mediterranean school'— writers and publicists who would continue to have difficulties controlling their metaphors well into the twentieth century."[8] Warner may have thus tried to distance himself from some of the inherently racialized Mediterranean expressions, but it didn't work, at least as far as Mike Davis was concerned. We know he blamed Warner for repackaging the Los Angeles region as "Our Mediterranean! Our Italy!" creating a faux landscape and a fictional history, shadowed by real racial injustice. No wonder Warner does not overuse the Italian metaphor!

So while Warner tried without complete success to pull back from his own leading metaphor, one of his contemporaries, the Caribbean travel writer Frederick Albion Ober, tried a different, more hypothetical tack in his 1892 *Our West Indian Neighbors*, subtitled *The Islands of the Caribbean Sea, "America's Mediterranean."* Ober, a naturalist and ornithologist who had an official government appointment as "Special Commissioner Sent by the World's Columbian Exposition to the West Indies," wrote several travel books, generally divided into multiple chapters representing the places he visited and, always richly, copiously illustrated.[9] Ober uses the Warnerian exclamation point to underscore the conjectural, imagined dimension of his Mediterraneanism, the source of the "myths of a drowned continent" (*OWI*, 2–3) underlying the Caribbean islands: "And what daring speculations do these protruding peaks of submerged mountains suggest! It is no new hypothesis, that they are the sole visible remains of a vast Caribbean continent, which once occupied what is now the basin of 'America's Mediterranean'—the 'Lost Atlantis,' . . . by a sort of poetic justice, it was in this island of Santo Domingo, where slavery was first introduced into America, that it was also first abolished" (*OWI*, 169). For Ober the speculative and hypothetical are the defining conditions of "America's Mediterranean," and we could go so far as to conjecture that they allow the poetic justice he finds in the history of Saint-Domingue slavery. "Toussaint l'Ouverture was Haiti's George Washington," he says, relying on that conjectural comparative formula we've seen before (*OWI*, 169). Reclus, who footnotes Ober several times as a source (*NG*, 12, 252), makes the same leap when he says, "By a sort of retributive justice, the negro race has even acquired political autonomy in the large island of Haiti" (*EI*, 9). Humboldt, too, had made his own similar prophetic finding in *Relation historique* about the African part of the Mediterranean basin, writing of Haiti, "*Il étoit reserve à notre siècle de voir s'accomplir cette prediction*" ("It was reserved for our age to see . . . a European colony of America transform itself into an African state"; *RH*, 4:158–59; *PN*, 3:430–33). So, too, Semple later, in a very different register, stresses the anticipatory quality of the California Pacific coast as a future predictor where "the US as a Pacific Ocean power" represents "the promise of a new historical era for the American Mediterranean" (*AH*, 398). All of these mediterraneanizers differently mobilize the kinds of "speculative thinking" that C. L. R. James associates with the black Jacobins, especially with Toussaint, his black Spartacus.

Accordingly, in the next section on *Ramona*, I take a speculative approach to the Helen Hunt Jackson node of the California Mediterranean network. Both she and her novel stand out as notable missing links in Warner's *Our Italy*, despite her fame at that very time in drawing crowds to the very locations, the inland regions around the San Gabriel valley, Pomona, and Pasadena, that are among those featured in the book. This, too, despite her friendship with Warner, dating to their days as acquaintances in the Northeast literary scene and as travelers in Southern California, and despite the fact that Remondino mentions both Warner and Jackson—on the same page, no less. Opening the chapter "Altitude and Southern California Resorts," Remondino praises both Jackson, who "has well said that, climatically speaking, the California of the South was an island on the land," and Warner, who is quoted with a line from *Our Italy*, "written under the inspiration of these unique climatic conditions" (*MS*, 129). The shifting presence and absence of these and other key figures in the California Mediterranean follow the pattern we've already seen with Humboldt, in which he regularly appears and disappears from the American Mediterranean networks. This is especially striking in the California context, where more places are named for him than in any other state, yet he has had to be repeatedly re-remembered. Here, too, race is the absent center of the story, for a mediterraneanizing lens in this case is about not seeing Indigenous Mexico in turn-of-the-century California. Likewise with *Ramona*: as a largely forgotten textual source of California place-names, or, Humboldt-like, a figurehead in the fantasy heritage, honored largely in the breach, the novel requires a speculative dimension to become part of the American Mediterranean.

Ramona, "Nuestra Novela" on America's Mediterranean Shore

This is a story of unrecognized translations and invisible translators: the best seller *Ramona* (fifteen thousand copies sold in the first ten months of publication) is, strangely, best known for its adaptation history, the afterlives rather than the work itself.[10] A fictional account of Indian oppression, legal and extralegal, set in and around Southern California, based in part on Jackson's 1883 *Report on the Conditions and Needs of the Mission Indians*, coauthored with the Los Angeles developer Abbott Kinney, the novel intertwines the history of Native American injustice with the plight of the Californios, Spanish-speaking descendants of the Mexican hidalgos who received large land tracts during the break-up of the missions—all folded within an interracial love story (the half-Indian, half-Scottish Ramona; the "pure Indian," Alessandro; and the aristocratic Californio, "a Mexican gentleman," Felipe). Jackson famously hoped *Ramona* would do for the Indian what "Mrs. Stowe had done for the Negro," but instead of consciousness-raising the novel spawned a Ramona industry.[11]

Jackson was barely in her grave (she died in October 1885) by the time that the search for the "original" Ramonas was on, almost overshadowing the novel with documentary, photographic, and testimonial evidence devoted to establishing the identity of the people and especially the places on which the novel was based. A "Ramona promotion of fantastic proportions" persisted throughout various boom periods of California tourism, 1885–1955 (*SC*, 73). The Home of Ramona brand of oranges advertised from 1900 to 1955 with a fruit-crate label of the Ramona home against a landscape backdrop that changed (like the adaptable American Mediterraneans) depending on the orange supplier (figures 25–26). *The Ramona Pageant*, the official California state outdoor play, has been staged annually since 1923 in Hemet, near the numerous reputed Ramona sites (Ramona's Home, Ramona's Marriage Place) in Southern California; and there are four US films, only two of which survive, the 1910 D. W. Griffith silent short starring Mary Pickford and Henry King's 1936 Loretta Young and Don Ameche hit, as well as several Spanish-language films, including Televisa's 2000 *Ramona* as a telenovela starring Kate del Castillo. Those are the recognized blockbusters of the *Ramona* performance and film history, notable as much for their ephemerality as for their local celebrity, regularly cited in the criticism.[12]

From the Mediterranean perspective, more important than the blockbusters is how *Ramona* imprinted on the built environment of California what was largely erased from the novel. In the many Mediterranean revival houses and suburban developments in California and on the many streets, businesses, and towns named Ramona, we can hear the twisted legacy of the Spanish (language and speakers) that Jackson effaced in the novel, along with her own role as translator. In this sense, the most enduring *Ramona* legacy is neither *The Ramona Pageant* nor the films but rather the spillover of the novel's suppressed, secret Spanishness onto the human geography of California.

Jackson herself, perhaps inadvertently, contributed to the problem when she said, "I do not dare to think I've written a second *Uncle Tom's Cabin*—but I do think I have written a story which will be a good stroke for the Indian cause." With this ambivalent nod to a famous predecessor, Jackson created what has become a virtual *Ramona* cliché, casting the shadow of "everybody's protest novel," as James Baldwin decried it, over her own. The comparison lives on, resurrected in the blurbs for the 2005 Modern Library edition of *Ramona*. The Jackson line, "I do not dare to think I've written a second *Uncle Tom's Cabin*," appears on the back cover, and on the front, Martí's version of that line from the 1888 preface to his Spanish translation, back-translated into English by Esther Allen as "Ramona is a second *Uncle Tom's Cabin*." At the same time, possibly inadvertently, Jackson further undercut her own protest novel and the role of the "Indian cause" in it when she incorporated without citations descriptions of places, people, and events from her own well-researched nonfiction. The result was both to foreground the fictionalized love story and the romanticized Spanish (Indian and Californio) past and to background the factual basis in contemporary Indian and Mexican injustice.[13]

Ramona silently, without attribution, adapts elements from Jackson's work on "Indian matters," including *Century of Dishonor*, her 1881 treatise against the record of US relations with American Indians past and present, and the 1883 *Report* coauthored with Abbott Kinney. The novel also contains no acknowledgment either of the extensive research Jackson did for both books in New York's Astor Library and Hubert Howe Bancroft's San Francisco archives or, most important, of her fieldwork on location in Southern California. Yet traces of the local histories she documented are found throughout *Ramona*, the murder of a Cahuilla Indian, Juan Diego, for example, providing the factual basis for the killing of Alessandro near the end of the novel. By another turn of the same screw, Jackson thus not only deflated herself, becoming one of the translation theorist Lawrence Venuti's "invisible translators," but also ironically set the stage for her own subsequent elevation by critics and historians, who gave her single-handed credit as source and creator of what was seen as a wholesale invention, California's Spanish fantasy heritage.[14]

Compounding the translational problem is the underrecognized role of Abbott Kinney, Jackson's coauthor of the 1883 *Report* and interpreter for her research trips on location in Southern California. Born in New Jersey, the wealthy real-estate developer, who lived in San Gabriel near Pasadena at Kinneloa (the name of his mansion, Kinney's Hill, in Hawaiian), shared Jackson's Indian reform politics, knew California land law, and, most important, knew Spanish. "She found out that I spoke Spanish, and as she was anxious to talk with Indians and Mexicans, and also to call upon some of the Spanish families at the old ranch-houses, she gently intimated that it would be a great favor to her if I would go and interpret for her" (qtd. in Phillips, *Helen Hunt Jackson*, 239). Jackson accepted the appointment as special commissioner of Indian affairs in Southern California provided Kinney be assigned as her co-agent and interpreter.[15] His translation work with the local Spanish-speaking people, Native American and Californios, whom Jackson interviewed, compensated for her own lack of Spanish, and they were also accompanied by an agency interpreter, Jesús López, as well as their driver, both of whom helped in Kinney's absence or when Kinney's Spanish proved insufficient.[16] Kinney's presence underscores the importance of Spanish-language sources, oral and written, to Jackson's *Ramona* project, as well as her whole Indian cause, yet he is remembered in the *Ramona* context mostly as Jackson's coauthor, less often as her interpreter, even less as one of the architects of the popular Mediterranean revival in Southern California.

So it takes a Mediterranean perspective to bring Kinney into the *Ramona* fold for what he is best known, the creation and development of "Venice of America," one of Southern California's "fanciest promotions." Sometimes called "Kinney's Folly," the opening of the beach town of Venice in 1905 brought to a 160-acre tract of ocean-side land near Los Angeles the canals, buildings, and amusements of Venice (including, as Carey McWilliams notes, a fleet of gondolas and gondoliers imported from Venice). A Kinney Company map details all the canals, now paved roads, and 1906 tourist postcards picture the gondolas in the main lagoon (figures 8 and 21). In planning Venice of America, Kinney incorporated several references to the community's Mediterranean namesake, from the Italianate architecture to his grand vision for Venice as a West Coast cultural mecca, site of an American cultural renaissance. Little of it survives today but the LA Historic Resources Inventory lists the Venice Arcades as Monument No. 532 in the style of "Mediterranean and Indigenous Revival Architecture, 1887–1952."[17] And Abbott Kinney Boulevard in the heart of Venice Beach honors his memory as millionaire entrepreneur and visionary. As a cultural ensemble all of this adds up to what one architectural guide to Italian Los Angeles calls "a Mediterranean symbiosis," in which genteel nineteenth-century enthusiasm for Italian culture converged seamlessly with the simultaneous resuscitation of the missions to produce a popular movement that lasted through the 1930s.[18]

A linchpin of that movement, Kinney's influence on architectural style outlasted his 1905 Venetian folly, but most important is how his underappreciated presence as Jackson's coauthor and interpreter in the *Ramona* network connects the novel to the American Mediterranean. His Spanish translation work for her and his popularization of the Italian tradition bring up the question of the languages of the American Mediterranean—and how the *Ramona* legacy favors Spanish with one notable exception, the Indian with the Italian name, Alessandro. Kinney points to the oddity of Alessandro's Italian name, which we'll return to later. As an understudied actor in the *Ramona* network, Kinney also underscores the ways the novel produces an "unrecognized adaptation" of Jackson's own research in the archives and on location. The film theorist Robert Stam coined that term to get around what he calls "the chimera of fidelity," and he proposes instead the idea of adaptation as translation, a means to "a much broader intertextual dialogism."[19] Gérard Genette once again enters the picture here as Stam's source for thinking as broadly as possible about transtextual relations, in Stam's translation: "all that which puts one text in relation, whether manifest or secret, with other texts" ("The Dialogics of Adaptation," 65). One of Genette's five types of transtextuality is paratextuality, which we've followed as a key formal element of the American Mediterranean, accompanied by its obvious or concealed, manifest or secret, relations to race. While the equation between adaptation and translation runs the danger of being possibly hopelessly broad, in this case the unrecognized adaptation points directly to those unmarked translations and invisible translators that together produced *Ramona*.

Ramona Afterlives I: Texts, Paratexts, Translation

The *Ramona* network is built on a text that expands and contracts over time as well as a rich paratextual record. In translational terms, what if we think of that text as itself an unrecognized adaptation? Following Jackson's own oft-quoted comment on the impact of "serious books," which people won't read, versus a novel "to move people's hearts," *Ramona* is read as a fictional counterpart to her various efforts to influence US Indian policy through her writing.[20] Several of the most memorable scenes in the novel were adapted from the places she visited and the interviews she conducted with the Coronel family (who led her to Rancho Camulos, one of the top two candidates for the prototype of the novel's setting) as well as others during her 1883 California trip for her *Century Magazine* series. Yet the novel contains no acknowledgment of any of these sources, nor of the Spanish that both her informants and her characters would have spoken. What's more, the "serious books" were soon added back in: *Ramona* editions less than two years after the novel appeared feature an appendix with the Jackson-Kinney *Report* and a reprinted *San Francisco Chronicle* article on Rancho Camulos, "Ramona's

Home: A Visit to the Camulos Ranch and to the Scenes Described by 'H.H.'"
(May 9, 1886). So what Jackson first removed from the novel was then restored in the form of those paratexts that haunt the novel with the memory
of earlier failures.[21] "Not one word for the Indians," she wrote to her friend
Charles Dudley Warner ("Dear C. D. W.") on October 2, 1884, a few months
after the novel had come out; "I put my heart and soul in the book for them.
It is a dead failure."[22]

Critics and readers have agreed with Jackson that *Ramona*'s fictionalized
portrait of the Californio past—"the half barbaric, half elegant, wholly generous and free-handed life led there by Mexican men and women of degree in
the early part of this century" (*R*, 11)—outflanks the factual brief on behalf of
the Indians. But Jackson's letters, beyond this one to C. D. W., part of the rich
paratextual record of the novel, further complicate that consensus. Writing
earlier to the *New York Independent* editor William Hayes Ward on January 1,
1884, she reported, "I am at work on a story—which I hope will do something
for the Indian cause; it is laid in So. California—and there is so much Mexican life in it, that I hope to get people so interested in it, before they suspect
anything Indian, that they will keep on." Here, the two groups—both linked
through the novel's land, citizenship, and race debates—are at odds, the Indian disguised by, hidden within, the Mexican. A month later, on February 5,
1884, her letter "To an intimate friend" (conjectured to be the critic and Emily
Dickinson editor Thomas Wentworth Higginson) suggests a more multilayered relation, cooperative and competitive, between the two groups:

> You know I have for three or four years longed to write a story that should
> "tell" on the Indian question.... Last spring in Southern California, I began to
> feel that ... the scene laid there—and the old Mexican life mixed in with just
> enough Indian to enable me to tell what had happened to them—would be the
> very perfection of coloring.... The success of it—if it succeeds—will be that
> I do not even suggest any Indian history,—till the interest is so aroused in the
> heroine—and hero—that people will not lay the book down. There is but one
> Indian in the story.[23]

Mixing the Mexican with the Indian, but just enough of the latter, meaning one, *Ramona* alternately conflates and collapses the histories of the two
aggrieved groups, the Indians and the Californios; they are both paired as
victims of American law and as racialized outsiders and treated as unstable
substitutes—covering for, both masking and displacing, one another.

The result of this merger of Indian and Mexican, the process of using
the terms interchangeably: the two, the plight of the Indians and "'the fine
old Spanish families,'" got "curiously mixed up" (*SC*, 76). It is hard to tell just

whose protest novel this is. First, the oft-noted contradictory racial politics of the novel produced Jackson's language of blood and race, her terminology for groups and naming of individuals that conflates an earlier romantic racialism with the emerging scientific racism of her time. Second, Jackson uses Californio memories of people and places to contextualize the exploitation of the Indians and reflect the intertwined histories of the two groups. Historians of race relations in California and the Southwest point to the uneven racialization of Mexicans and Indians, both subject to different degrees and kinds of discrimination in legal and land rights after 1848. Given that context, Jackson's comparison doesn't do justice to either group. In this she participates in the "common tendency" in the post-1848 period after the Treaty of Guadalupe-Hidalgo ended the Mexican War to see conquered people and places of the Southwest as "interchangeable identifiers and metaphors."[24]

So, too, the Spanish both groups, Indian and Mexican, would have spoken goes unrecognized in *Ramona*. Barely a word of Spanish is used in the novel, other than the titles *Señora*, *Señorita*, and *Señor*—in contrast even to Warner's occasional Spanish thrown in to foreignize *Our Italy*. It is simply understood but unremarked that Spanish is the language of all the novel's Mexican and Indian characters. Nobody actually speaks it; rather, spoken Spanish is rendered as formal, old-fashioned English, one perhaps modeled, the Jackson biographer Kate Phillips suggests, on the English, "quaint, simple, stately," of Susette LaFlesche (also known as Bright Eyes), the translator of the Ponca chief Standing Bear, whose lectures Jackson credits with her awakening as an Indian reformer. The novel's Indians, like those Indian communities that persisted at the secularized missions, are understood to be Spanish speaking, even the Italian-named Alessandro. His strange (mis)naming has been noted since the novel first appeared, sometimes attributed to Jackson's concern that American readers wouldn't know how to pronounce the Spanish.[25] Jackson has Alessandro give Ramona an alternative name, an "Indian name," "Majel," for wood dove (and she joins in, suggesting the feminine "Majella"), because he finds it hard to say Ramona (*R*, 196). But of course the native name doesn't stick either in the novel, titled *Ramona* after all, or in its afterlives. Only the white Americans, the invaders who follow in the wake of what the novel calls the "conquering" of Mexico and California (*R*, 13), speak in dialect, reflecting their linguistic foreignness in places of origin outside the state.

Jackson thus taps into the potential for American multilingualism beyond the *mañana* talk of the California Mediterranean but truncates that possibility. Speaking to Aunt Ri, the main dialect character who comes to sympathize with the Indian condition, Ramona is left in a void of untranslatability. "'Ah, Señora, I cannot talk in the English speech; only in Spanish.' 'Spanish, eh? Yer mean Mexican?'" (*R*, 282). Conflating language with identity, this line sees through the Spanish talk to the Mexican within and distorts both, in an unexpected turn of the screw on the standard elision of the Mexican subject by the Spanish heritage. Or as McWilliams puts it, "the restored Mission is a much better, less embarrassing symbol of the past than the Mexican field worker or the ragamuffin pachuco of Los Angeles" in the present (*SC*, 83).

The language politics of the novel are surely muted, present only in a few moments of resentment against the Americans that bookend the novel. In the beginning we hear of "the near and evident danger of an English-speaking people's possessing the land" (*R*, 22), and at the close, just before the happy ending when Felipe contemplates escape with Ramona to Mexico: "The methods, aims, and standards of the fast incoming Americans were to him odious. . . . Even the Spanish tongue was less and less spoken" (*R*, 359). The unspoken Spanish of the main characters, hidden within their heightened English, may be all the more audible given Jackson's own attraction, expressed in her own voice in her *Century* article "Echoes in the City of Angels," to "the soft Spanish speech continually heard . . . which seems bewilderingly un-American." The promise of the foreign as much as the threat of the American can be heard in that "bewilderingly un-American"—or as she wrote to Kinney of Rancho Camulos, "all as Mexican and un-American as heart could wish."[26] In this push-pull of identity and difference, language played a pivotal role. Spanish was both essential and dispensable. Jackson's just barely audible "soft Spanish speech" is only one example of the ambivalent foreignizing at play in the novel.

This fundamental irony leads to the problem with Jackson as invisible translator of the voices of the informants and friends she interviewed in Southern California, themselves unacknowledged "ghostwriters and protagonists."[27] Jackson disappears her informants and herself; when the "Spanish speaking people" (the subtitle of McWilliams's *North from Mexico*) go unrecognized, so does she as their translator. As well recognized as her sources later became, thanks to the voluminous authentication literature documenting the original *Ramona* sites and settings, in the novel they are silently incorporated in the *testimonio* tradition that the historian Hubert Howe Bancroft, in whose San Francisco library Jackson worked, had pioneered as a compiler of state history. When in the early 1870s he sent interviewers out to gather oral histories from the pre-statehood gentry of California, Bancroft generally omitted the circumstances of recording and translating his informants (Padilla, *My History Not Yours*, 28). Jackson herself became a Bancroft-esque editor of testimonial voices in the form of a novel. We don't hear what she describes in her letters, how Antonio Coronel spoke Spanish, translated, according to

Jackson, by his wife Doña Mariana in the "soft, Spanish-voiced broken English," as delightful to her ear as "the soft bastard Latin" of Italian to Byron's.[28] Yet there's an abiding concern throughout the *Ramona* network, the novel, and its afterlives, with testimony in several senses: reproducing the voices of the Californios is the most obvious and critical, but also the search for the "real" Ramona and her places is testimonially based, shaped by the desire for documented sources that attest or bear witness to the novel's authenticity.

Simultaneously, the endless search for the *Ramona* originals, both the people and places, was the unintended consequence of Jackson's disappearing of both her informants and her own translation as keys to the novel's writing and reading. In fictionalizing these people and places, the novel ironically set in motion the search for their factual originals. But the strategy backfired, in that Jackson's Indians competed with her Californios, as the source of the originals, and both groups themselves in turn faded away, were disappeared, superseded by the places they were believed to have inhabited. D. W. Griffith singled out Rancho Camulos, where he shot his 1910 film on location, itself unusual at that time and, a first in film history, with a special screen credit to the location, as a virtual star of the film. The historian William Deverell notes how "nonpersons" dominate the fantasy heritage, focused on Spanish-style roofs and porches, tile and decoration, rather than Mexican people.[29] The basic *Ramona* plot is similarly a familiar one of displaced persons, the Indians by the Spanish-speaking people and both by the Americans, but with a twist: the people are displaced by the places that are identified with and substitute for them. Jackson may have wanted *Ramona* to be "a second *Uncle Tom's Cabin*," but the novel turned out to be no "otra *Cabaña*," either for the Indians or for the Californios.[30] The novel failed as a brief on behalf of either group. Instead, it produced a regional history for the nation with the Californio rancho in the starring role, much as and perhaps even more than the Mississippi River is said to be a character in Huck Finn or Yoknapatawpha County as the center of William Faulkner's Mississippi.

This is not the contradiction it may sound like: the local place evokes a national time, a stage in the assumed developmental timeline of the nation. Moreover, easterners like Jackson and Warner, instrumental in the invention of Mediterranean California, produced a lot of the Ramonana. As Kevin Starr says, *Ramona* was a "Pacific Coast extension of the larger process of the New England mind Mediterraneanizing." A culture industry arose for the preservation and revival of the "dying" Mexican-Spanish culture, producing a predominantly Anglo-made golden age past for the region and, by extension, the nation. The result was a geographical place called California, with the names of *Ramona* characters imprinted on the built environment and in the place-name literature, even while disappearing the people who continued to live their history in that place. Whether these authenticating places are celebrated as the real, decried as "dishonest architecture," inventions that provide a fantasy heritage, or studied as "memory places," stages on which living memories are practiced, performed, and perfected, together these sites have produced and become living translations of the novel.[31] As a kind of *tableau vivant* in and of the landscape, holding out the promise of finding time past in present space, the *Ramona* place-based afterlives, in the form of the Mediterranean revival architecture as well as the place-names in the built environment of Southern California, eclipse all of its other translations.

Ramona Afterlives II: Names on the Land and in the Place-Name Literature

The most common, visible, and enduring of the *Ramona* adaptations are the California place-names that originated with the novel. The films, plays, and pageant are all more ephemeral in contrast to the many Ramona streets, schools, and parks in California (and some scattered elsewhere in the nation)—not to mention all the Ramonas and Alessandros in the handbooks of California place-names, which often preserve those places even after their names are changed. There are Ramona motels, mobile home parks, real-estate developments, a town near San Diego named Ramona (home of the Ramona Pioneer Historical Society), and, according to McWilliams in 1983, the name Ramona appears in the corporate title of fifty or more businesses in Los Angeles. The Ramona-Alessandro Elementary School is located on Ramona Avenue in San Bernadino. Ramona brands include Ramona's Chile Rellenos and Ramona Lemons. (For Home of Ramona brand of oranges, see figures 25 and 26.) The Ramona place-names are not only located all over the state but also inscribed in the corresponding literature, the handbooks of California place-names, the guides to the origin, meanings, etymology, and pronunciation of geographical names. In this literature, the process set in motion by the novel has come full circle so that entries on Ramona and Alessandro are no longer the proper names of persons but rather of places.

The California place-name literature sheds light specifically on the significance of naming in the novel and broadly on how the text illuminates the history and perceptions of Spanish language (use and learning) in the US from 1884 to the present. More broadly, still, this is the unfinished history of Spanish in the US. What's striking, William Deverell says, about racial tensions during the early years of California statehood, roughly the period of the novel, is how "the place also witnessed a curious conflict over names—wherein disputes

over naming reveal deeper antagonisms."[32] We know how that conflict—
Ramona or Majel/Majella, Alessandro or Alejandro—shadows the novel, never
at the center but always present, unresolved, at the edges. As an unrecognized
translation of testimonial voices, the novel occludes both informant and translator so that places rather than people move to the center of consciousness in
the novel's afterlives. It's in this sense a history of mis- and un-translation (as a
symptom of those tensions, not as a flag of the missing "faithful" translation)
grounded in the complex of tensions (over ethnicity, race, and class) among
Indians, Mexicans, and Anglos in California and the West.

In post-1848 California, these relations were in flux and reflected both
the tendency to use Mexico and Mexicans interchangeably and the need to
make distinctions between things Mexican and Spanish. In order for Anglo
Californians to invent the Spanish fantasy heritage, the basis of the "historical
morality tale of the great Carey McWilliams," Deverell says, they needed to
distinguish present-day Mexicans (racial and economic others within the nation) from the Spanish past that, Deverell notes dryly, hadn't existed for hundreds of years. So the elite Californios, whose status, in the immediate aftermath of the 1848 Treaty of Guadalupe-Hidalgo, was already rapidly eroding
through land-title and citizenship challenges, became the temporary cultural
stand-ins for the missing Spanish. Making them Spanish could make them
less Mexican—by definition, Deverell says. By the time of the Los Angeles
boom of the 1880s and '90s, the Californios were, at least as images in the
Anglo mind, simultaneously exoticized as foreign, mourned as shadows of a
bygone past, and defined as not quite white or American.[33]

It's again the threat and promise of the foreign, Spanish as both essential and dispensable. Jackson's paean of praise for the "soft Spanish speech"
that she heard in the greater Los Angeles area and then made barely audible
in *Ramona* is just one example of the ambivalent foreignizing in the popular *mañana* language of Mediterranean California. Tracking the *Ramona*
translations in the "names on the land" does not add up to a homogeneous
English-only history but instead reveals alternative bi- and multilingual futures that still today haven't yet been fully realized. Explicit discussions of
Spanish-language learning sometimes accompany the place-names, and
some of the place-name books cover both Spanish- and Indigenous-language
names. In all cases, there's a long history and historiography embedded in
the place-names themselves, inscribed on the environment, and transcribed
in the place-name literature. The epigraph to Deverell's *Whitewashed Adobe*
cites Richard Rodriguez's timeline in *Days of Obligation*: it took one hundred
years for La Ciudad de Nuestra Señora la Reina de los Angeles de Porciuncula
to become LA.[34]

The Ramona-Alessandro entries are a good guide to why and how the state place-names are so enduring. Each entry tracks changes in usage over time as well as new information, the entries preserve the name changes and their errors, obsolete names are included as appendices (allowing for the nonextant to be treated as equivalent evidence), and sources are generally credited in bibliographies at the end and regularly include literature as one among equals. The bibliographic citations are often haphazard and incomplete, ironically reinforcing the need for future studies. More than this, the subject of geographical nomenclature is itself constitutionally incomplete. Not only are places with names once unknown revealed over time but also the names of places often change with time, and new information about them is always being found. A tradition of correction, revision, and preservation thus emerged in the place-name literature.

To call these books dictionaries doesn't do justice to their historical scope and conceptual scale. Place-name study in the United States has developed broadly as a resource for geographical, historical, and linguistic knowledge of regional and national toponymy. It's inherently multilingual and comparative, alternating between local and national scales and perspectives. The aims and aspirations of place-name scholars go beyond etymology, the study of the origin and meaning of geographical names identified with the dictionary genre, to a more thoroughgoing historical and historiographical mission. The literary traces in California toponymy are as critical as the more standard geographical sources of maps, atlases, gazetteers, newspapers, and periodicals. The novelist and historian George R. Stewart, founding member of the American Names Society, says it all with the title of his 1945 book, *Names on the Land: A Historical Account of Place-Naming in the United States.*

The most visible of the place-name guides, Erwin G. Gudde's *California Place Names*, was designed as an ongoing record to be updated over time. The Gudde book is actually two different ones, a scholarly "big book," titled *California Place Names: The Origin and Etymology of Current Geographical Names*, which appeared in four editions (1949, 1960, 1969, 1998), and a pocket-size "small book" for a popular readership, titled *1000 California Place Names: Their Origin and Meaning*, which also went into several editions (1947, 1949, 1959); after Gudde's death, the linguist William Bright revised the third edition in the retitled *1500 California Place Names* (1998).[35] The first one, the 1947 pocket guide that preceded by two years and presaged the big book, is a preview, an abridged version, based on research done for the scholarly volume— and thus features the popular-scholarly crossover characteristic of most place-name studies. The new, expanded (to a "dynamic" 1,500 place names) "pocket" version of the classic, according to the University of California Press promotional material, "is not only bigger but better." The UC Press website explains that this handbook focuses on two sorts of names: those that are well known as destinations or geographical features of the state (La Jolla, Tahoe, Alcatraz) and, most important from a translation perspective, "those that demand attention because of their problematic origins, whether Spanish like Bodega and Chamisal or Native American like Aguanga and Siskiyou." This edition is expanded especially with names of Native American origin, reflecting Bright's own expertise as author of *Native American Placenames of the Southwest* (2004; rpt. 2013), giving us, again according to the promotional paratexts, "a much deeper appreciation of the tangled ancestry many California names embody."[36]

From its first appearance in 1949, the big book has served as a model for all state place-name dictionaries.[37] Both Gudde and Bright in their introductions stress that the book, in all its editions, can never be considered "definitive," in the sense of being complete, inclusive and up-to-date (as a geographical gazetteer would). Gudde's preface to the second edition comments that "fortunately the majority of readers of the first edition realized that only positive criticism is of any value," and that the new edition was revised in light of their corrections and suggestions—("Prefatory Note to Second Edition," *California Place Names*, xii–xiii); the 1969 third edition includes a reference list of obsolete names, in response to "the most common objection to the first edition . . . that it contained no obsolete names—a 'geographical dictionary' should include vanished names as well as living ones" ("Prefatory Note to Third Edition," *California Place Names*, vii). The tradition of correction and revision in the Gudde-Bright series is also critical to the rest of the place-name literature. It tells a history of mistranslation, either by perpetuating or by incorporating and updating it.

In the *Ramona* context, Gudde, the industry standard, widely reviewed and revered, represents the most common legacy of both correction and preservation. The two place-names, Ramona and Alessandro, follow the format used for all entries, customized through the same shorthand references to the novel and its adaptations. All the "Ramona" entries in Gudde's three popular editions start with the county location and then date the place-name in relation to the novel: in *1000 California Place Names*, "**Ramona**: [San Diego Co.]. Named soon after 1884 when Helen Hunt Jackson's sentimental novel was at the height of its popularity" (66). Then updating Gudde, Bright's *1500 Names* expands the Ramona entries and adds an Alessandro entry. For the Ramona entry, more detail is added from both text and context: "Named soon after 1884 when Helen Hunt Jackson's sentimental novel was at the height of its popularity. The novel's heroine was a young woman of Cahuilla Indian descent, and an outdoor Ramona Pageant is still staged annually at Hemet. The Spanish name Ramona is the feminine counterpart of *Ramon*, 'Raymond'" (122). Bright added pronunciations to his edition as well as other correctives: "**Alessandro** (al uh ZAN droh) [Riverside Co.]. Named in 1887 after the Indian hero in Helen Hunt Jackson's romantic novel *Ramona*. Jackson perhaps confused *Alessandro*, the Italian equivalent of *Alexander*, with the Spanish *Alejandro*" (13). The 2004 edition corrected the date: "Alessandro . . . The name was applied to the Santa Fe station in 1888 for the Indian hero in Helen Hunt Jackson's sentimental romance *Ramona*, then at the height of its popularity."[38] Beyond basic correctives, the revised and expanded entries show how the form, a bare-bones alphabetical list of place-names, was itself adapted across time to include historical, temporal, as well as spatial detail.

So the Ramona-Alessandro entries incorporate some self-correction, reflecting challenges to the names in the novel, primarily Alessandro, that were made almost as soon as the novel was published. The Spanish-Italian slippage was noted very early on, by Charles Fletcher Lummis and other Ramona-ites on the authentication trail. Lummis, the best known, famous for his flamboyant dressing up as a gaucho, was also a Spanish-fluent promoter of Spanish speaking in Southern California as well as an advocate for Native American causes, via his magazine *Land of Sunshine* (later *Out West*) and civic organizations such as the Landmarks Club he founded in 1895. Lummis, even more than Jackson, with her reformist politics, and Warner, with his sometimes-qualified romantic racialism, openly defended the "mañana habit" in a 1909 piece in *Out West* as "a matter not of race, nor of speech, but of climate." Here, in "The Making of Los Angeles," Lummis connected the "glamour of California" to "the glamour made by histories you did not know, by people whose language you can't understand, of a life which seemed romantic."[39] As city editor for the *Los Angeles Times* and librarian of Los Angeles Public Library, he helped popularize the idea of Los Angeles as a multicultural city and fought a running battle against efforts to erase or bastardize Spanish street and place-names in California.

The Lummis critique in *Land of Sunshine* (1895) of "Mrs. Jackson's use of the Italian instead of the Spanish form of the name [Alessandro]—one of the few inaccuracies of her 'local color'"—is especially pointed, in contrast, for example, to the skeletal entry in one of the earliest place-names studies, Nellie Van de Grift Sanchez's *Spanish and Indian Place Names of California* (1914): "**Alessandro** (Alexander). This place is in Riverside County. This form of the name, used by Helen Hunt Jackson in her famous book, Ramona, is Italian. The Spanish form is Alejandro." On Ramona, Sanchez says: "Ramona (a Christian name), well known as that of the heroine of Mrs. Helen Hunt

Jackson's romance." The Lummis critique has had staying power, recycled in the postwar AAA guide, *The Dictionary of California Land Names*, where he is quoted as having once said of Helen Hunt Jackson's *Ramona*: "It has always been a fly in my ointment that the proper names in that noble book are so much misspelled—and to me absurd. 'Alessandro' is not Spanish but Italian. It ought to be Alejandro."[40] Theories about Jackson's Italian Indian name have also been recirculated then and now, usually speculating on her concern about American problems with Spanish pronunciation as well as her knowledge of Italian and her ignorance of Spanish.

The details of grammar, gender, and translation that appear over time in the entries for both Ramona and Alessandro raise different issues. Bright's revised Gudde entry, adding the feminine form to the derivation of Ramona ("the Spanish name Ramona is the feminine equivalent of Ramon, 'Raymond'") refers back to an earlier pattern of revision in the place-name literature and even earlier in the Ramonana. The timeline includes George Wharton James's 1909 *Through Ramona's Country* ("It is by no means an uncommon Spanish name, many girls bearing it. It is the feminine form of Ramon"), the 1916 *Moreno's Dictionary of Spanish-Named California Cities and Towns* ("**Ramona__**[Rahmoh'-nah]. Feminine of Raymond [Ramon])," and the 1925 *A Pronouncing Dictionary of California Names in English and Spanish* ("**Ramona** [Rah-moh'-nah]. Feminine of Raymond").[41] The repeated references in both the Alessandro and Ramona entries make an apparent appeal to linguistic accuracy that is not false per se but rather differently misleading in both cases.

The point is not to challenge their accuracy but rather to focus our attention on how the entries themselves function as translations of *Ramona*, how the dictionary definitions take part in the circulation of the work. From this networked perspective, the gendered grammar of the Spanish "Ramona" as the feminine of "Ramon" is essentially irrelevant to the novel and seemingly points to a distinction that doesn't make much of a difference either to the work or to its adaptations. The opposite is true of the Alessandro commentary, which circulates as a possible explanation for a recognized anomaly in suggestive ways through the broad *Ramona* text-network. As place-names, both show what could be called strategic mistranslation-ism, or how alternate translations come to be accepted gradually over time, afterlives that don't supplant but are incorporated into the original. Put another way, the Ramona-Alessandro place-names, unlike the displaced persons of the novel, tell the story of how originals are succeeded but not displaced.

The novel may thus make nothing of the grammatical gender of the feminine Ramona, but naming and the language of the names become an identity issue. Gender brings up and complicates the long California history of what

McWilliams calls "the distinction, always shadowy between Indian and Mexican" (*SC*, 47). As we've seen, Alessandro calls Ramona by an "Indian" name, Majel, "in the Luiseno tongue," which he translates as the wood dove (*R*, 181). She suggests further changing it to Majella, and he agrees, repeatedly saying that it's the name Ramona that is "hard for my tongue" (*R*, 196). Whether Majella, the name Ramona prefers, is meant to sound to her and the reader as more Spanish or more feminine, it is unclear how "Indian" it is. Although there is apparently a "Lake Majella" in Monterey, named by two "lady visitors" in July 1885 (just a month before Jackson died), neither Majel nor Majella appears in Bright's *Native American Placenames*.[42] Neither the Spanish nor the Indian names can be said to do any straightforward or one-dimensional cultural work, either positive or negative.

Still, the false definitional precision of the feminine Ramona carries real cultural weight; Ramona's identity as a Spanish speaker is inscribed in her name and reinforced by her identification at the novel's end with Mexico. Historically, in the post-1848 period of the novel's setting, Mexico became American (ours literally in the variations on the formula "Our Mexico") at the same time that Mexican people themselves were demonized, racialized, and foreignized. The tendency to see American expansion as both a national and a racial process of interchanging identities—people and place, race and nation—was recast by the California boom of the 1880s into the need to differentiate those interchangeable or joint identities, Mexican from American and Spanish. Put another way, Deverell argues, the Mexican history of the US that extended back before the founding of the missions and forward beyond the Mexican-American War was Americanized, sanitized for domestic consumption, by circuiting through Spain. What was forgotten, or whitewashed, in the process was the racial violence of both the past and the present, against both Mexicans and Indians, now also interchangeable identifiers. The two terms, McWilliams says, were used "interchangeably or jointly, as in such frequently encountered expressions as a 'Mexican Indian woman'" (*SC*, 47). It is no wonder that so many of the California place-name books list both Spanish and Indian in their titles. This tradition encompasses Nellie Sanchez's *Spanish and Indian Place Names of California*, Gertrude Mott's *A Handbook for Californiacs: A Key to the Meaning and Pronunciation of Spanish and Indian Place Names*, and Laura Kelly McNary's *California Spanish and Indian Place Names*. When they invoke the two naming traditions, they do so not to highlight either their identity or their difference but to demonstrate their interrelation. And grammatical gender, it turns out, is a critical bridge between the two.

Further, the place-name books come with quite a bit of paratextual material. Most open with an introduction or foreword that functions almost as a manifesto (too self-aggrandizing a term for their tone but not inaccurate for their aims). No matter how short, these openers serve as a kind of mission statement or brief on behalf of the purpose of place-naming and place-name study. They endorse different conceptions of the historical consciousness produced by place-names, oriented toward both space and time through language. A sampling of these paratextual statements suggests the complex historicizing that develops, attuned to changes within and over time, corrective and revisionist as well as preservationist. There is the basic question of what makes a name (official names, government documents, published maps, "cluster" or "group" names, literary or fictional names, "folk names," "transfer names"). And then there is the matter of history; the timeline; major dates, events, and figures; the historical narratives that emerge from the place-name work. While they endorse different approaches to historicizing through place, the place-name literature provides a counterweight to English-only or to *mañana*-Spanish conceptions of American literature. A brief look at each of the four representative books, those that circulate most widely in the literature (Gudde, Sanchez, Mott, Hanna), will give a solid sense of the genre and its relation to space and time through language. Together they subscribe to a historical linguistics that documents and honors language change, preserving the errors and the correctives alike.

Gudde sets the standard in the scholarly *California Place Names*: "My purpose was not only to present the etymology and meaning of the place names but to bring out in the stories of those names the whole range of California history . . . Our names are an essential part of our living presence, and in their stories are reflected all phases of the nature of the country and of the history of the people" ("Introduction," Third Edition, xiii–xiv). Gudde ranges widely beyond California to provide a thumbnail sketch of the nation's history, with footnotes to the errors and revisions, starting from the Indians: "A great many Indian place names, though actually Indian, were not bestowed upon features by the natives but by the white conquerors. Many others arose doubtless when Spanish or Americans misinterpreted Indian words as names of places, and these were then often accepted by the Indians" (xiv). From there the timeline moves to the "first period" of European naming from 1542, to the Spanish and Mexican land-grant period, to the "American occupation" and the less interesting present. The length of an entry does not necessarily reflect the importance of the place, Gudde remarks: "Names applied in the broad daylight of history require less space than names whose origin is lost in the dusk before the coming of the white man" ("Introduction," Third Edition, xviii). Throughout, Gudde taps the potential of place-names to tell an intertwined regional and national history that moves according to a different logic, with multiple boundaries, perspectives, and actors, from the conventional progression of the nation: "To show when, how, and by whom these names were applied, to tell their meaning, their origin, and their evolution, their connection with our national history, their relation to the California landscape and the California people—this is the purpose of the book" ("Introduction," Third Edition, xv).

Before Gudde, earlier place-name books focused on the histories revealed and obscured by mistranslation. Nellie Sanchez's 1914 *Spanish and Indian Place Names of California* (which Gudde cites in the introduction as "well known" in the context at the time of the "meager" number of printed works dealing with place-names [*California Place Names*, xxiv]) trades on a kind of linguistic imperial nostalgia, trained on the old Spanish with a nod to Indian names. Sanchez notes, "We of California are doubly rich in the matter of names," with both "Indian nomenclature" and the heritage of "those bold adventurers from Castile." But Californians have been squandering "this priceless heritage" of the "Spanish pioneers," the missionaries and soldiers who established the naming history and practices of California (*Spanish and Indian Place Names*, 2), with all the translation errors in those names. She continues: "There are a number [of names] that appear to be of Anglo-Saxon parentage, but are in reality to be counted among those that suffered the regrettable fate of translation into English from the original Spanish" (3). All the regrettable translations issue in different ways from the gulf between the old and the modern: "Among our Spanish names there is a certain class given to places in modern times by Americans in a praiseworthy attempt to preserve the flavor of the old days. Unfortunately, an insufficient knowledge of the syntax and etymology of the Spanish language had resulted in some improper combinations" (7). The old is real, the modern faulty: "Between this class of modern Spanish names, more or less faulty in construction, given by 'Spaniards from Kansas,' . . . and the real old names of the Spanish epoch . . . , there is an immense gulf" (8). And the Sanchez solution? "In the numerous quotations that are used in this book, the language of the original has generally been retained, with no attempt to change the form of expression" (8). Sanchez endorses her place-name guide as a historical account valuable for fidelity to the sources and the structure of the stories (the "stories of the origin of some of our place names" that are "retold . . . , as far as possible, in the language of their founders . . ."), arranged by geographical location, (beginning with San Diego as the most logical point, since it was there that the first mission was established), and following the course of Spanish Empire" (4–5). Sanchez is an originalist when it comes to language and an imperialist when it comes to history.[43]

Gertrude Mott's *A Handbook for Californiacs: A Key to the Meaning and Pronunciation of Spanish and Indian Place Names* (1926) opens with a foreword by Herbert E. Bolton, the prominent Borderlands historian, then director of the Bancroft Library at the University of California.[44] In it, he includes both the Spanish and the Indians as, admittedly, unequal partners in Borderlands history:

> Spain effectively and permanently colonized half of the Western hemisphere. . . . Not the least of her contributions to California civilization are the geographical and place names which she spread so liberally over our map. . . . Unfortunately many of these musical words are badly mangled in the lips of our readers and of visitors to our state, and their rich significance is lost to them through ignorance of their historic or symbolic import. Realizing this, . . . Mrs. Mott has prepared this guide to the correct pronunciation and the meaning of California geographical and place names of Spanish origin. In the list she has included, also, a few names bequeathed to us by the oldest Californians, the Indians. (vii–viii)

Certified by the Bolton seal of approval, Mott's *Handbook* gives Californiacs a key to their fractured linguistic history.

Around the same time as the first Gudde big book in 1949, Phil Townsend Hanna's *The Dictionary of California Land Names* (1946) is a good example of both kinds of place-name studies, those that recirculate the same irrelevant or misinformation and others that include or stress correctives. Compiler Hanna both distances himself from and embraces a history of mistranslation: "Names of the American period, as a rule, are elusive, vexing and exasperating. They are, at times, likewise ludicrous. To a larger extent, perhaps, than the names of the Spanish period, they are obsolete. However, if the work of the place-name student is to be of service as accessory to history it must throw light on obsolete as well as current names, thereby making the descriptive as well as historical writings of half a century and more ago comprehensible to the modern student."[45] Published by the Automobile Club of Southern California, Hanna's dictionary also exemplifies the multipurpose, almost multigeneric range of place-name books, at once dictionaries, travel and sightseeing guides, and works of history and historical linguistics.

Gudde, Sanchez, Mott, and Hanna stake out the language poles, and their associated values, aesthetic and political, that would organize California place-name literature. At one end is the recovery project of the original Spanish of Sanchez's "Spanish pioneers," at the other the modern mixed Spanish-Indian names or variants, often with untraceable origins, and in-between the "neo-Spanish-style" or "derived," even "contrived," names (from Spanish and American Indian languages).[46] Reflecting the twin aims of the dictionary genre, all the works document both pronunciation and historical etymology, while they also adapt the short form of the alphabetical list by adding to the entries narrative detail and updating any errors. Whether the uses of translation error are embraced or rejected, these are all unfinished histories, dynamic and open to change. The multiple editions of the Gudde-Bright series reflect that uncompleted project, the ongoing work of place-name identification and documentation. They do so as a record of what's missing as much as of what remains.

Finally, some of the more recent guides pay attention to the question of language learning, in sync with their view that California place-names draw on living languages. Bright stresses in the preface that his *1500 California Place Names* isn't a simple expansion of Gudde but a new work, based on "fresh data and more reliable information on names of Native American origin," gathered from research by linguists and anthropologists working with "living speakers of California Indian languages" (2). California place-names are a good place to start studying Spanish, according to Barbara Marinacci and Rudy Marinacci's *California's Spanish Place Names*, which opens with a how-to section and includes an appendix with a short guide to Spanish grammar. Published in 2005, their book as a whole might be taken as a brief on behalf of learning to read and speak Spanish, "decidedly California's second language" (9), part of its past and the future, too. Speculating on the first California constitution, which included a bilingual requirement for all public documents, repealed a few years later, the authors write, "It may be that California is well on the way again to becoming a two-language culture, as it was for the incoming *Yanquis* more than a century ago" (136). The permanent loss of language that might have been the legacy of that first state document is updated as an unfinished past, the gateway to a possible future. Thus attuned to linguistic change, the historical consciousness promulgated by California place-name handbooks tracks a past defined by the multiplicity of language use and envisions a future produced by that ongoing process of becoming.

Mediterraneanizing with Martí

We've come pretty far from California's Mediterranean shore (Remondino), and now, to conclude this part of the book, we go even farther, three thousand miles away to New York City. There José Martí, writing during the late 1880s for a Spanish-speaking audience in the US, the Caribbean, and Latin America, stakes out his own philosophy of translation with his *Ramona*.[47] Translating Jackson's 1884 novel into Spanish, Martí's *Ramona* (1888) provides a bridge between the 1890s Mediterranean California and the 1940s Caribbean. Starting right with the title, Martí's translation suggests the sweeping adaptation he made: hers is titled *Ramona: A Story*, his *Ramona: Novela americana*. If Martí's view of translation is capacious—"traducir *es transpensar*" (his emphasis; "to translate is *to think through/across*"), he wrote—his *Ramona* is clearly that and more.[48] One of only five novels Martí translated into Spanish, Jackson's North American romance of Indian reform was transformed into what he calls in his substantial *Prólogo* to *Ramona* "*nuestra novela*" ("our novel"), "una obra que en nuestros países de América pudiera ser de verdadera resurrección" ("a work that in our countries of America could be a true resurrection"; 203). Martí's *Ramona* starts with a look back, as do so many others, Jackson included, to the shadow text of *Uncle Tom's Cabin*. But when Martí called his *Ramona* "otra 'Cabaña'" ("another *Uncle Tom's Cabin*") speaking out in favor of the Indians as "la Beecher" did for the Negroes—"*Ramona . . . es otra 'Cabaña'*" (199)—he also looked forward to both the limits and possibilities of the multiple racial and national aspirations of *nuestra América*. Two figures, that of the composite author-translator and his main character, whom he calls a "mestiza arrogante" ("arrogant mestiza"; 204), provide the key to his translation-as-adaptation.

Translation for Martí provides the means of thinking in terms of composite forms and collective identifications. As a *novela americana*, the Spanish *Ramona* acts on the promise of resurrection, giving Jackson's novel a new, transnational "American" being. The grammatical sign of his translational thinking is the Martíean signature pronoun "our," the *nuestra* that Martí uses so distinctively and idiosyncratically. Anticipating his famous 1891 essay "Nuestra América" (Our America)—dedicated to imagining a collective "American" identity, reflecting the intertwined hemispheric histories (aboriginal, slave, European) of the New World—his introduction, written three years earlier, repeatedly recasts *Ramona* as *nuestra novela*. And Martí's Jackson, despite "el haber nacido en Norte América" ("the fact of having been born in North America"), serves as an authorial conduit, who "in her famous *A Century of Dishonor* was as passionate as our eloquence and piercing as our prickly pears [arrebatada como nuestra elocuencia y punzante como nuestras tunas]; who in her solemn verses has the serene clarity of our nights and the purple and blue of our ipomeas [la claridad serena de nuestras noches y el morado y azul de nuestras ipomeas],—she paints with American light our panorama, drama, and temperament [con luz americana paisajes, drama y caracteres nuestros]" (Prólogo, *Ramona*, 204). "As [*Como*] Ticknor wrote the history of Spanish literature," Martí speculates, toward the end of the introduction, "Helen Hunt Jackson, with more fire and knowledge, has perhaps written in *Ramona* our novel [ha escritos quizás en *Ramona* nuestra novela]" (Prólogo, *Ramona*, 204). Six "ours" and two "Americas" in the short course of a few sentences join with the comparative "as" (as passionate, as piercing) to link ours with theirs. The total is greater than the sum of the parts: a conditional and prophetic *Ramona* in *nuestra América*, a work, Martí says, in the conditional, that "could be" ("*pudiera*") a true resurrection and is "perhaps" ("*quizás*") ours (Prólogo, *Ramona*, 203).

So it is, counterfactually, Jackson's North American novel that may be *nuestra novela*. Martí's stress on the plural possessive "our" gestures toward a multidirectional trans-American genealogy. The *Ramona* lineage is grounded not only in North America (alluding to George Ticknor's three-volume *History of Spanish Literature*, published in New York and London, 1849, soon translated into Spanish as well as French and German) but also in a hemispheric feminist-sentimentalist tradition. Here another space-time swerve is necessary to recognize this nineteenth-century network. On the occasion of a new 1973 Cuban edition of Martí's *Ramona*, the Cuban intellectual-activist Roberto Fernández Retamar, working under the auspices of the Casa de las Américas, celebrated with his own essay, published in 1978, suggestively titled "Sobre *Ramona* por Helen Hunt Jackson y José Martí" (On *Ramona* by Helen Hunt Jackson and José Martí). Creating a composite author-figure, Jackson-Martí, Fernández Retamar salutes "el combate contra la esclavitud de los negros y contra el brutal trato dado a los indigénas americanos [the struggle against the enslavement of blacks and against the brutal treatment of indigenous Americans] . . . iba a encarnar, en nuestro continente, en cuatro novelas estimables [embodied, in our continent, in four estimable novels]" by "cuatro singulares mujeres americanas del siglo pasado" ("four singular American women from the past century"; 700). His list: *Sab* (1841) by the Cuban Gertrudis Gómez de Avellaneda (1814–73) and *La cabaña del tío Tom* (1852) by the North American Harriet Beecher Stowe (1811–96), . . . *Ramona* (1884) by the North American Helen Hunt Jackson (1830–85), and *Aves sin nido* (1889) by the Peruvian Clorinda Matto de Turner (1854–1909).[49] It's thanks to Fernández Retamar in the 1970s that Martí belatedly takes his place in a nineteenth-century literary history of feminist, anticolonial activism in the Americas.

At the center of this hemispheric network is the traveling *Ramona*, coauthored by a North American sentimentalist and by a, perhaps *the*, Cuban nationalist. Fernández Retamar calls the novel "una obra *transpensada*, recreada por José Martí" ("a *thought-through* work recreated by José Martí"), "una obra que debemos considerar *también* suya" ("a work that we must consider as *also* his") and thus a work important "al desarrollo de la novela hispanoamericana" ("to the development of the Hispanoamerican novel"; 704–5; emphasis original). This process of *transpensamiento* (703, emphasis original), which might be translated both as a thinking *through* and *across*, looks back to Martí's own conception of himself as translator of *Ramona*. The translation from his perspective is the product of more than one author and belongs to more than a single national literary tradition. A new and different work from the original, it elevates the role of translation to active participant in, rather than mere footnote to, the production of literary and cultural meaning. *Nuestra novela*, like *nuestra América*, are composites, volatile and unstable products of linguistically, ethnically, and culturally mixed cultures.

Martí's *Ramona: Novela americana* is thus more than literally a translation; rather a better word might be "transculturation," the Cuban anthropologist Fernando Ortiz's term, coined in 1947, for the multidirectional relations of contact in the colonial world, colony-to-metropole, core-to-periphery.[50] To use Ortiz's term for the process of cultures meeting in the colonial contact zone makes Martí's transculturated *Ramona* an anticipatory work, looking forward to the concept of the contact zone that wouldn't emerge until the new waves of decolonization in the late 1940s. If the process of translating makes *Ramona* "our novel," then Martí's translation shifts its space-time coordinates and actually returns the novel to its invented Latin American beginnings in the fiction of Matto and Avellaneda. Only when *Ramona* is transculturated and counterfactually returned, repatriated to what becomes, after the fact, its linguistic and cultural origins, might it truly become *nuestra novela*. Put another way, it takes the circuitous route of translation to complete that process of return. Understood as repatriated back rather than exported to, the transculturated novel and its composite author together break out of the various local critical categories and national debates—sentimental versus political, artist versus propagandist, antislavery versus Indian reform—that have heretofore isolated its and her component parts.

Ortiz also brings Martí into the 1940s with a long essay, "Cuba, Martí and the Race Problem," translated into English in *Phylon* (1942), based on a speech he gave on July 9, 1941, in the Municipal Palace in Havana.[51] Ortiz heralds Martí for tracing "the immense parabola of racism in Cuba": he had to confront the race problem that threatened "to incapacitate them all for national integration"; "he had to seek in the ideology of his era the weapons with which to destroy the old and prejudicial myths; and he had to anticipate the future, projecting the political perspective toward a positive, social solution of racial conflicts" (256). Ortiz's Martí, like Walter Benjamin's Angel of History, faces both backward and forward, and thus he "traversed the entire parabola of the revolutionary thought of his era . . . from the analysis of the subjugation of some races by others to the social decadence of racism" (256). Another way to describe the parabola is through the Mediterranean continuum, where, as we've seen, race is both shallowly submerged and invisibly marked.

Likewise, Martí's *Ramona* is differently raced from the *Uncle Tom's Cabin* of the Indian that it is for Jackson and others, writing in English in the US. Rather, it is the story of what he calls in his introduction "*la mestiza arrogante*," "the arrogant *mestiza* whose attachment to her Indian lover endures through persecution and death . . . until the victorious blond race casts them out" ("la mestiza arrogante que en la persecución y en la muerte va cosida a su indio . . . hasta que los echa, . . . la vencedora raza rubia"; Prólogo, *Ramona*, 204). Whereas the novel calls her a "half-breed" with "alien and mongrel blood" (*R*, 30, 234), Martí's mestiza arrogante, the product of mixed Indian and white heritage, is instead the implied ideal subject and physical embodiment of the revolutionary interracial collectivity he calls, using the feminine, "*nuestra América mestiza*." As such, Martí's Ramona owes her mixed heritage to the Latin-American conception of *mestizaje*, long identified with the fraught notion of racial mixture. The racial valence of the term is critical to the rich and troubled story of mestizaje in the Americas, where it is associated with the double legacy of colonial histories of conquest and slavery and their aftermath (the erasure of blackness and disappearance of the Indian, through outright genocide or a process of temporally subsuming the Indian as "heroic past" to the mestizo as "heroic present," as well as the drive toward "new and often utopian possibilities of aggregation").[52] So, too, with the related adjective *mestizo*, a word important to Martí and one that has always been especially problematic for his English translators, sometimes translated as "half breed," sometimes left in the original Spanish, as in "our *mestizo* America."

Both terms are left untranslated in a key passage in the 1971 English translation of "Calibán: Apuntes sobre la cultura de nuestra América" ("Caliban: Notes toward a Discussion of Culture in Our America"), Fernández Retamar's classic essay, published in Spanish in 1971 by Casa de las Américas, where he famously asks, "What is our history, what is our culture, if not the history and culture of Caliban?"[53] His answer is to credit Martí with originating a "Calibanesque vision of the culture we call 'Our America'" ("su vision calibanesca de la cultura de lo que llamó 'nuestra América'"; "Caliban: Notes," 20; "Calibán: Apuntes," 56): "in the colonial world there exists a case unique to the entire planet: a vast zone for which *mestizaje* is not an accident but rather the essence, the central line, ourselves, 'our *mestizo* America'" ("Caliban: Notes," 4). Focusing on "*mestizo*," Fernández Retamar says that "Martí, with his excellent knowledge of the language, employed this specific adjective as the distinctive sign of our culture—a culture of descendants, both ethnically and culturally speaking, of aborigines, Africans, and Europeans" ("Caliban: Notes," 4). What draws Martí into the circuitous route of translation, then, is the half-spoken name of "race," both disreputable and with the potential for collective identification across the hemisphere's languages and borders.

When Martí called his *Ramona* "otra *Cabaña*," he used the machinery of translation to recognize himself and his twin sisters, Jackson-Stowe, as together a composite author-figure whose work locates race at the borders of more than one language, national culture, and ethnic group. And, further, when he calls Ramona, against the Jacksonian grain, the mestiza arrogante, Martí tapped what would become the vexed discourse of mestizaje. Tensions between race and culture, biology and ideology, and the uneven presence and absence of the primary "racial" groups—absorption of the Indigenous, disappearance of blackness—(Rafael Pérez-Torres, Nestor Canclini) reflect the conflicted past of *mestizaje* as well as the debates over its uses in Latin American, Latino, and Indigenous contexts and studies. With typical Martíean foresight, the way Ortiz says he traversed the entire parabola of revolutionary thought, this later cultural nexus can be glimpsed retrospectively in the late nineteenth-century politics of race in Cuba. Then and now, Martí is celebrated both as an advocate for independence beyond race and as a champion of the interracial movement, especially that led by Antonio Maceo and other black leaders. "There is no racial hatred, because there are no races," he famously wrote, in "Nuestra América."[54] But two years later, in "Mi Raza" ("My Race"), published on April 16, 1893, in *Patria*, founded by Martí in New York as the organ of the recently created Partido Revolucionario Cubano, he complicated that categorical statement in the Cuban context, twice asserting there will never be "race war" in Cuba (319, 320), where the Republic "from its first independent constitution on April 10, in Guáimaro, never spoke of whites or blacks" (320). Two years later still, his death on the battlefield in the war for independence against Spain guaranteed his permanent place as the martyred father of Cuba.

The tensions between race consciousness and race neutrality in Martí's construction of Cuban revolution sum up the oft-noted race problem of his Cuban nationalism. Whenever Martí resurfaces, through Ortiz in the 1940s and Retamar in the 1970s, he provides an updated flash point for new racial conflicts of the future. We'll see how this born-again Martí informs even the work of US-based writers interested in the Gulf-Caribbean during the 1940s, when the Mediterranean metaphor resurfaced in relation to the Caribbean. The 1890s network of Martí's *Ramona*, then, brings us back to the American Mediterranean through Cuba, one locus of new-world slavery for Humboldt.[55] We know that Humboldt took the specter of Haiti in Cuba and around the basin as a potential prophecy of future slave emancipation, black revolution. Moving to the Caribbean 1940s in the next and final section of the book will fill out that speculative Mediterranean palimpsest across time, space, and language—from the Humboldtian beginnings to their ongoing fulfillment in the decolonizing 1940s.

4

1940s Gulf-Caribbean Mediterraneans

It's no surprise that Roberto Fernández Retamar should have made José Martí the centerpiece of a foundational essay on the Calibanesque culture of Our America, but the Caribbean-Mediterranean connection he makes in the process may be more unexpected. Commenting etymologically on Caliban as "Shakespeare's anagram for 'cannibal,'" he notes, "that comes in turn from the word *carib*," which itself refers to the Carib Indians, whose "name lives on in the name Caribbean Sea (referred to genially by some as the American Mediterranean, just as if we were to call the Mediterranean the Caribbean of Europe)" ("Caliban," 6). The wry humor of the reference here is as striking as the fleeting parenthetical is typical of the American Mediterranean on-again, off-again presence. Starting with Humboldt, we know how the term tends to operate at the paratextual fringes, always threatening to vaporize, circulating like a translation without an original. Retamar's Martí thus makes a Mediterranean bridge between the California 1890s and the Caribbean 1940s, much as Martí's *Ramona* does in the reverse.

What makes the 1940s such a fertile American Mediterranean moment? We know that a substantial cluster of popular cultural and scholarly works looks back, during this decade across the Caribbean and the US, to reassess the transoceanic history of slavery and emancipation, slave revolt and national revolution. What could be called the Martíean 1890s, a palimpsest of histories, geographies, and languages of new-world colonial conquest and slavery, reappear in the 1940s in a range of genres across the disciplines, including anthropology, fiction, film, and history in Spanish, French, and English, by a variety of writers and artists, both well- and little-known. Some works use the Mediterranean term or concept (Carpentier, Roberts) but most don't (C. L. R. James, Du Bois, Street). All draw on and adapt other nations' histories to narrate their own during this revisionist decade. They orient themselves around different places, primarily Haiti, Cuba, and the US, as well as different times, key flash points being the 1790s Haitian Revolution, the last of the Cuban wars for independence (1895–98, culminating in the failed Ten Years' War, 1868–78 and the Little War, 1879–80), and the US Reconstruction.

Race questions underlie the particular histories that are associated with each region. Different Greco-Roman Mediterranean traditions are also invoked, the seemingly raceless, conquest-based slavery of the Roman empire and the figure of Spartacus the most prominent keys to representing slave revolt, with its intense race consciousness, in the New World.[1] The 1940s text-network of forgotten pasts, unfinished revolutions, and speculative futures also turns *translatio imperii* on its head with the Jamesian figure of "black Spartacus"—an epithet for Toussaint L'Ouverture—who, crossing the Atlantic back to France and reshaping, temporarily, French revolutionary politics, brings classical slave revolt into the American Mediterranean to produce a revolutionary countergeography. The 1940s Caribbean conjuncture recalls, rewrites more internationally, the California 1890s as well as individual island histories of slavery and independence. These pasts function as a fulcrum for later cultural memories of unfinished projects of emancipation and revolution. Tracing the literatures of these often-asymmetrical histories sheds new light on the making of race and anti-imperial politics in locations across the Americas.

The Black Jacobins in the Mediterranean of the West

Of the many ways of framing studies of Caribbean writing, one of the most fruitful in recent years has been the "extended" Caribbean, a trans-American, transoceanic frame that emphasizes connections and networks across a region that extends from New York to Rio. A literary geography that tracks the multidirectional movement of people, ideas, and goods from north to south, from X to Y, such a region has no fixed boundaries: what might be included will change according to focus and time period.[2] The related concept of the "long" unit of time, derived from Fernand Braudel's work on the "longue durée" and the Mediterranean—his magnum opus, *The Mediterranean*, published in 1949—also comes into the picture here.[3] The invention of a Caribbean Mediterranean during the long 1940s, extending back to the 1930s and forward to the 1950s, produced a striking flowering of experimental literary-historical cultural production in New York, New Orleans, Cuba, Jamaica, and Trinidad. This was not the usual US-centric history of civil rights, the legal struggle over race relations at home, but something different, hemispheric and transnational. Nor was it the parochial, island-based approach to the Caribbean as "a geographical area fraught with cultural divides" that are primarily "linguistic," or European-derived ethnic and racial boundaries.[4] Instead, during the era of both world war and worldwide decolonization, writers of popular history and historical fiction, among other genres, drew on emerging global decolonization movements (the spirit of the 1955 Bandung Conference before the fact), working locally toward deimperialization in unlikely interregional networks, from French Saint-Domingue to New Orleans; Laurel, Mississippi, to Oriente, Cuba, and Pensacola, Florida, to the hills of Jamaica and points both north-south and east-west.

These writings of the 1940s display the uses of failed revolutions in the past, especially Haiti and Cuba (C. L. R. James, Roberts, Street) but also US Reconstruction (Du Bois, Street), to predict, will into being, the yet-to-come decolonizing of the future. Accordingly, these Caribbean-Mediterranean text-networks move dynamically along the scales of space, time, and language. To map their interconnections, we turn first to two unlikely bedfellows: W. Adolphe Roberts, who first coins the phrase "Mediterranean of the West" in his pioneering study *The Caribbean: The Story of Our Sea of Destiny* (1940), and later invokes Martí in *The Single Star* (1949), a novel set in Jamaica and Cuba in the late 1890s during the Cuban War of Independence, and C. L. R. James, who never uses either the Mediterranean name or the concept.[5] Together they mark the two ends of the long 1940s timeline, James's 1938 *The Black Jacobins* near the start and Roberts's 1949 *The Single Star* near the close, as well as the major places and associated languages, James/Haiti/French and Roberts/Cuba/Spanish. Both James and Roberts write mostly from locations that are neither their own nor the setting of their key mediterraneanized works, Roberts in New York and Washington, DC (as well as New Orleans and Kingston), and James in the English seaside town of Brighton. Finally, both are also speculative thinkers in their own right, thinkers who underline the counterfactual, hypothetical imagination required to find the Mediterranean in the Americas.

Their vision departs radically, though, from the garden-variety, US-based speculation of Frederick Ober. We have seen how he waxes eloquent in his 1904 travelogue, *Our West Indian Neighbors: The Islands of the Caribbean Sea, "America's Mediterranean,"* about "the daring speculations" suggested by the chain of islands that "take in the Virgin Isles and the Caribbees" and "protrude like gigantic stepping-stones above the blue waters. . . . The sole visible remains of a vast Caribbean continent, which once occupied what is now the basin of 'America's Mediterranean'—the 'Lost Atlantis' . . . has long been the 'happy hunting ground' of scientists from the time of Humboldt to the present" (3). In contrast to Ober's possessive "Our West Indian Neighbors" and "America's Mediterranean," identified with the mythic "Lost Atlantis," Roberts's "Mediterranean of the West" is ground zero for the "Story of Our Sea of Destiny," the subtitle of his introduction to *The Caribbean* (1940). The book as a whole is his history of the Caribbean *from* the Caribbean, in Peter Hulme's words, "the first historical expression of a pan-Caribbean historical consciousness."[6] It is a history that self-consciously relies on the hypothetical.

Roberts opens his book on that history with an introduction titled "Mediterranean of the West," accompanied by a map titled *The Caribbean Area* (figure 5). The first of multiple maps detailing the region across time, this map, read not geographically and topographically but skewed impressionistically, produces "an imaginative parallel with the Mediterranean," which depends on "a distortion of the Americas": "America north of the Isthmus of Panama becomes an aggregate of Europe and the islands of the Mediterranean"; "Asia has vanished in the Atlantic . . . precisely where the lost continent of Atlantis is thought to have been"; "tilt the map slightly upside down," and "Puerto Rico is Crete, and Hispaniola a Greece torn from the mainland. . . . The multitudinous Cuban cays and the Isle of Pines are Sardinia and Corsica smashed to fragments" (*C*, 18–19). The net result of this extended, and violent, inverted parallel: with "a little poetical license . . . the two seas . . . can be rated as counterparts, while the imperial implications take on a startling resemblance" (*C*, 18). Landlocked seas for Roberts are contact zones, "magnets" for nations striving to dominate as a single, imperial hegemon "those inland oceans" (*C*,13). The imperial resemblance—"South America, to the Conquistadores, was the Dark Continent" (*C*, 19)—is summed up in the closing lines as "the conflict for power" that is both "the destiny of the sea" and "our sea of destiny" (*C*, 19).

Roberts's mediterraneanized Caribbean, produced by hypothetical distortion and poetic license, reflects a disjunctive parallel, how the Mediterranean does *not* fit the Caribbean. The map that illustrates his chapter makes the point visually and unmistakably (figure 5). A map with an inset, conventionally used to show scale, either overview or close-up of a section, is in this case cartographically nonconforming: the main map is labeled "The Caribbean Proper" with a small inset, a mini map labeled "Mediterranean Sea." "Between the Americas . . . lies our own Caribbean. Held in the embrace of two continents, the Caribbean is the key to both" (*C*, 13). The point of the comparison is its reversal, "our own Caribbean" overturning the Mediterranean model. The "hemisphere with the older civilization" may start as the model but under the pressure of the imaginative parallel, the Caribbean becomes the main event to the miniaturized Mediterranean. The rest of the maps in the book tell the story of our sea of destiny from preconquest and colonization to 1940 (figures 6–7).

Roberts's history that makes the Caribbean Mediterranean a space-time of reversals points back to the question I raised in the preface of whether *invention* or *discovery* more aptly terms the project of this book. That question, deeply interwoven with the historiography on the "discovery" and/or the "conquest" of the Americas, is key to Roberts's last lines in the introduction on the Caribbean destiny: "After they realized that America was a new world and not the Indies, the discoverers shaped their course by the dream, or the theory—whichever one prefers—that the glories of their old hemisphere would be repeated here" (*TC*, 19). The ultimate fate of that dream is the open-ended history of the Mediterranean of the West. The name itself, characteristic of the fleeting mention of the American Mediterranean proper, is used only twice in *The Caribbean*, once characteristically, paratextually in a title, and again at the very end of the last chapter on "the Caribbean today," in 1940 (see map, figure 7): "The ideas advanced in the latter half of this chapter are speculations, not prophecies. . . . One thing is sure: the Caribbean is the Mediterranean of the West, and if the present war reaches the New World, or totalitarianism dominates the Old, the sea's strategic importance will be greater than at any time in the 448 years since the coming of Columbus" (*TC*, 342). However it turns out, this resolutely unfinished history depends on visualizing the comparison between the Caribbean and the Mediterranean.

Two years before Roberts's book, another West Indian, C. L. R. James, then living abroad in England, produced his own, even more sweepingly revolutionary history of the Caribbean, *The Black Jacobins* (1938). Writing from the exile in which West Indians are said, invariably, to transcend their island identity, both the English-speaking white Jamaican and the black Trinidadian stress the speculative dimension of their historical projects. James comes into the picture here in part through Roberts, one of the "West Indian visionaries . . . , who took note of the topographical analogy between the American archipelago of the Caribbean and the Mediterranean archipelago of the Greek islands and on that basis projected a cultural analogy."[7] While Roberts emphasizes the spatial imagination, James makes a temporal transposition from the revolutionary struggles of *The Black Jacobins*, the events in 1790s Saint-Domingue, or as he calls it, San Domingo, to the as-yet unfinished history of world deimperialization.

The textual timeline of *The Black Jacobins*, its editions, prefaces, appendix, and commentary, comprises an extended network of its own.[8] The 1938 book ends famously prophetically, "The imperialists [who] envisage an eternity of African exploitation" did not foresee that "the blacks of Africa are more advanced, nearer ready than were the slaves of San Domingo" (*BJ*, 376). Later, in the 1963 revised edition of *The Black Jacobins*, James widens the prediction, paratextually, with an appendix, "From Toussaint L'Ouverture to Fidel Castro," that pinpoints the now-extended location and time of his project: "What took place in French San Domingo in 1792–1804 reappeared in Cuba in 1958" (*BJ*, 392). Later, still, in his 1971 Atlanta "Lectures on *The Black Jacobins*," James reasserts the Haiti-Africa conjuncture: "I wrote the book in order that people should think about the African revolution and get their minds right about what was bound to happen in Africa."[9] This leap into futurity, the whole oceanic space-time transposition, "thinking about what is going to happen as a result of what you see around you" ("Lectures," 72), he ultimately labels "speculative thought": "unless, in the words of Hegel, you are doing speculative thought, you are not doing any thought at all" ("Lectures," 74). Like Roberts's imaginative distortion and poetical license, James's speculative thought underwrites their oceanic histories of the revolutionary Caribbean, from Columbus to Castro.[10] They share a particular skeptical take on their own conjectural enterprise, the limits and possibilities of transposing other regional and global histories, including those of the classical Mediterranean, to the nations, empires, and languages of the trans-Atlantic-and-Pacific Americas.

Following their lead, this fourth part of the book jumps off speculatively from the extended or greater Mediterranean as a frame for the 1930s and '40s era of both world war and worldwide decolonization. The main question is which Mediterranean matched specific national contexts. The ocean studies scholar Rolf Petri notes that the German imagination of Mediterranean-ness focused on Greek antiquity, the Italian on the Roman Empire, while the French was more multifaceted. These national dimensions of the Mediterranean metaphor make visible the different Greeces and Romes of the extended Caribbean, their different historiographies and historical consciousness. Concomitantly, the greater Mediterranean frames the international anticolonialism of the 1930s and '40s through a critical awareness of the colonial languages and nationalist struggles for self-determination throughout the Caribbean.[11]

That perspective underwrites the network of texts and contexts for part 4. Their space-timeline centers in the long decade of world war and decolonization in Cuba, Haiti, and the US South, then radiates out, looking backward to key events of the 1790s and 1890s, and forward to their still unfinished status in the future of the 1960s–1970s. There is a critical linguistic dimension to this text-network, which both uses and comments on what Fernández Retamar calls the "three great colonial languages of the Caribbean," where each language takes on different geopolitical functions in relation to their different imperial contexts ("Caliban," 13). Spanish, the language of the colonizer, becomes an instrument of liberation for Martí, French a Janus-faced language of revolution and counterrevolution for James and Roberts, and English, the omnipresent shadow, looming over all of these periods of colonial domination and resistance. As historians of language, they point back to Reclus, who we know predicted in the late 1890s that English would not become the dominant force in Spanish America that some argued it would. Thinking this way through a three-dimensional grid makes language into a shuttle or conveyance for different space-times.

To model a way of moving dynamically along all three of these scales—space, time, and language—this part will follow a cluster of networks centered around the literary geographies of Cuba and Haiti, from the 1930s through the 1970s. First, Martí, remembered surprisingly, in the 1940s US (by Roberts and others), as well as, more obviously, in Cuba (by Ortiz, Carpentier, Fernández Retamar, and others), turns out to be the linchpin for one network. He occupies the center, a figure of translation where one island history of unfinished revolution becomes the model for a larger whole. Cuba becomes the Caribbean, the Caribbean a mediterraneanized sea, and Spanish meets up with English as two of the three colonial languages of the greater Caribbean. Second, James's *The Black Jacobins* creates a text-network of its own, extending from the 1938 first edition to the 1971 Atlanta Lectures. Drilling down further in time, the 1938 *Black Jacobins* brings in Du Bois's *Black Reconstruction in America*, published three years earlier in 1935, and later, Carpentier's *El reino de este mundo* (*The Kingdom of This World*; 1949), the novel written by a Cuban about the Haitian Revolution, in which the famous preface on *lo real maravilloso* also contains his single reference to "el Mediterráneo Caribe." Finally, a brief look at the Spartacus complex in fiction and film of the 1960s will conclude part 4, followed by an epilogue on Braudel's Mediterranean to close the book.

Network I: Martí, Roberts, Street

New York City in the late 1930s and '40s may seem an unlikely location for two writers, one a Jamaican in exile, and the other a US Southerner from Lebanon, Mississippi, to produce popular novels set in Cuba with a starring role for José Martí. Both lived and worked in the New York City literary world, but they didn't apparently cross paths. By 1936 when Street had his first major success, the well-reviewed book of essays *Look Away!*, Roberts was on the verge of leaving town for San Juan, New Orleans, and ultimately Jamaica. Both relative unknowns to a US reading audience today, their work deserves at least a modest revival. Their shared location during this era, when Du Bois and James took different transnational routes to what they signaled as alternative histories of "black" Reconstruction and the "black" Jacobins, is my impetus. All four writers take part in the period's historical reassessment of slavery and emancipation, revolt and revolution, not only as transnational and translingual but also as anticolonial and historicist. Taken together, they ultimately link the Caribbean with the Pacific, making good, in the middle of the so-called American Century, on Ellen Churchill Semple's prediction in 1903 of "the US as a Pacific Ocean power," "the promise of a new historical era for the American Mediterranean" (*AH*, 398).

Roberts and Street never met but come together in both the time and place when and where each wrote and set his defining historical fiction: 1940s New York City and 1890s Cuba. In his 1962 autobiography, *These Many Years*, in a chapter titled "1939," Roberts remembers the moment when "it came to me that I must write the history of the entire Caribbean, from the discovery by Christopher Columbus up to the present day" (*TMY*, 283). This became his Caribbean book, with its centerpiece, the distorted map of the Mediterranean of the West, which he followed with a trilogy of novels he called his New Orleans historical series: *Royal Street* (1944), *Brave Mardi Gras* (1946), and *Creole Dusk* (1948). Set in the 1840s, 1860s, and 1880s respectively, the novels might also be called "Mediterranean" in their oceanic account of a nineteenth-century Creole family in New Orleans, using the city at the center of Roberts's Mediterranean of the West as a gateway to overlapping spaces and times of circulation of people and goods—up the Mississippi River, across the Atlantic Ocean to Europe and Africa, and from the Gulf of Mexico to Havana, Port-au-Prince, and Panama. While in New York City during the wartime decade of the 1940s, James Street, Baptist preacher and journalist, wrote his own series of historical novels, set in Lebanon, Mississippi, between 1794 and 1896. Street's Lebanon, his own version of Faulkner's Yoknapatawpha, is based on Laurel, Mississippi, where he grew up, the center of what became known as the Free State of Jones, a dissident county that rebelled against the Confederacy during the Civil War. Both Roberts and Street end up in Cuba, their historical novels concluding with Roberts's *The Single Star: A Novel of Cuba in the '90s* (1949), which dramatizes the role of expatriate Southerners who became Jamaican planters and fighters in the Cuban War of Independence—framed with an epigraph by José Martí, Cuban poet-patriot killed in the war—and Street's *Mingo Dabney* (1950), which puts his American hero in 1895 Cuba, crossing paths with none other than the revolutionary martyr Martí.

To speak of Martí as Roberts and Street do, at this point in time from a US perspective, not that of nuestra América, but the America "que no es nuestra" ("which is not ours"; translation mine), is as counterintuitive as it turns out to make complete contextual sense. When Ortiz published his essay, "Cuba, Martí and the Race Problem," translated into English in *Phylon* (1942), the editors footnoted the very first line, explaining that "José Julian Martí y Perez is not well known in America" (253). The footnote provides what they considered essential biographical information, covering his life in New York, where "with Maximo Gómez and Antonio Maceo, he began the Cuban Revolution," and ending with his death in Cuba on May 19, 1895. These are the very historical figures that Roberts and Street feature in their novels, raising for us the question of how and why those US-based writers knew enough to incorporate in their fiction Martí and "his great work of organizing and directing Cuban independence," along with "his philosophy of race relations," as the footnote puts it (253). The Ortiz connection through this translated speech of 1941 is a clue, an indicator, a flash point, that I'll continue to return to throughout this section.

These two unsung novels, not Cuban but of Cuba, are paradigms of the mediterraneanizing that puts Du Bois and James in the same broad context as Roberts and Street—not to mention Faulkner and even, by contrast, Margaret Mitchell. An unlikely ensemble, they create a network through which we can rethink how and why the 1930s and '40s became a moment for the reinterpretation of slavery's afterlives, the dreams and failure(s) of emancipation in the hemisphere and beyond. Roberts joins Street in late nineteenth-century Cuba, the seemingly improbable location at which their Southern family histories conclude: the sagas of Street's Dabneys of Lebanon, Mississippi, and Roberts's Oliviers of New Orleans, as well as the Lloyds of Jamaica, break off before (Street) or just as (Roberts) the Spanish-American War ends with the defeat of Spain and the neocolonial triumph of the US. In short, the Roberts-Street histories end *in media res*, before the moment of *Cuba libre*, pointing to the yet-to-come decolonization that was around the corner in the 1940s. This speculative future based on the past as prophecy was the locus of how both Du Bois and James represented the history of black Reconstruction and the black Jacobins during these years.

Roberts / Jamaica, Street / Laurel, Mississippi: 1890s / 1940s Cuba

Of the two undersung authors, Street was read at the time as a Faulkner *manqué*, not really a modernist but instead a garden-variety best seller, with novels adapted into Hollywood films, whereas Roberts was not nearly as popular or well known but was the more serious and explicitly politically committed writer. Both used the same kind of formula fiction, also known as bodice rippers, historical novels spiked with romance and sex, to work out the racial dynamics of a Creole planter (Roberts) or yeoman farmer (Street) class that could potentially produce leaders for a dissident postwar South (Street) or for the decolonization and independence of Jamaica and elsewhere (Roberts). Together they were a rarity—cosmopolitan locals and writers of historical fiction with a hemispheric sweep in the radical tradition of Du Bois and James. In contrast to the small world of Margaret Mitchell's Tara and Atlanta in *Gone with the Wind*, inflated to epic proportions on the big screen, they told an Americas history of slavery and emancipation that predated the founding of the US and extended beyond its eventual continental borders to the Caribbean.

A quick description of the two historical series by Street and Roberts gives a sense of how both writers superimposed the late 1940s onto the late 1890s and infused locally popular genres—history and fiction—with an internationalist anticolonialism. Street's pentalogy opens with *Oh, Promised Land* (1940), set in Georgia and Mississippi from 1759 until a few years after the Louisiana Purchase, a crossroads of empire and home to a polyglot mix of settlers, Indians, and slaves. The rest of the series dramatizes conflicts over land, goods, and slaves among the Indigenous Creeks and the English, French, Spanish, and Americans, stressing the long history of free thinking among the independent-minded, sometimes antislavery, always anti-Negro hill country farmers of Jones County (its name came from the Revolutionary War hero John Paul Jones, whose motto was "I have not yet begun to fight"). The 1942 Civil War novel *Tap Roots* (of which Street says in the foreword, "If in this story, you miss the oft-told tale of the Civil War of Gettysburg and Lee, then I am glad") follows the ill-fated Free State of Jones, one of many communities in the Deep South that, according to Street, defied the Confederacy, to its end in the defeat of the Dabney hero modeled on Newt Knight, the historical leader of Jones County's rebellion against the Confederacy ("a splendid nonconformist who thought the struggle was a rich man's war and a poor man's fight"). A movie version of *Tap Roots*, starring Susan Hayward, Van Heflin, and Boris Karloff, was made in 1948. The fifth and final novel, *Mingo Dabney*, follows the last of the Dabneys, Mingo (named for his grandfather's friend and ally the Choctaw Tishomingo), to Cuba, where he joins the Cuban *mambí* army and seeks the hand of the female revolutionary La Entorcha Blanca (whom he had met, seemingly improbably, in the fourth novel, in Lebanon, where she had been left for her own protection by Martí, on a mission to raise funds and recruits for Cuba).[12]

Roberts explores the same networks of race, nation, and empire as Street does but reverses the origin and route of his Southern families: while Street's Dabneys go to Cuba from the US, Roberts follows the triumphs and tragedies (mostly the latter) across three generations of Creole protagonists, fleeing the Haitian Revolution, like so many of the Caribbean master class, going from Saint-Domingue to Cuba and the US, where they are embroiled in nationalist schemes with transnational, multilingual, and cross-racial underpinnings. Roberts's historical series of the 1940s starts with the nonfiction *The Caribbean* and ends with a novel, *The Single Star*, circuiting through "old New Orleans" in the aftermath of the Haitian Revolution, to Haiti and Santo Domingo (1844) during the struggle for independence, to Panama and the French canal project under Ferdinand de Lesseps (late 1880s), and finally full circle to Jamaica by way of Cuba and the war for independence from Spain (1898). Roberts's final novel of the decade, published in 1949, *The Single Star* extends the New Orleans trilogy to the 1890s, when the Jamaican Stephen Lloyd (son of disillusioned ex-Confederate Southerners) joins Cuban revolutionaries Miguel and Ines (her *nom de guerre*, *La Estrella*, after the single star on the Cuban flag) Carmona on a secret journey to Cuba, where he serves in the Cuban army against Spain. The novel is framed with an epigraph by José Martí: "The day will come when we shall place, on the strongest fort [Morro Castle, Havana] of our country, the flag of the single star."[13]

Roberts fuses Martí's Cuba as an unfinished revolutionary model with the then-coming independence of Jamaica, much as Street does with 1895 Cuba as an inspiration for the dissident South of white supporters of antiracism, if not black civil rights. Both writers implicitly harken back and forward to James's *Black Jacobins*, both the 1938 edition, which makes the Haitian Revolution a predictor of the decolonization of Africa, and the second edition of 1963, with the appendix, "From Toussaint L'Ouverture to Fidel Castro," which "attempts for the future of the West Indies, all of them, what was done for Africa in 1938" (*BJ*, 391, preface to the 1963 edition, vii). Roberts and Street locate themselves in the same sphere of world conflict and decolonization as James and Du Bois, transposing the emerging independence struggles of the 1930s–1940s world onto different times and places. For Du Bois and Street, the long fetch of slavery and incomplete emancipation in the US is the critical history. For Street, Roberts, and James, the mediterraneanized Gulf-Caribbean is part of a larger region with a shared geography and history, not a part of England or a European appendage, but rather Caribbean—and the Caribbean was American, in the broadest sense of the word.

The question is: how and why did their 1940s turn 1890s Cuba in the extended Gulf-Caribbean into Roberts's Mediterranean of the West, a model space-time for alternative hemispheric histories of race and revolution, empire and nation? Notably, when Roberts and Street displace the issues of the 1940s time of writing back to the era of the Cuban War of Independence in

1895, their novels close without resolution, breaking off before the December 10, 1898, Treaty of Paris formally concluded the Spanish-American War. Rather than political certainties, they carry back from the 1890s and earlier an open-ended Caribbean history of multiple, failed revolutions, linking ongoing unfinished revolution in the eighteenth (Haiti) and nineteenth (Cuba) centuries to world decolonization in the 1940s and after. In turn this timeline intersects with their own political projects, Roberts's for Jamaican independence, Street's for an alternative history of a dissident South. Both espouse explicit pro–self-determination, nationalist and antiimperialist views by looking backward to that earlier moment of "America's unfinished revolution" (the subtitle of Eric Foner's magisterial study of Reconstruction).[14]

As mediterraneanizers, transposing imperial histories around the Gulf-Caribbean, Roberts and Street work simultaneously across space, time, and language, often comparing asymmetrical units—Anglophone Jamaica with Hispanophone Cuba, the fictional Lebanon, Mississippi, with the historical Cuba. As novelists they give us a model of disjunctive comparative history that resembles what the historian Rebecca Scott characterizes in *Degrees of Freedom* as "something else": in her hands parallel and divergent histories of two of the most important post-emancipation societies in the late nineteenth-century Gulf, Louisiana, and Cuba; in their hands fictional histories of the Cuban wars for independence, echoing other Caribbean and Latin American liberation movements from Simón Bolívar forward. Together these entangled histories are made into uneven analogues for 1940s deimperialization.[15]

Reflecting another type of asymmetry, what Talal Asad calls "the inequality of languages," the multilingual Americas—particularly questions of linguistic and cultural translation—are the starting point, ground zero, for Roberts and Street as they layer the histories of other times and places onto their own presents.[16] Both novels interweave Spanish and English, focusing on names of people and places as indicators of the limits and possibilities of translation, tracing both proper names and noms de guerre (most striking: Roberts's La Entorcha and Street's La Estrella, the two female love interests, both revolutionary symbols struggling to be or not to be fully sexualized partners to the heroes). Both novels share a geo-temporal imaginary in which the moment of Cuba in 1895 links to the US of the Civil War, Reconstruction, and the global 1940s, as well as to Haiti and Jamaica (much as James links the Cuban past prophetically with its future through the Haitian Revolution), while Cuba also works in disjunctive parallel with Lebanon (Street) and the Caribbean Sea has a Jamaican/Mediterranean counterpoint (Roberts). Racial comparisons and contrasts are made, more or less systematically, between the places, their histories, movements, and politics. The race question also surfaces through the names and terms mobilized by all sides as well as through contradictions in the hero's conversion to the cause of Cuban independence (*cherchez la femme!*) and the implied or explicit relationship with the US. Both writers inhabit and reveal the conditions that enable, that produce, the 1940s conjuncture of mediterraneanized thinking: anticolonial nationalisms and translingual, transnational movements.

When Ortiz remembered Martí in the 1940s *Phylon* essay, a translation of a speech in Havana, he centered on the race problem, framed by the memory of his own boyhood as a Spanish speaker in "an insular city on the Mediterranean," where he knew "but one Negro," his French-speaking black friend, born a slave in Nubia and brought to Spain and freed ("Cuba," 254). "He was the only boy in the *colegio* who spoke French and I was, in that school on the Mediterranean isle, the only pupil who knew how to speak Spanish fluently" (254). The race-language link here taps the contradictions Ortiz documents in Martí's "sensitivity to the parabola of racism" throughout his career as a revolutionary (255). Ortiz and his black friend were treated as relatively superior at school because of their foreign language skills, but the children would call him "*Cabeza de Moro* (Moor's head)" and "demon" (because they had been taught that the devil is black). Still, Ortiz concludes, the meaning of his skin color went no deeper. Shortly afterward, though, when he was fourteen, he first heard his "racist grandfather," a Spanish loyalist, denigrate Martí as "a mulatto inside" (254). Language politics and race politics both conflicted and cooperated in the "revolutionary jungle" (254) of Ortiz's Cuba.

The novels bear out these contradictions at every level. This starts with their fictional adaptations that repeatedly reference the same group of historical figures and events: from the geography of Cuba and its relation to the 1895 war for independence (the hills of Oriente, the battles of Baire, Mal Tiempo, San Juan Hill, the *trochas*, trails built by the Spanish to isolate east from west) to the *reconcentrados* of Valeriano Weyler ("the Butcher"), the concentration camps in garrison towns in which the urban Cuban population was herded toward the end of the war. Both novels feature, more or less fleetingly, their own Martís, along with other major Cuban leaders, Antonio Maceo and Máximo Gómez, "calling the roll of Cuba's idols" (*MD*, 30). Roberts's novel moves from Jamaica to Cuba after the death, on May 19, 1895, of "the immaculate Martí [who] was taken from us in the first weeks of the war" (*SS*, 110), and the death, slightly later, on December 7, 1896, of Maceo, "the Bronze Titan." In contrast Street keeps Martí alive long enough to stage US encounters with his work for the revolution, fundraising and recruiting, in Lebanon and Cuba. Both Martís, though, yoke the physical frailty to the political and rhetorical strength for which the writer was famous: from the "puny body" of the "little man" with the limp from the "Spanish shackles" (*MD*, 27–28) emerges the voice and the cry of the "unconquered and unconquerable revolutionist," "Independence or death!" (*SS*, 40).

While Martí functions for both writers as model martyr, his Cuba the prototype for the unfinished revolutions of Jamaica (Roberts) and the renegade, hill-country South (Street), the novels part ways in assessing the role of race in shaping these histories. *The Single Star* lionizes "the Apostle" as the lone political figure with "the power to convince every type of Cuban, white or colored" (*SS*, 40)—"thousands rushed to enlist because the blood of Martí had flowed" (*SS*, 110)—but strategically dispenses almost as quickly with Maceo as with Martí. The critical role of Afro-Cubans in the 1895–98 War of Independence is sidestepped in Roberts's novel, more focused on championing the white Creole leadership of the Cuban independence movement as analogue for Jamaica. Hence the novel's racially equivocal epitaph on Maceo: "History did not show his equal among generals of Negro blood, and few of any race that could be called his superiors. In losing him the Cuban cause had suffered a terrible blow" (*SS*, 110). Despite the fact that half of Maceo's soldiers were black, "the whites expressed themselves with intenser feeling about the genius of the mulatto chieftain, the negroes hesitating as though they feared they might be accused of praising him simply because he had been colored" (*SS*, 110). However qualified this final summation of Maceo's role may be, the novel rejects the colonial viewpoint of the Jamaican planter class, both pro-English ("Jamaica must never desert the Empire!" [*SS*, 22]) and marked by overt racial fear of "turning the country into a second Haiti" ("Was it possible or even desirable in a country like Jamaica to bar the colored man?" [*SS*, 63–64]). Stephen Lloyd, with his US Southern roots and an internationalist bent (he chose to go to university in Montreal), differs from "the Jamaican Creoles [who] knew little and cared less about what was happening in Cuba barely a hundred miles away" (*SS*, 21). Hispanophone Cuba is Roberts's limited test case for Jamaican independence. Beyond this, Roberts's "Creole romance" does not go, turning away from racial politics in favor of making the anticolonial argument against Britain, itself a challenge for an intensely Anglophilic planter class.[17]

In contrast, for Street other Martís and Maceos emerge, differing mainly along lines of race. The final two novels of the Street series, *Mingo Dabney* in 1950 and, the year before, *Tomorrow We Reap* (co-written with James Childers), depict Martí's organizing work in Florida and Mississippi in 1893, "beating the bushes for nickels and dimes," before recounting the death of "the prophet . . . killed at a place called Dos Ríos!" (*MD*, 97). In *Tomorrow We Reap*, addressing Cuban tobacco factory workers and Mississippi valley folks alike in Lebanon, Martí calls for money and arms, a practical activist as well as "poet and mystic."[18] Street's Martí also speaks inconvenient truths to the people as well as to power. Working to explain to an audience of local Southern skeptics in "a valley of provincials," why "a revolutionist is interested in . . . Lebanon," "the internationalist was appalled . . . at American insularity," Martí says, "The South, whether you gentlemen agree or not, is a colony of the United States, and my country is a colony of Spain. We've had four hundred years of exploitation; you've had only thirty. . . Have you ever considered the similarity between your South and my Cuba? We each are an agrarian society . . . cursed with one crop, burdened by race antagonisms, poverty, and ignorance" (*TWR*, 131, 105). Despite the provincials' resistance to "the foreigner's misconception of hegemony in the valley" (*TWR*, 106), they ultimately adopt his revolution as their own ("aid to Cuba became a cause in the valley, a new thing to talk about. A box supper was given at the Free Church and a raffle at the Odd Fellows Hall" [*TWR*, 138]), pushed most pointedly by Martí's assurances about Cuban racial politics. "Will Cuba accept Negro soldiers?" asks an elderly black man, to which Martí replies, "We ask for men, sir. . . . It is the promise of liberated Cuba to the slaves of Spain" (*TWR*, 107–8).

But if in contrast to the situation at home, the cry "Not in *our* Cuba!" inspires a small interracial army of US volunteers from Street's Lebanon to enlist for Cuban freedom, once in Cuba in Street's fifth novel, Antonio Maceo is pointedly racialized, alternately called the Bronze Titan, the Brown One, the Nigra. *Mingo Dabney* portrays him ambiguously as a reluctant conscript in a white man's world, a soldier who favors silk underwear, his "hair and lips . . . the only visible indications of his Negroid heritage, and yet Africa was the explanation of the pride and sensitiveness of Antonio Maceo. He never allowed himself to forget he was neither black nor white in a society where white was the color of the overlords" (*MD*, 183). Street's Maceo ultimately finds a pressure point where Cuban and US racial views meet and collide. "Mingo Dabney was a Southerner and Antonio Macéo was a mulatto" (*MD*, 187). Mingo "understood the implication" (47) but believes Maceo's color makes no difference (he wants "to seal a brotherhood not rip it further apart" [*MD*, 187]); his fellow American volunteer sets the record straight. "You can say 'Negro' all you please, but you still think 'nigra.' Americans just ain't color-blind yet" (*MD*, 205). Maceo's death at the end and his clandestine burial (with Mingo's help) near Punta Brava, which, as the historical record indicates, deprived the Spanish of the evidence of his body, conclude without resolving the racial conflict of the emerging nation: Martí's aspirational post-race equality versus Maceo's life, "a slave to caste" (*Mingo*, 188) within "the gap of color" (*MD*, 184).

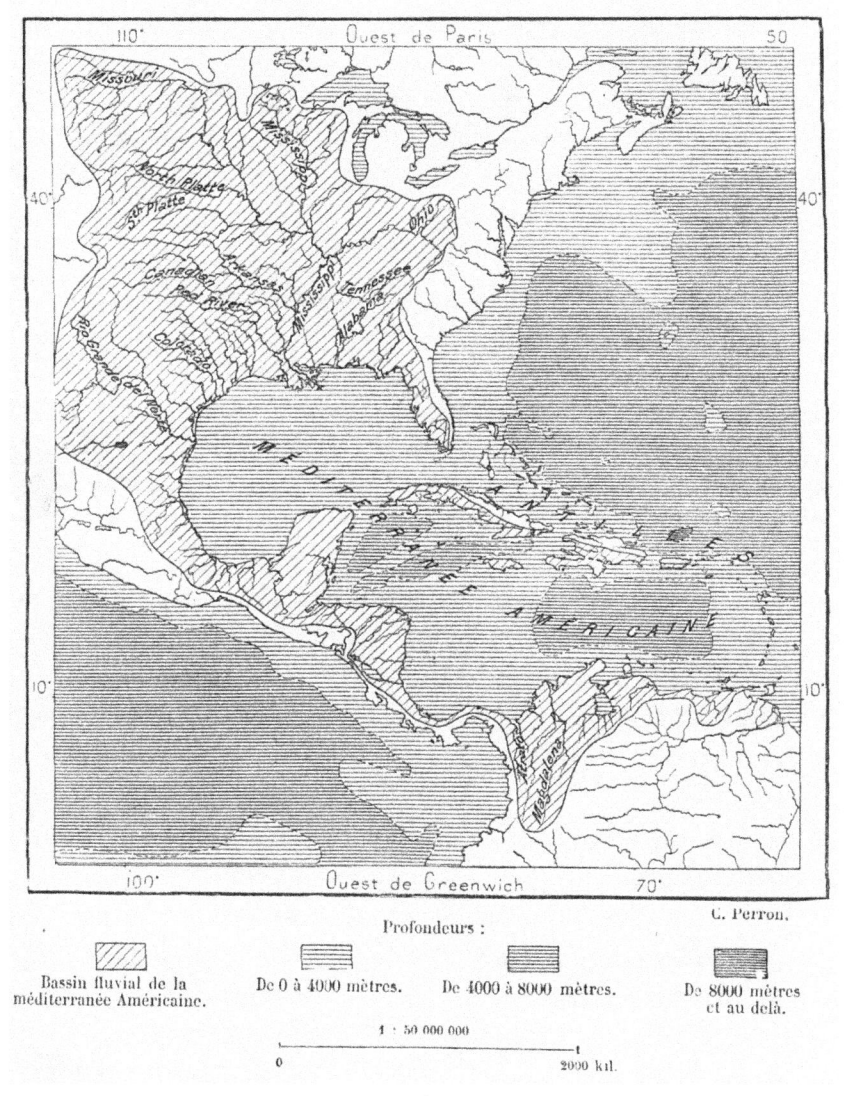

FIGURE 1. *Méditerranée américaine* (1891). From Élisée Reclus, *Nouvelle géographie universelle* (Paris: Hachette, 1876), 629. *"La double méditerranée américaine,—golfe du mexique et mer des Caraïbes"* (1). This map displays watersheds draining to the sea and accompanies the comparisons made in the text between the catchment basins of the Gulf of Mexico and the Caribbean Sea. An illustration of physical geography, it is twinned with one of several maps throughout the volume showing the human geography of the dominant races in the region (figures 2–3).

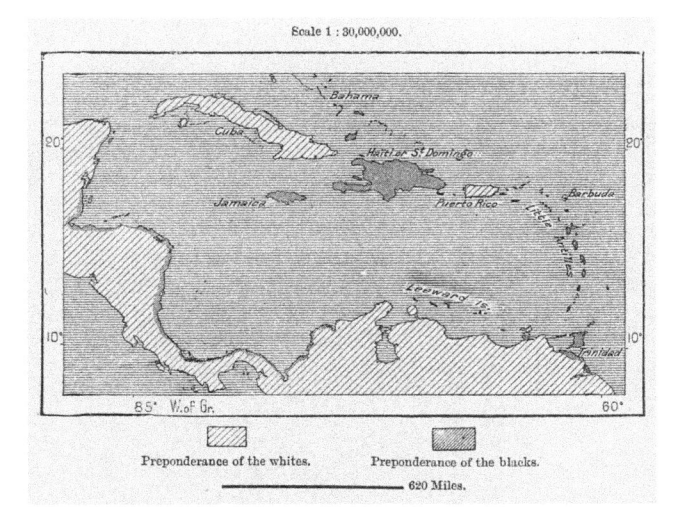

Scale 1 : 30,000,000.

Preponderance of the whites. Preponderance of the blacks.

620 Miles.

FIGURE 2. *Preponderance of the White and Black Races in the West Indies* (1897). From Élisée Reclus, *The Earth and Its Inhabitants, North America*, ed. A. H. Keane, vol. 2, *Mexico, Central America, West Indies* (New York: D. Appleton, 1897), 352. "The majority are half-breeds, people of colour . . . a complete fusion has taken place, to such an extent that, of the five million inhabitants of the Antilles, at least three million belong to the mulatto element" (351–52). The illustrations both reduce and amplify the complexities, the ambiguities, and contradictions of Reclus's account of race in *La Méditerranée américaine*. The maps simplify by separating out and isolating competing elements ("races" as a single metric in figures 2–3), whereas the engravings, from unpeopled landscape panoramas, viewed from a distance, to small-scale human figures grouped in middle-ground images of urban and rural scenes, to close-up ethnographic portraits, enshrine and deepen the racial contradictions (figures 16–20).

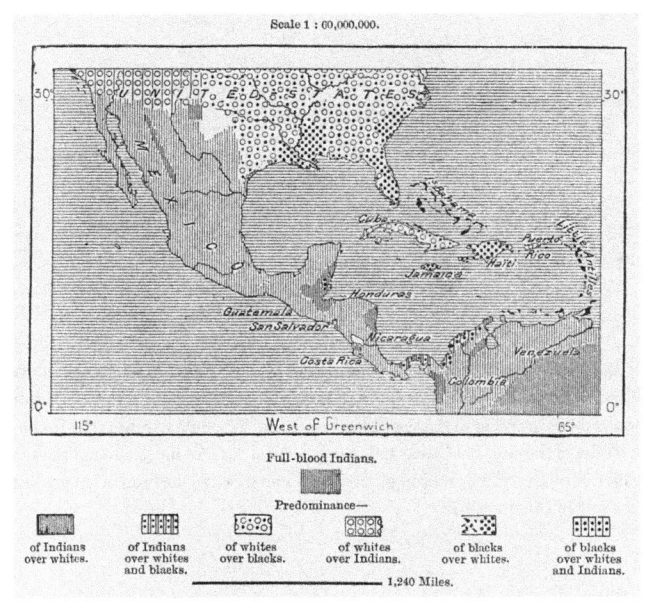

Scale 1 : 60,000,000.

Full-blood Indians.

Predominance—

of Indians over whites. of Indians over whites and blacks. of whites over blacks. of whites over Indians. of blacks over whites. of blacks over whites and Indians.

1,240 Miles.

FIGURE 3. *Predominant Races in Central America* (1897). From Élisée Reclus, *The Earth and Its Inhabitants, North America*, ed. A. H. Keane, vol. 2, *Mexico, Central America, West Indies* (New York: D. Appleton, 1897), 11. "It is noteworthy that the Indian type of features is perpetuated from generation to generation. However white the complexion may become, . . . certain Maya traits [are preserved] by which [the Yucatan Mestizo] may be at once recognized" (155). The text can both reinforce and contradict the illustrations—and vice versa.

FIGURE 4. *Puget Sound—The "American Mediterranean"* (1910). From Otis M. Moore, compiler, *Washington Illustrated: Including View of the Puget Sound Country and Seattle* . . . (Seattle: Puget Sound Bureau of Information, 1901?). Photograph: Manuscripts, Archives, and Special Collections, Washington State University Digital Libraries Collections. The opening sentence on the page facing the map reads: "The 'American Mediterranean' it has been aptly termed—for beauty of scenery and facilities, for commerce unexcelled—penetrating the state of Washington for a distance approximately two hundred miles, east and south, and occupying the very central portion of that section of the state known as Western Washington" (n.p.).

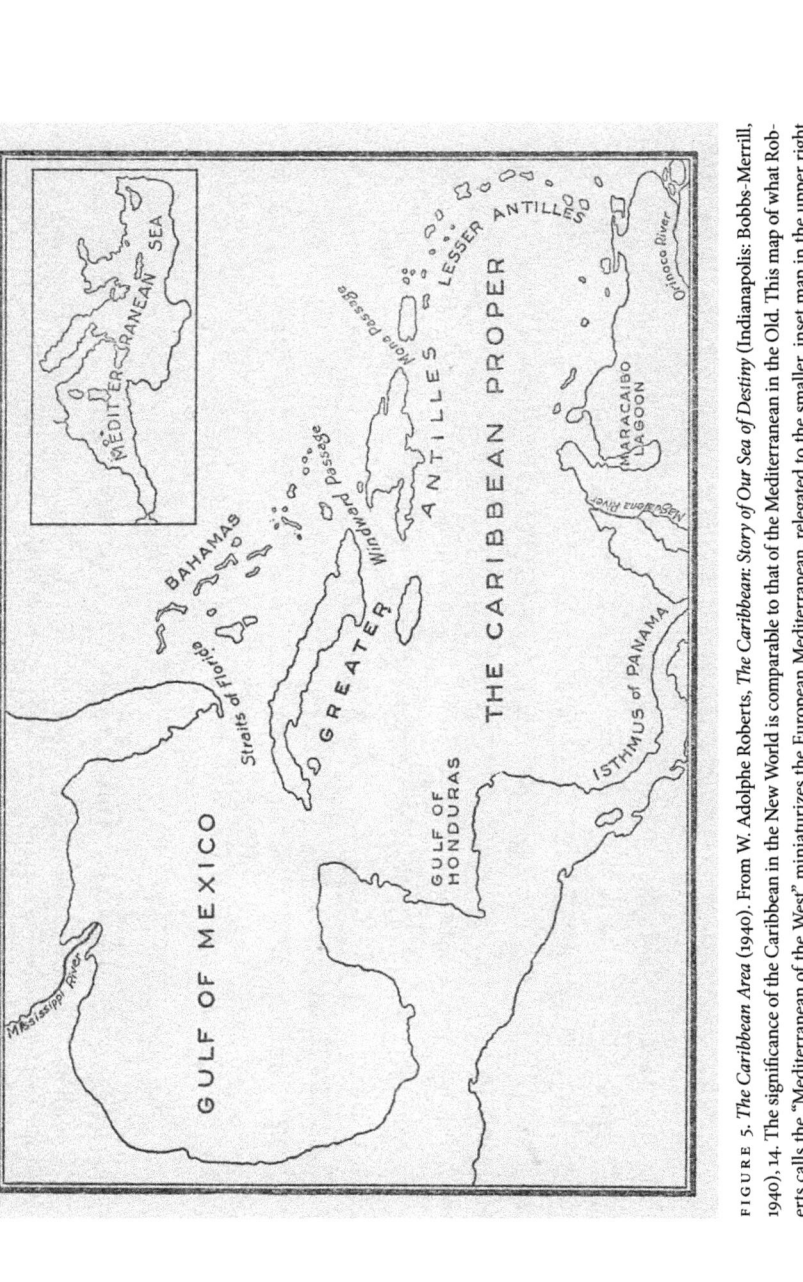

FIGURE 5. *The Caribbean Area* (1940). From W. Adolphe Roberts, *The Caribbean: Story of Our Sea of Destiny* (Indianapolis: Bobbs-Merrill, 1940), 14. The significance of the Caribbean in the New World is comparable to that of the Mediterranean in the Old. This map of what Roberts calls the "Mediterranean of the West" miniaturizes the European Mediterranean, relegated to the smaller, inset map in the upper right corner of the primary map of *The Caribbean Area*. The point of the comparison is its reversal. The older classical Mediterranean may start as the model but under the pressure of the imaginative parallel, the Caribbean becomes the main event to the miniaturized Mediterranean.

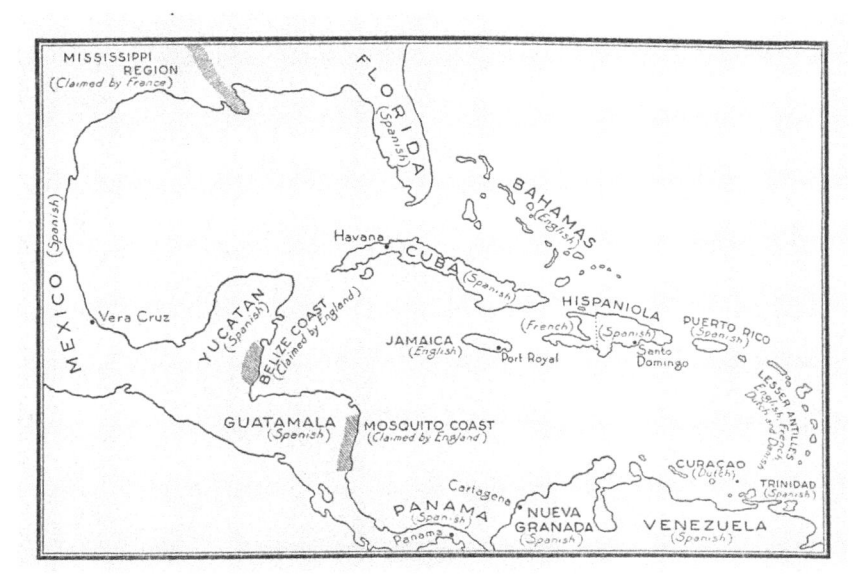

F I G U R E 6. *The Caribbean in 1700* (1940). From W. Adolphe Roberts, *The Caribbean: Story of Our Sea of Destiny* (Indianapolis: Bobbs-Merrill, 1940), 176. Key historical events are superimposed on the template map of the Caribbean, showing "the story of our sea of destiny" across space and time. This map of *The Caribbean in 1700* identifies the key places in the region as colonial possessions of the European powers, including Florida (Spanish), Hispaniola (French and Spanish), the Lesser Antilles (English, French, Dutch, and Danish), and places "claimed by" England and France.

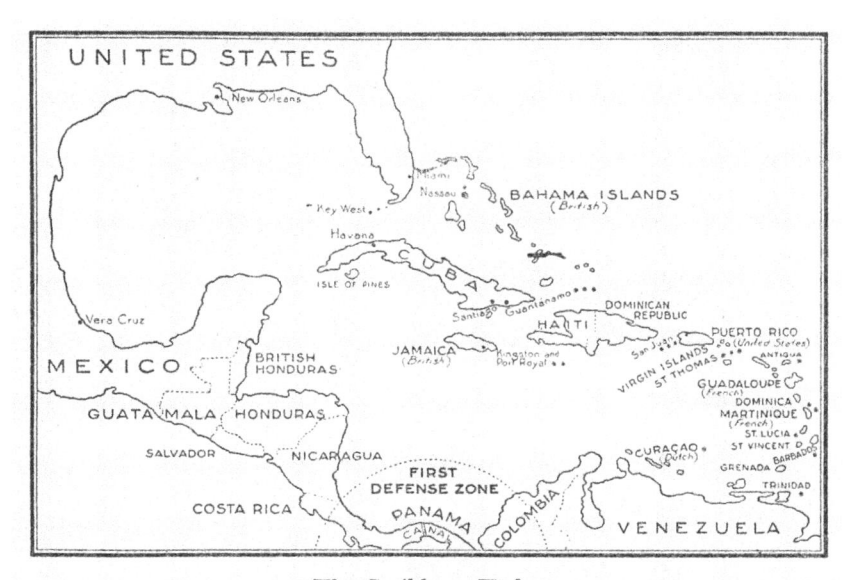

The Caribbean Today

*** Existing United States bases.
 ** Essential bases now in foreign hands.
  * Secondary foreign bases.

F I G U R E 7. *The Caribbean Today* (1940). From W. Adolphe Roberts, *The Caribbean: Story of Our Sea of Destiny* (Indianapolis: Bobbs-Merrill, 1940), 339. This final map closes Roberts's book with "some issues of 1940," focused on the US as dominant power in the region, as measured by "existing naval bases," including Guantánamo.

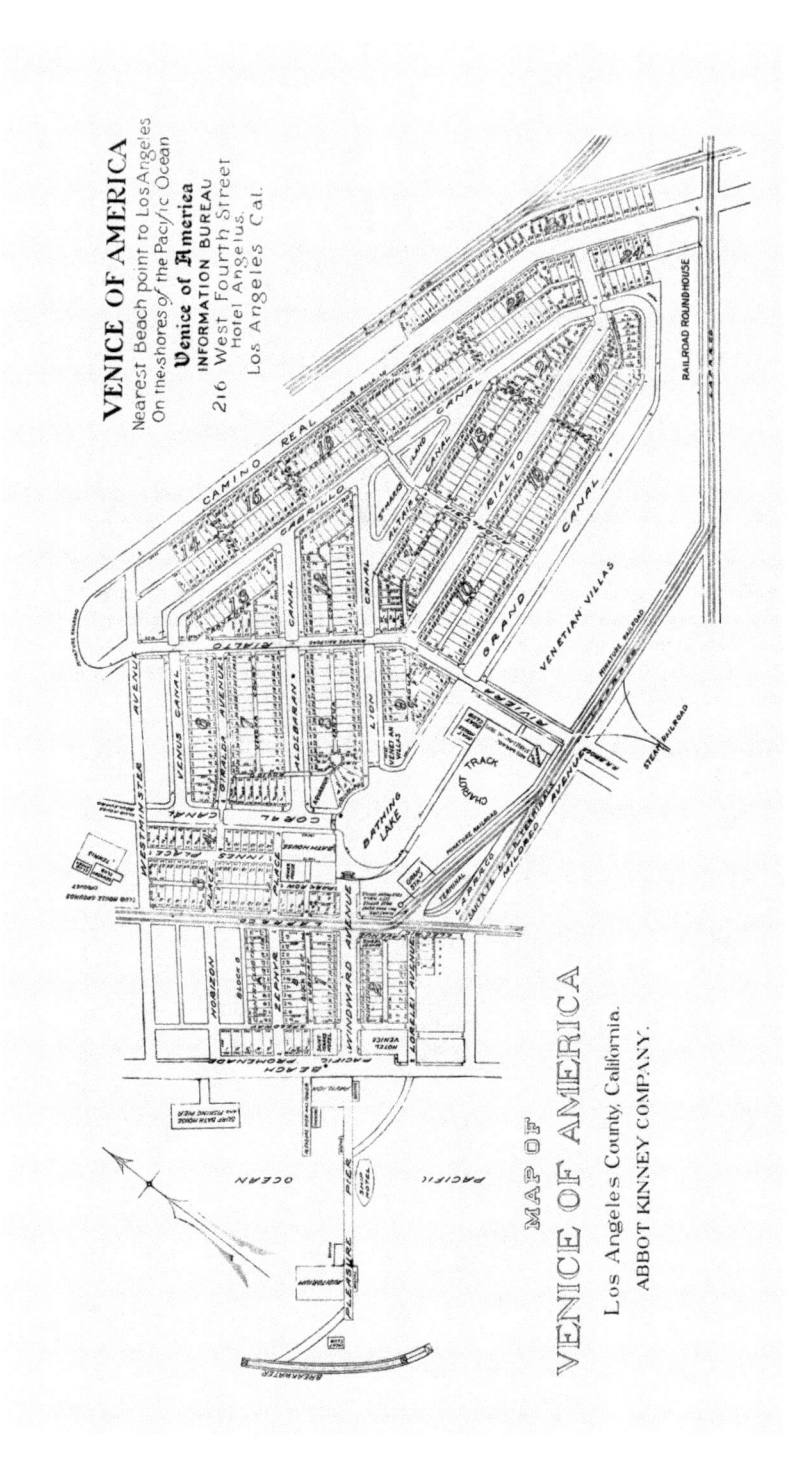

FIGURE 8. *Venice of America*, historical map no. 450, the Abbott Kinney Company (1905). From *Venice Canals*, *Community of Venice, Los Angeles, Los Angeles County, CA*, Library of Congress, Prints and Photographs Division, Historic American Engineering Record (HAER CAL,19-LOSAN,74). Photograph: Library of Congress, Washington, DC. The Los Angeles real-estate developer Abbott Kinney, one of the architects of the popular Mediterranean revival in Southern California, was best known for the creation and development of "Venice of America." Sometimes derided as "Kinney's Folly," Venice featured a network of canals detailed here in a Kinney Company map, now all paved roads. The canals were one of several references to the community's Mediterranean namesake, from the Italianate architecture to Kinney's grand vision for Venice as a West Coast cultural mecca, site of an American cultural renaissance.

FIGURE 9. *Scenes in Montecito and Los Angeles.* From Charles Dudley Warner, *Our Italy* (Hartford, CT: American Publishing, 1891), 13. The illustrations are both typical of the highly conventionalized American Mediterranean representation of a picturesque landscape, depicted from a distance or enclosed in ornate frames. Human inhabitants are either absent or dwarfed by the landscape, and when depicted, they resemble the travelers and tourists of Warner's audience.

FIGURE 10. *Midwinter, Pasadena.* From Charles Dudley Warner, *Our Italy* (Hartford, CT: American Publishing, 1891), 53. The ratio and scale of landscape to human figures shift with the perspective of the panorama. The panoramas that take a midrange perspective feature human inhabitants at work and leisure. Agricultural work dominates in scenes of raisin-curing, orchard irrigation, and packing cherries. Female figures dominate the leisure scenes.

FIGURE 11. *Laguna, from the Southeast*. From Charles Dudley Warner, *Our Italy* (Hartford, CT: American Publishing, 1891), 159. The drawings, often taken from photographs, typically present either a landscape, viewed from a distance (bird's-eye view, panoramic, *vue générale*), with small-scale human subjects, or with no inhabitants at all. This long-perspective view shows in crude stereotypes the hardscrabble life of the Zuñis at a desert pueblo in Laguna. The wide angle creates a division in the viewer's attention between the figures in the foreground and the rows of buildings that ring the desert background.

FIGURE 12. *Terraced Houses, Pueblo of Laguna*. From Charles Dudley Warner, *Our Italy* (Hartford, CT: American Publishing, 1891), 167. This illustration reinforces the contradictions of race in Warner's Mediterraneanism. The viewer's focus is on the desert setting and terraced houses rather than the human figures, themselves stereotypes, including the seated child and the women carrying pottery jars on their heads in the foreground of the illustrations. In contrast, Warner's text is more nuanced and self-reflective, glosses over "the idle drudgery of their semi-savage condition," the village, "without water or street commissioners," "swarming" with "litters of children," in part by comparing the place with a Syrian village and other Mediterranean analogues (*OI*, 168–69). "The resemblance was completed by the figures of the women . . . , carrying on the head a water jar, and holding together by one hand the mantle worn like a Spanish *rebozo*" (*OI*, 165–66).

FIGURE 13. *In and around Los Angeles, Cal.* From P. C. Remondino, *The Mediterranean Shores of America* (Philadelphia: F. A. Davis, 1892), 75. Photograph: Young Research Library, University of California, Los Angeles. Like many American Mediterranean books, Remondino's sells itself on the title page as "fully illustrated" and features stylized landscape scenes, with inset close-ups of both places and people, framed in decorative circles and squares.

FIGURE 14. *Scenes at and near Yuma*. From P. C. Remondino, *The Mediterranean Shores of America* (Philadelphia: F. A. Davis, 1892), 85. Photograph: Young Research Library, University of California, Los Angeles. A Yuma Indian, close to naked, holding bow and arrow, gazing intently off to the distance, is featured along with fully clothed figures, perhaps tourists, seated, gazing idly at the landscape near a railroad bridge, and standing in front of a hotel.

FIGURE 15. *Panoramic View of San Francisco, from California and Powell Streets, Looking toward the Bay*. From W. C. Riley, *Puget Sound, the American Mediterranean, and Pacific Coast* (Saint Paul, MN, 1892). Photograph: The Bancroft Library, University of California, Berkeley (F897.P9R9). One of the more lavish panoramas, printed as plates on one side of a folded strip attached to the cover of this fifteen-page pamphlet of illustrations with captions, but no text. The pamphlet moves up the Pacific Coast from Los Angeles and San Francisco to Victoria, British Columbia; with images in-between of a Chinese theater, restaurant, and temple in Portland; hops harvesting in the Puyallup Valley, Washington; glaciers of Mt. Tacoma, Washington; and of course Puget Sound. This panorama, divided into two separate planes, features a 180° view of the San Francisco Bay on the top plane, with more static urban and rural scapes of both nature and culture, labeled "Tropical Plants and Historical Buildings, California," on the bottom. The pamphlet captures the length of the Mediterranean Pacific and thus conveys the sweep of the American Mediterranean, a region both invented and discovered that went all the way from the Atlantic to the Pacific Ocean.

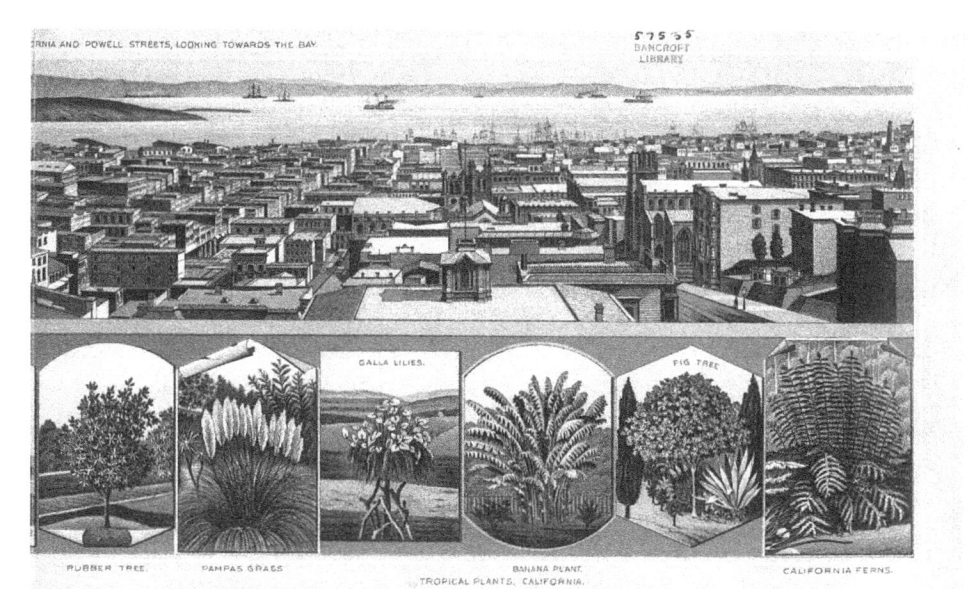

GALLA LILIES.

FIG TREE

RUBBER TREE.   PAMPAS GRASS.   BANANA PLANT.   CALIFORNIA FERNS.

TROPICAL PLANTS, CALIFORNIA.

FIGURE 16. *Panamá: Vue panoramique, prise du Mont Angon.* From Élisée Reclus, *Nouvelle géographie universelle: La terre et les hommes,* vol. 17, *Indes occidentales: Mexique, Isthmes Américains, Antilles* (Paris: Hachette, 1891), 601. A long-perspective view of the uninhabited landscape that echoes the structure of each chapter, opening with "Physical Features," "Climate," and "Flora and Fauna" before moving to "Inhabitants" and "Topography."

FIGURE 17. *Paysage de Panamá: D'après une photographie communiqué par la Compagnie du canal de Panamá.*" From Élisée Reclus, *Nouvelle géographie universelle: La terre et les hommes,* vol. 17, *Indes occidentales: Mexique, Isthmes Américains, Antilles* (Paris: Hachette, 1891), 577. A midrange view of the Panama countryside that shows men at work, this one taken from a photograph produced by *la Compagnie du canal de Panamá* and evoking similar images of work on the canal.

FIGURE 18. *Types de la Martinique—Nègre chasseur de serpents et Négresse charbonniére* (The snake-catcher and charcoal girl, Martinique). From Élisée Reclus, *Nouvelle géographie universelle: La terre et les hommes*, vol. 17, *Indes occidentales: Mexique, Isthmes Américains* (Paris: Hachette, 1891), 647. A close-up, ethnographic portrait of local inhabitants identified with their work. Paired male and female figures in native garb are included in illustrations throughout Reclus's volume.

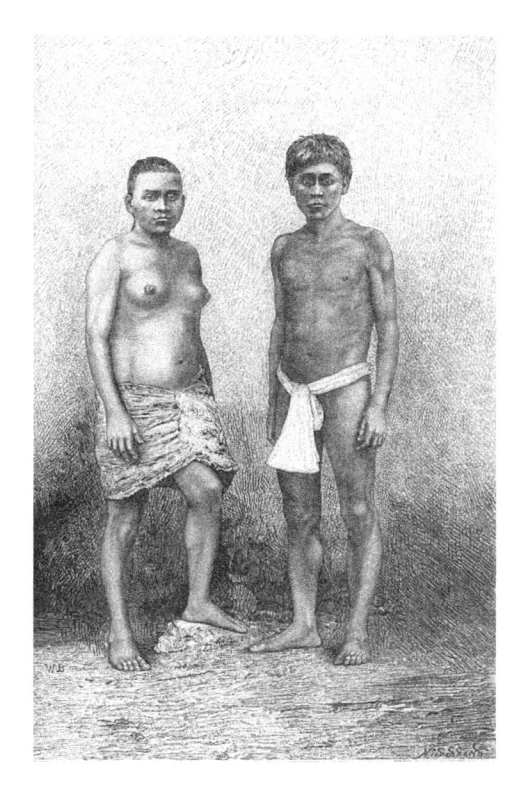

FIGURE 19. *Jeunes Indiens talamancas,* From Élisée Reclus, *Nouvelle géographie universelle: La terre et les hommes*, vol. 17, *Indes occidentales: Mexique, Isthmes Américains, Antilles* (Paris: Hachette, 1891), 553. "*Indiens*" are the only human figures portrayed as half-naked in the ethnographic portraits throughout Reclus's volume. The text on the facing page devotes equal attention to their looks and their language, concluding that their linguistic origins especially argue against the hypothesis of a Nahuatl provenance.

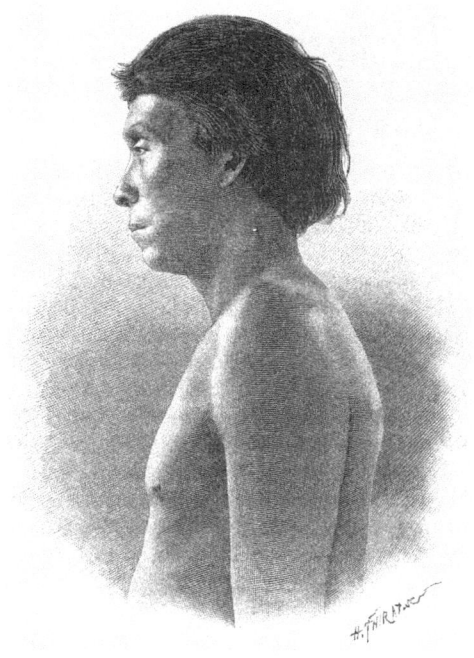

FIGURE 20. *Indien guatuso*, From Élisée Reclus, *Nouvelle géographie universelle: La terre et les hommes*, vol. 17, *Indes occidentales: Mexique, Isthmes Américains, Antilles* (Paris: Hachette, 1891), 555. An unusual close-up, with the subject in profile, rather than full frontal. The French text underscores the humanity of the Guatusos: "Ces indigènes non pas las férocité qu'on leur attribua jadis: l'homme blanc . . . est bien autrement dangereux" (555). The A. H. Keane English translation omits "l'homme blanc," the white man ("Nor are the Guatusos ferocious savages, as formerly asserted; on the contrary, most of them have been exterminated by the Nicaraguan and Costa Rican Ladinos engaged in collecting rubber" [*EI*, 304]). Together, the illustration and both versions convey the multiple contradictions of Reclus's work.

On the Lagoon, Venice, Cal.

FIGURE 21. (top) *Across the Lagoon, Venice Calif.* (1906); (bottom) *On the Lagoon, Venice Cal.* (1906). From Werner von Boltenstern Postcard Collection (Coll. 042), Department of Archives and Special Collections, William H. Hannon Library. Photograph: Loyola Marymount University. The opening of the beach town of Venice in 1905 brought to a 160-acre tract of ocean-side land near Los Angeles the canals, buildings, and amusements of Venice, including a fleet of gondolas and gondoliers imported from Venice. Visitors rented canoes or hired gondoliers at the lagoon boathouse. Today the lagoon is the paved Venice circle.

FIGURE 22. *Puget Sound, the Mediterranean of America.* Travel advertisement, Northern Pacific Railway / Yellowstone Park Line (1906). Ads like this one, aimed at middle-class travelers enjoying the leisure time of the extended summer vacation that became part of many US school calendars around 1900, were designed to attract attention to the Mediterranean character of the climate, commerce, and culture of the Pacific coast. The Northern Pacific Railway quotes an unnamed "eminent physician," testifying to the benefits of "our Northern Pacific Coast country." Like figures 4 and 15, Puget Sound is the location identified as "The Mediterranean of America."

FIGURE 23. *Porto Rico Cruise.* Ad, Atlantic, Gulf and West Indies Steamship Lines (AGWI), *Country Life in America,* ed. Liberty Hyde Bailey and Henry Hodgman Saylor, vols. 25–27 (February 1915), 89. The Atlantic, Gulf and West Indies Steamship Lines touted the Gulf-Caribbean waters and ports for their proximity to New York, their "superb climate" and "fascinating things to do and see." The AGWI logo prominently features "American Mediterranean."

Good Bye to Winter

QUAINT scenes and balmy air are waiting for you along the fascinating shores of the American Mediterranean. There is Nassau in the Bahamas, the seat of the British Colonial Government, only three days from New York by luxurious twin screw steamers of the Ward Line, where the average winter temperature is only 72°. It is a paradise of beautiful flowers and vegetation, with golf, tennis, bathing and all outdoor sports. First cabin tours, $25.00 and up.

FIGURE 24. *Good Bye to Winter.* Ad, Atlantic, Gulf and West Indies Steamship Lines (AGWI), *Country Life in America,* ed. Liberty Hyde Bailey and Henry Hodgman Saylor, vols. 25–27 (November 1913), 104. The destinations "along the fascinating shores of the American Mediterranean" include Florida, Puerto Rico, Bahamas, Texas, Mexico, along with Cuba. "Havana, the Paris of the Western Hemisphere, with its wonderful Cuban climate and interesting ways and by-ways," is depicted in the circular inset of old cobblestone streets.

FIGURE 25. *Home of Ramona Brand* (1900). The Jay T. Last Collection of Graphic Arts and Social History. Photograph: Huntington Digital Library, Huntington Library, San Marino, California. The Home of Ramona brand of oranges advertised from 1900 to 1955 with a fruit-crate label of the Ramona home against a landscape backdrop that changed (like the adaptable American Mediterraneans) depending on the orange supplier. This fruit-crate label advertises "Fancy California Oranges," grown by U. F. del Valle in Camulos, Ventura County, California, one of the locations said to be the home of Ramona. The yellow-stucco, Spanish-style house with a porch and red roof dominates the landscape.

FIGURE 26. *Home of Ramona Brand* (ca. 1906–55). Citrus Label Collection, Schmidt Litho. Co. (printer), Prints and Ephemera. Photograph: Huntington Digital Library, Huntington Library, San Marino, California. This version of the fruit-crate label, advertising "Valencias" (top right corner) with wrapped Sunkist orange logo (bottom left), "Grown & Packed by Piru Citrus Assn., Piru, Ventura County, Calif.," adds a whole layer of landscape to the earlier version. Here the image of the ranch house with wide porch in the foreground is pictured against the backdrop of the Sierra Mountains and spreading orange groves. The landscape dominates, much as the stage and screen adaptations of Helen Hunt Jackson's novel *Ramona* are dwarfed by all the Ramonas in the built environment of Southern California.

Roberts's Cuba thus speaks to Jamaican conceptions of race, political leadership, and the anticolonial project in an age of transition between empires, while Street makes "a bunch of Cuban galoots trying to start a revolution" (*MD*, 24) into a reproach and call to arms to the US South. For both writers, in the place and time of both the setting and the writing of their texts, the United States replaces imperial Europe as the global hegemon. Roberts: Miguel the Cuban revolutionary asks, "Is this not an inevitable phase of what American statesmen used to call their country's 'manifest destiny' to control the New World north of Panama?" and answers himself, "American intervention would rid us of Spain . . . but we might only be exchanging masters" (*SS*, 89). Street: Maceo warns Mingo, "The money lords of your country have determined a policy of aggressive imperialism. They call it manifest destiny and speak eloquently of service to the weak" (*MD*, 182). The liberation struggles of the 1890s and the 1940s—some nationalist and multiracial but not anticolonial, some anticolonial but not antiracist—are shadowed by the specter of the US with its long-standing "tremendous political urge toward the Caribbean Sea" (*SS*, 89). Roberts and Street use the same, overlapping imperial histories to negotiate from their different political locations in the 1940s, the Jamaican nationalist speaking in a postcolonial climate attuned to West Indian federation (debates over Jamaican nationalism—independent self-government or a larger transregional collectivity), and the dissident Southerner speaking against white supremacy and for racial equality as the civil rights movement is just emerging nationally.

Underlying all of these representational differences are strategies of translation that also differ dramatically in these novels, both of which endorse a transregional and translational sensibility but with conflicting outcomes. Proper names bring up nicknames, assumed names, *noms de guerre* and their provenance, all marked differentially by race and gender in both novels, which come to different, equally inconclusive conclusions. *La Entorcha* and *La Estrella* are linked by the same romantic plot conflict encoded in the alternation between their *noms de guerre* (*La Entorcha Blanca* alluding to the prematurely white hair of this symbolic "living torch" [*MD*, 53], *La Estrella* "signifying the star!" [*SS*, 56] of the Cuban flag to come) and their birth names: are they "enraptured apostles" of revolution" (*MD*, 32), "pledged to Cuba" (*SS*, 362), or are they women, candidates for love and wifehood? While the novels end with different romantic resolutions (marriage of our hero and Rafaela/La Entorcha, parting of the ways for Inés/La Estrella and Esteban/Stephen), both leave the political plot unresolved, the future for Cuban independence still open-ended.

Similarly, the writers part ways in their final take on the limits and possibilities of the translation zone. Street has a kind of exuberant practice, if not a philosophy, of language, staging linguistic and cultural contact, especially through names and naming practices, in a changing constellation of Spanish and English as both reciprocal and unequal. Roberts's approach to the translingual is more formulaic, standard literary procedure for this kind of tropical historical romance, interweaving into the English text the occasional untranslated Spanish phrase for foreignizing effect. With the obligatory nod to Spanish and some French words in the original (sometimes accompanied by translations, sometimes not) as a familiar Latinizing gesture in his "novel of Cuba in the 1890s" (the subtitle), Roberts doesn't pursue either the sociopolitical contexts for or the implications of the power of languages—in contrast to his own earlier practice in the New Orleans trilogy, where, for example, the historical shift from Spanish and French empires to US control is encoded in the changing street names of New Orleans.

The Single Star doesn't take its language politics as seriously as Roberts does elsewhere. He gives Stephen Lloyd a "linguistic flexibility" (fluent in several languages, including French, reflecting his maternal New Orleans roots, he learned rudimentary Spanish at McGill University and quickly becomes fluent in Cuba), but it doesn't go much further than to advance the plot, dramatizing his role as spy for the Cuban army through all his assumed names (Captain Lloyd, Captain Dixie, Esteban Yo-eed, Jerome Beaulieu, El Inglesito).[19] He calls his horse "Arawak, the name of the aboriginal tribe Columbus had found in Jamaica" (*SS*, 229), but this is a throwaway detail, like other translingual glimmers in the novel that just don't pan out. The hero's English name, "translated" into the "Spanish form" by the Cuban female guerilla leader Inés (La Estrella) Carmona, is Esteban Yo-eed (*SS*, 57). She also teases him with the name "Inglesito" ("You're going to find that every Cuban soldier calls you Inglesito—the little Englishman—the diminutive being friendly and having nothing to do with stature. Nor can you persuade them a Jamaican is not necessarily an Englishman" [*SS*, 57]). Yet the power of English as a dominant language is neither disrupted nor challenged—nor at least defamiliarized as it is with Street's "El Dabney." Estrella gives Stephen the hispanicized name "Esteban Yo-eed," but it reflects her "quaint" (*SS*, 37) pronunciation rather than the creative act of a linguistic equal: "I'd not get it right in a year. Will you let me translate it? The Spanish form is Esteban . . . though she slurred the first E and brought out the name as though it were Stéban" (*SS*, 57). The string of aliases and nicknames turns out be just that—a list of names assumed and readily reversed when needed toward the end of the novel. After all the nominal role and code switching, Stephen Lloyd returns to Jamaica, to his own name, to his sweetheart of past days, and resumes his life there, virtually unchanged.

Street, who experiments with a variety of translational approaches, goes much further than Roberts in elaborating the Spanish-English network of his novel. Street's Mingo, named for the Indian friend of his grandfather, who worked on an alphabet for his native Chocktaw, speaks no Spanish when he goes to Cuba, but thrown into the language and culture of the contact zone, he steps into an ongoing process of transculturation. This term of Ortiz's rejects the top-down model of one-way cultural transference (acculturation, deculturation) in favor of a multidirectional import/export process in which both center and periphery exchange and are changed by the cultural production of the other. In this moment of overturning the *translatio imperii*, Ortiz's term gives an ethnographic name to the colonial encounters Street imagines. From the Ortiz perspective of a native anthropologist with a deep literary sensibility, involved in the political struggles of his nation, Street's novelistic attention to languages may approximate the engaged ethnography that defines *Cuban Counterpoint*.[20]

For Street's Mingo, Cuba presents a scene of transculturation first and foremost in linguistic terms. Mingo embraces the diminutive Minguillo, given to him (like Inglesito to Stephen Lloyd) by the woman he loves, Rafaela/La Entorcha, accepting it (unlike Lloyd) simultaneously as Spanish ("Mingo was a very common name in medieval Spain. A peasant name"), Cuban ("We Cubans often take a name and make it little. Sometimes we almost turn it into music. . . . The sound of the name, . . . in its Cuban beauty, brought a quick gasp to Mingo Dabney, a boldness to his heart"), and Choctaw, a springboard back to the Indigenous origin of his name in Lebanon (*MD*, 39–40). Steeped in Mississippi valley folk culture, he adapts the popular legend and work song "John Henry" he remembers from Lebanon to the world of his Cuban troop, "the *impedimenta* of Macéo's army" (*MD*, 174), scorned as "ragtail" camp followers, ox drivers, and scavengers, not fighters, "thieves and brigands and cutthroats," "stealing and robbing to help supply Macéo" (*MD*, 174). Whereas Roberts defines the term *impedimenta* with little fanfare and no italics ("unarmed men, swelled by overage servants and an occasional refugee woman, were known as the impedimenta" [*SS*, 205]), Street sets off the term with italics and uses it to plumb the contradictions, linguistic and cultural, that emerge when Lebanon encounters Cuba in the asymmetrical relations of the contact zone.

Street's *impedimenta* adapt Mingo's song, "tapped their feet and repeated the words, with no idea of their meaning," interweaving their Spanish with his English to retrofit the lyrics: "*Viva* John Henry!" (*MD*, 211–12) and "John Henry! *Grillos*! El Dabney's *Grillos*!" (*MD*, 221). Here they riff on the names "El Dabney" has given them and them him. In a signal of more transculturation, we first hear of the newly hispanicized "El Dabney" from the "Haitians in this part of Cuba," whose "drums are always talking" (*MD*, 121): "A *gringo* was with Macéo's *impedimenta*. They called him El Dabney" (*MD*, 203). In turn, the *impedimenta* adopt his term "*grillos*," christening them "crickets" ("El Dabney was making a joke. He was calling them *grillos*. Crickets, eh? Hissing bugs. . . . They hissed the sound. John Henry! *Grillos!*" [*MD*, 221]) as a self-mocking term of endearment. El Dabney's Spanish slang creates a new consciousness of names: "The Spaniards called them lice and leeches, but El Dabney called them *grillos*. There is unity in a name, and pride if the name is given in affection. . . . They whispered the names among themselves and . . . were proud even to have names" (*MD*, 221).

Not only the names themselves but also their circulation through "the talking drums of Haiti" (*MD*, 104) dramatize both Street's engagement with a pan-Caribbean consciousness and his attention to race matters. When the drums are first introduced as Mingo and the other Southerners enlisting for Cuba libre are sailing on the *Virginius* near the western tip of Haiti, they hear rhythmic pounding but can't make out what the drums are saying: "I've never known a white man who could read them," Mingo is told by the ship captain (*MD*, 104). Nowhere is Street's investment in the language of race more evident than in the uses of *mambí* (which is introduced on shipboard along with the drums), a derogatory term of the Spanish for Cuban rebels that became a badge of honor. "It was a new word to Mingo, and the sailors weren't sure of its meaning. . . . A Mambi is a poor Cuban who farms and fights and tries to live. . . . *Mambi* means dirt. Just common clay. The Garlics started it and now the Cubans are proud of it" (*MD*, 80). Typically for Street's brand of transculturation, he brings this cultural encounter unexpectedly from a colonial periphery to what amounts to another periphery back home: "'I'll be damned,' Mingo said. 'Sort of like the Yankees starting Johnny Reb, and wishing they hadn't'" (*MD*, 80). Also perhaps typical of either the inconsistent editing or Street's own unsystematic Spanish usage, the term *mambí* does not always have the accent nor is it always italicized. Whatever the source, the fundamental instability of these racialized names defines both their linguistic and their cultural locations.

Finally, the multidirectional counterpoint of languages and cultures indicates the logic of the comparative location across space and time, the layered places and histories of both Roberts's and Street's novels. Their mobile settings in Jamaica/Haiti/Cuba and Cuba/US pinpoint unlikely geo-historical comparisons among uneven regions and revolutions, empires and nations. Most striking is Roberts's mediterraneanizing speculation in *The Single Star*, when en route from Jamaica to Cuba, Stephen recounts to Inés and her brother:

"Think of the whole expanse of water bounded by eastern Cuba, Haiti and Jamaica as a little sea within the Caribbean. On certain old maps it is called the Jamaica Sea, and it merits a name of its own no less than the Aegean and the Tyrrhenian Seas in the Mediterranean. This is our region's womb of history" (SS, 85). Echoing a similar line in *The Caribbean* ("the potent womb, our sea of destiny, the Mediterranean of the West"), this is the novel's vision of the Caribbean as a whole, a hypothetical Jamaica Sea connecting Caribbean concerns of 1898 and 1949 to a much longer, hemispheric prehistory (*C*, 19).

Stephen recalls that they are currently retracing the course followed by Diego Mendez four hundred years earlier when he set out to find help after Columbus was wrecked on the north Jamaican coast during his last voyage. This was the path of a military expedition sent by the governor of Jamaica to aid French planters during the slave revolt led by Toussaint L'Ouverture. In reverse the French traveled along the same route as refugees after the success of that revolt, and very recently, in 1895, José Martí and Máximo Gómez had returned to Cuba via this route to join the insurrection. As Roberts's novel notes, "The conquistadores and the buccaneers and the warring admirals from Europe criss-crossed it in their different periods" (SS, 85). With this space-timeline Roberts makes his Caribbean a crossroad of past and future imperial control and resistance, from the Spanish and British to the looming US: "The United States has always had a tremendous political urge toward the Caribbean Sea (SS, 89), and again, "the history of the United States points to an inevitable ambition to control our Caribbean Sea" (SS, 200). The sea as a mediterranean womb of history holds in suspense the possibility of the future independence of Cuba, as well as that of all the Antilles, not yet foreclosed in 1895 as it would be by 1949.

The layered times and places create a literary palimpsest of revolutionary history in the Caribbean, Latin America, and the US, from the 1940s back to the nineteenth century and earlier (Simón Bolívar to George Washington), anticipating through historical revolution, especially failed or unfinished revolutions of the past, a future world not yet foreseen in the present. Roberts: "Men from Simón Bolívar's fatherland had a special duty to fight in wars of liberation" (SS, 239). And Street: "We are entering Act Three of the greatest drama of all times—the drama of the American Revolution" (*TR*, 183–84). For both Roberts and Street, the Cuban War of Independence 1895–98 refers back to another layer in Cuba's ongoing struggle against Spain, the earlier, unsuccessful Ten Years' War of 1868–78. In turn, the transculturated legacy of Cuba's unfinished revolution looks forward to different possible futures for Roberts's Jamaica and Street's US South. "The past history of our struggle," according to Roberts's Cuban heroine, reveals this moment as "the second revolution. The original one failed in 1878 after lasting a decade. We call it the Ten Years' War" (*SS*, 39). "To tell this story," Street explains in the acknowledgments to *Mingo Dabney*, "I shifted the *Virginius* episode from the Cuban Revolution of 1868–78 to the Revolution of 1895–98," transposing the failed shipment of recruits and arms that brings Mingo to Cuba from one era to the other. The acknowledgments page, itself dated "Chapel Hill, N.C. January 5, 1950," marks another endpoint of this unfinished history (*MD*, n.p.).

And the revolutionary era of the 1890s, the authors know from their perspective of the 1940s, will also fail, thanks to the intervention of the US. Further transposed to the "far future Jamaica," Stephen Lloyd argues, as we've already seen, "American intervention would rid us of Spain, but . . . we might only be exchanging masters" (*SS*, 89), and even more pointedly, some nations can "enjoy a Caribbean revolution without getting fanatical. . . . But I'm a West Indian colonial. Liberty for these islands is what I want and not the exchanging of one imperial system for another" (*SS*, 217). Transposed to the US, the Cuban model with, not despite, all its limits and failed promises becomes a source for resurrecting and redeeming the multiple failures of the Civil War in what would be another American Revolution. Once an unconquered commander in the Confederate navy, the captain of the doomed *Virginius* had followed the "Confederate mirage" (*MD*, 20), just as the Dabneys of Lebanon had made their Mississippi valley a sanctuary for Southern "Unionists, Abolitionists and slavery-haters" that risked battle with the Confederacy and lost (*TR*, foreword, n.p.). In the conflict of Reconstruction, "the Dabneys were defeated again [in] a deal that took Union soldiers out of the South and changed the land from a conquered province into a colony, sealing the Negro in a far room of the house still divided" (*TWR*, 2). The redemption for these compound losses: "we are ready for a new act" in "the drama of the American Revolution" (*TR*, 184).

So the revolutionary times and places in these 1940s novels are doubly doubled, using the hemispheric past to point to Jamaica and the US South as analogous, open-ended, unfinished revolutionary points yet to come—and showing how at certain key conjunctures some nations need other nations' histories to tell their own. Finally, the language of self-determination common to both writers during this decade—Roberts's "if Jamaica should ever demand self-government from England" (*SS*, 178) and Street's elegy to "the South of revolution and rebellion" (*TWR*, 18), a Confederate dissident's history of "passive resistance" (*TR*, 311), "passive insurrection" (*TR*, 337)—is notably out of time, untimely, not part of the 1890s Cuban rebellion but of the 1940s and beyond. We can hear the echoes of the postwar struggle for decolonization and civil rights in Roberts on Teddy Roosevelt's racism as he plans the charge on San Juan Hill and Street on the Free State of Jones as a "white republic" (*TR*, 407). In both cases the raising of the US flag over the not-yet free states (in Mississippi, in Cuba) signals a reference to the Declaration of Independence more relevant to the 1940s than to either the US Civil War or the Cuban 1890s.

Splendid Failures and Unfinished Revolutions I

To explain such a striking level of similarity between the two novels, literary critics would usually look for lines of contact between Street and Roberts. There is (as yet) no evidence that they knew of each other or their work, so it may just be that 1949 was a relatively good year for popular novels set in Cuba—or more broadly, as a *New York Times* review of Roberts's *Single Star* puts it, "the over-production of bosomy, swashbuckling novels of the Spanish Main."[21] There is also biographical evidence for why these two individual writers were drawn to that popular form. Roberts says in his autobiography (in a chapter titled "The Shaping of a Nation," on the 1940s in New Orleans) that he had promised himself for years to write a historical novel about the Cuban War of Independence and that a research trip to Cuba in November 1948 ("I retraced the route followed by the US expeditionary force . . . to San Juan Hill in 1898") clarified how and why turn-of-the-century Cuba finally provided the model closest to his aspirations for Jamaican independence (*TMY*, 319). "Jamaicans were Caribbean by temperament," he explains, addressing the question of Jamaican self-government versus federation. "In the long run we would react more like Cubans than like Englishmen or West Africans" (*TMY*, 317). He notes "with deep satisfaction" his award by the Cuban government of the *Orden Nacional de Mérito: Carlos Manuel de Céspedes*, "the highest decoration ever awarded by Cuba to a foreigner," given specifically for his two books, *The Single Star* and *The Caribbean* (*TMY*, 321). Here and in all his writings of this decade, Roberts works through the ambiguities of his own position as a white Jamaican nationalist within the large international community of black Jamaicans in New York, a journalist-novelist-historian of the "Mediterranean of the West" writing in the context of US race relations and global decolonization (whose work once appeared in an anthology of Negro writing).

In contrast, Street leaves less of a written autobiographical trail than Roberts, but we know that he wrote two essay collections on the South, *Look Away! A Dixie Notebook* (1936) and the posthumously published *James Street's South* (1955) in which he blended personal memories of his Southern boyhood with journalistic coverage of contemporary events and politics in the region. In both collections he repeatedly condemned racial violence (the Elaine massacre during the "Red Summer" of 1919, a series of lynchings in southern Mississippi) and wrote movingly on black migration, forced and voluntary (in two chapters: "The First Exodus," on the early nineteenth-century internal slave trade and the supposed, little-known slave origins in Dutch Haarlem of the anthem "Dixie," and "The Last Exodus," on black South Carolinians walking to Harlem in the wake of "Judge Lynch's" ride through the region).[22] Street had already signaled much of this history in his fiction, and like Roberts, worked through the ambiguities of his position as a critic and champion of his global South, with the language of the decolonizing 1940s projected backward in his historical series on the 1890s and earlier.

So whether or not Roberts and Street knew one another is less important than their individual responses to the prevailing historical conditions, the network that, first, enabled the production of works by these two writers and others and, second, made them more or less visible. Together Roberts and Street show us something we didn't know about that moment of the 1940s. Why remember Cuba 1895, the war for independence, and 1898, the Cuban-Spanish-American War, during the 1940s, the decade of World War II? What was Cuba to the US? Street and Roberts challenge the assumption that "to the American popular eye, prerevolutionary Cuba was the island of sin," a center of gambling and prostitution controlled by the Mafia in cahoots with a corrupt government. Instead, their Cuban novels, culminating two blockbuster series of historical fiction, present an imagined crossroads where the multiple times, places, and languages of the revolutionary Americas meet to produce a history of the present. Their Cuba is not the gangster-strongman outpost of Fulgencio Batista and Lucky Luciano that it was in the mainstream US press and cultural imaginary of the time.[23] Their Cuban potboilers also run counter to the contemporary "bosomy, swashbuckling novels of Spanish Main," showing how a slightly different popular cultural strain, their adaptation of historical formula fiction, could espouse speculative histories and alternative historiographies. Read as indicators of the 1940s zeitgeist just prior to the decade of the 1959 Cuban Revolution, they depict the Cuban War of Independence from Spain as a revolutionary struggle for self-government (Roberts's Jamaica) and self-determination (Street's antiracist if not pro–civil rights South), in perfect step with the decolonizing energies of the time and almost anticipating, if not prophesying, Castro in 1959.

As a group of unlikely bedfellows, Roberts and Street join forces with Du Bois and James, as they actively shaped and were shaped by a history of pre– and post–world war struggles over racial equality, national and regional self-determination, and global deimperialization. Their work, extending domestically to the "I'll take my stand" school of Faulkner and other Southern studies regulars, rejects Margaret Mitchell's hermetically sealed South in favor of an extended Gulf-Caribbean. Different transoceanic accounts of geopolitical conflicts, their historical writing provides models for adapting intensely local histories through a transnational historical consciousness. In them, the South becomes a point of connection among spaces, times, and languages of an Americas Mediterranean that reaches oceanically from the Mississippi River across the Gulf and the Atlantic to Europe and Africa. Unlike the majority US-centric view that sees the histories of the intercolonial slave trade and the Civil War and Reconstruction through the lens of one end point—the struggle for civil rights in the US—these midcentury writers looked through a comparative prism to mine the past for a history of the present as a series of possibilities foreclosed but not ended. They used the "splendid failures" (Du Bois's term for Reconstruction, which could just as easily be the failed southern rebellion against the Confederacy or the Ten Years' War, 1868–78, in Cuba—or for that matter the 1895 War for Independence) of the past to imagine, predict, and will into being new futures.[24] These writings of the 1940s exist in a constellation of "unfinished revolutions" (Foner, *Reconstruction*) that appear and reappear at critical historical conjunctures, most strikingly in James's *Black Jacobins* text-network, to which we turn next.

Network II: Carpentier, Du Bois, James

This section focuses on another Cuban, US, and West Indian cluster, perhaps even more loosely interconnected than the previous trio. Carpentier plays a role analogous to Roberts as the originator of "*el Mediterráneo Caribe*," his Mediterranean of the West, coined in the famous preface to his 1949 *El reino de este mundo*, the only sustained representation of the Haitian Revolution in Spanish-Caribbean literature. Carpentier is known for his *poética del Mediterráneo Caribe*, so called in homage to this invented oceanic name, used once, paratextually, in the *El reino* prologue.[25] Like Roberts, Carpentier associates that extended Caribbean, the "epoch" of a new-world historico-literary consciousness, with the time and name of Martí: "During that same epoch in the Caribbean Mediterranean, José Martí appears and is capable of writing one of the best essays about the French impressionists that has ever appeared in any language."[26] This is all he says, invoking Martí in a long list of Latin American writers and artists inspired not by Europe but by the style, the particular literary historical trajectories of their own world. The Caribbean-Mediterranean-Martí equation would not be particularly memorable outside this network.

Not only is that equation a mere onetime mention, made in a paratext, but also the *El reino* preface itself has an unusually ephemeral textual history of appearing and disappearing. First, revised and expanded, the preface was published separately in 1967 under the title *"De lo real maravilloso americano"* and translated into English in 1995 as "On the Marvelous Real in America."[27] Second, the original preface was omitted from some later Spanish editions of the novel as well as the English translations, starting with Harriet de Onís's, published in 1957. The preface in short and long forms is usually read as a declaration of American independence from European surrealism and a manifesto for *lo real maravilloso americano*, based on the cultural expressions, oral and performative traditions, of nonwhite, Indigenous, and Black new-world populations. In yet another paratext, the first of two footnotes to the expanded, essay version of the prologue, Carpentier updates and complicates this reading:

> I turn here to the text of the prologue for the first edition of my novel *The Kingdom of this World* (1949), which did not appear in later editions, even though I still consider it to be, except for certain details, as pertinent now as it was then. Surrealism no longer constitutes for us a process of erroneously directed imitation, as it did so acutely even fifteen years ago. However, we are left with a very different sort of *marvelous real*, which . . . is beginning to proliferate in the fiction of some young novelists on our continent. ("On the Marvelous Real," 83)

The passage of time has both changed and reinforced the standing of the original, which now circulates almost as though a new and separate work, complete with a new title, "Prólogo a la primera edición de *El reino de este mundo*." Now referring back to the past, original edition, distinguished by that birth order, the new prologue is identical to yet differentiated from its predecessor. The best way to describe it is as one of the afterlives of the original, to use Walter Benjamin's term for translations.[28] The expanded version with a different title and additional footnotes, *"De lo real maravilloso americano,"* is another one. Carpentier's preface, like other American Mediterranean locators, thus tells a story of paratexts within paratexts.

How does this intertextual history of appearing and disappearing interrelate with the transnational history of revolution in both versions of the prologue, which invoke the "Faustian presence of the Indian and the black man" ("On the Marvelous Real," 88), associated first with the Haitian uprisings, heralded by the revolution in France and an Africanist language of vodou drumming, then with "all of America" ("certain synchronisms, American, timeless, relating this to that, yesterday to today," ["On the Marvelous Real," 84])? We can best answer that question by looking back to the 1930s, when Du Bois and James produced their own revolutionary histories, moving between or among Haiti, Africa, Europe, and the Americas, Du Bois's centered on black Reconstruction in the US and James's on the black Jacobins in Haiti.

Du Bois / America's Unfinished Revolution ::
James / San Domingo Revolution

James's foundational statement of the when, where, how, and why of *The Black Jacobins* comes not in the text "proper," neither the 1938 nor the 1963 version, but paratextually, at the opening of the preface to the 1963 Vintage edition. There he starts by looking immediately to the appendix at the end of the book. The "Appendix, 'From Toussaint L'Ouverture to Fidel Castro,'" extends, again paratextually, the book's history of the present, to make a sweeping space-time transposition. "What took place in French San Domingo in 1792–1804 reappeared in Cuba in 1958. . . . Castro's revolution is of the twentieth century as much as Toussaint's was of the eighteenth. But despite the distance of over a century and a half, both are West Indian. . . . West Indians first became aware of themselves as a people in the Haitian Revolution" (*BJ*, 391–92). Linking 1804 Haiti to 1958 Cuba as well as the beginning and ending of his book and its own history from 1938 to 1963, James bookends both his text and its contexts in a notably open-ended way. The series of oceanic transferences through which the Black Jacobins—in Robin Blackburn's apt formulation, "both the book and the historical force that it named"—come to predict revolution in other times and places produce an unfinished, prophetic history.[29]

Although the prediction of something coming in Africa at the end of the 1938 *Black Jacobins*, the decolonization that the imperialists did not foresee, had happened by 1963, it was critical for James to retain in the revised edition the original sense of multilayered, proleptic conditionality embedded in the 1938 ending. Instead of updating the past, changing his own book, he used various paratextual means, mainly the footnotes and appendix, to bring the book, now recontextualized, into its future, his present. Another way to think of this process is as a translation that multiplies the original. David Scott, who calls the 1963 edition "an event," is one of a handful of critics who focus on the texts as a series of translations, in response to different historical moments, both of themselves and of the Haitian Revolution itself.[30] Scott focuses on the revisions (from a narrative of romance to one of tragedy) that create 1938 anew in 1963. In so doing, James operates very much in the spirit of the translator's task according to Benjamin, an organic one of ensuring the future life of a literary work through new versions that succeed but do not supplant it.

The multiple acts of translating that constitute *The Black Jacobins* include, conventionally, the sources in the bibliography, some in French, some already in translation. Further, as a work of self-translation, it encompasses not only the two editions, the two prefaces, the added appendix, and updated bibliography but also passages in the 1963 text, usually in footnote form, where James comments self-consciously on his perceptions of history and his own process of writing ("This statement has been criticized. I stand by it. C. L. R. J." [*BJ*, 88]). The timeline of 1938–63 (roughly the same period that Carpentier's Caribbean Mediterranean is circulating in the form of the revised *El reino* prologue) also reaches out to related texts, including James's play, *Toussaint L'Ouverture*, produced in 1936 with Paul Robeson in the lead and revised by James in the 1970s under the title *The Black Jacobins*, and James's 1971 "Lectures on *The Black Jacobins*," a Summer Research Symposium at the Institute of the Black World, in Atlanta. In addition to "How I Wrote *The Black Jacobins*" and "How I Would Rewrite *The Black Jacobins*," those lectures include a third, "*The Black Jacobins* and *Black Reconstruction*: A Comparative Analysis." The comparison in the last lecture is partly James's form of self-criticism across time: had he written a book more suited to 1971, it would, strangely enough, have resembled Du Bois's in 1935. The connection is a corrective, Du Bois showing James how all revolt against constituted authority "has to begin from below" by "the people down below" (*BJ*, 105), the "obscure creatures," obscure not only in San Domingo but also in Watts, Detroit, Cleveland, and Harlem (*BJ*, 106). James brings Du Bois into his history of the present and in the process brings out the international dimension of *Black Reconstruction*.

More fundamentally, James points to Du Bois as an otherwise unlikely node in the *Black Jacobins* network, with *Black Reconstruction* neither featured in the text nor the bibliography but proximate in time. The books share some historiographical methods. Du Bois's bibliography, like James's, is annotated and organized to show the specific position of the writer's racial politics, from "Standard—Anti-Negro" to those who "write sympathetically," to "the standard works of Negro historians" (*BR*, 731, 733, 735). James's annotated bibliography similarly interweaves assessment of the sources (their "unscrupulousness," "brazenness," [*BJ*, 380, 382], the books that are "biased" but "indispensable" [*BJ*, 381]). Most important, to put Du Bois in the James orbit emphasizes the worlding of his intensely local history, narrated around the black and white proletariat in specific Southern states and regions. In two famous chapters at the end, "Back toward Slavery" and "The Propaganda of History," Du Bois puts *Black Reconstruction in America, 1860–1880*, in the worldwide context of 1935, and it is that shift in space and time that comes into focus through the James network.

To get a sense of the charged context of the decolonizing transnationalism of the 1930s and beyond, we need look no further than the penultimate chapter, "Back toward Slavery," on "a new dictatorship of property in the South through the color line" (*BR*, 707): "The unending tragedy of Reconstruction is the utter inability of the American mind to grasp its . . . national and world-wide implications. . . . We are still too blind and infatuated to conceive of the emancipation of the laboring class in half the nation as a revolution comparable to the upheavals in France in the past, and in Russia, Spain, India, and China today" (*BR*, 708). Du Bois's massive space-time shift here, the equivalent of James's own ("what took place in French San Domingo in 1792–1804 reappeared in Cuba in 1958"), locates the specific nature of the speculative black history both narrate. While both have been criticized for their reliance on secondary sources (Du Bois's in English, with one French source by Randolph Desdunes; James's in English and French), they nonetheless achieve an original synthesis based on multiple acts of translation across different places, times, and languages. The black Reconstruction-Jacobins text-network that extends from Du Bois 1935 to James 1971 envisions alternative futures emerging from prematurely foreclosed possibilities, the "splendid failures" (*Black Reconstruction*, 708) and "unfinished revolutions" (Foner, *Reconstruction*) of the past.

It is clear, starting right from the 1938 edition, that what James had in mind with *The Black Jacobins* was to write proleptically about the "San Domingo Revolution" as the "preparation for . . . the revolution in Africa" ("Lectures," 72). Whereas in 1938 he makes this point directly only at the very end of the text, it becomes increasingly prominent in the second edition, in the paratextual form of new footnotes, added between 1962 and 1971, which confirm and deepen the original claim. The 1963 revised version makes a point of keeping unchanged the predictive and contested nature of the Haiti-Africa comparison. "I have retained the concluding pages," James writes in the preface to the revised edition, "which envisage and were intended to stimulate the coming emancipation of Africa" (*BJ*, vii). "I wrote my book with the African revolution in mind," James reiterates in his 1971 Atlanta lecture, "How I Wrote *The Black Jacobins*": "It seems that those who come from a small island always think of a revolution in very wide terms. . . . You can't begin to think of a little revolution in a small island" ("Lectures," 74). Playing with scale and scope here, James widens the historical perspective both spatially and temporally, in a way that mocks the concept of Haiti as, in the historian David Geggus's words, a "small-scale affair" and the unexamined equation between size and power that undergirds such claustrophobic (self-enclosed, self-confirming, self-limiting) comparisons.[31]

Part of what makes *The Black Jacobins* an exemplary and lasting work of historical criticism, then, is the self-consciousness with which James connects the story of Toussaint to the emerging, still-unfinished stories of his own times (the postwar decolonization of Africa, the sixties spread of radicalism and revolutionary consciousness around the world) and by extension to our time—as well as times yet to come. James's "West Indies," located in the paratexts of the 1963 edition, make their own massive moves of oceanic transposition, a complex set of space-time shifts and transferences. Beginning with the preface to the 1938 first edition and ending with the famous 1963 appendix, what preserves the relevance, even contemporaneity of *The Black Jacobins*, is the prolepsis characteristic of unfinished or *as yet* unfulfilled history. So the space of *The Black Jacobins*, both the book and the force it names, is notably transnational and multilingual while their time is if anything even more multidimensional. Linking the Haitian Revolution and African decolonization in the 1938 edition and then linking Haiti to the Cuban Revolution in the 1963 appendix, James stresses the disjoint space-time of the "Caribbean quest for national identity": "In a scattered series of disparate islands, the process consists of a series of unco-ordinated periods of drift, punctuated by spurts, leaps and catastrophes" (*BJ*, 391). This explains why the Haitian Revolution has produced such a traveling history, and why Haiti poses so insistently the question of why some nations need other nations' histories to tell their own.

The layers of time are made even more visible in the footnotes added to the revised edition, which reinforce the conditional prophecy of the original open ending by both retaining and updating it. The additional footnotes confirm and extend, noticeably still at the margins, the closing argument of the first edition, predicting that what happened in Haiti would also happen in Africa. A group of new footnotes (eight total) comment on the time of the writing, both the first and the revised edition, some noting simply "written in 1938" (used twice, *BJ*, 55, 265) or "written, it must be remembered, in 1938" (*BJ*, 82), others noting, "Still true, in 1961" (*BJ*, 43), and others explicitly articulating in spatiotemporal terms the significance of this layering of times. "Such observations, written in 1938, were intended to use the San Domingo revolution as a forecast of the future of colonial Africa" (*BJ*, 18). So what was forecast in 1938 remains present in 1963, still future facing despite the passage of time, alongside another new forecast, made like the first, at the margins of the text, that "what took place in French San Domingo in 1792–1804 reappeared in Cuba in 1958" (*BJ*, 391). The effect is to create a series of interdependent conjunctures joined by the anticipatory sense of "something coming."[32] The revisionist thinking in the book itself is most present subtextually on the margins, grammatically in various comparative structures and modes, and paratextually in the prefaces and appendix that frame the whole.

In this sense the paratexts, including the prefaces and appendix as well as the footnotes, are not appendages but defining forces within the text-network of *The Black Jacobins*. Only there, only paratextually, are we told the how and why of the whole. "I have retained the concluding pages," quoting again from the preface to the revised edition, "which envisage and were intended to stimulate the coming emancipation of Africa. They are a part of the history of our time" (*BJ*, vii). "They," the pages, are part of the history of our time, a speculative, conjectural history that depends on a sense of continuing prolepsis. "We were all quite certain that after the coming war," James writes in 1971 referring back to the 1930s as though they were yet to happen, "the African would emerge as an independent force in history." "That is why I wrote the book," he reiterates, "in order that people should think about the African revolution and get their minds right about what was bound to happen in Africa" ("Lectures," 72–73). "Would emerge," "should think," and "bound to happen": the verbs express a counterfactual and hypothetical, an outcome both open and imminent. Rather than revising this central argument of the original, either in 1963 or in 1971, to acknowledge African decolonization, James lets the prediction stand on its own unfinished terms.

When readers follow the footnote trail and look back to the text that James emphasizes, in the 1963 preface and the Atlanta lectures of 1971, as retained, unchanged, we find more conditional if/thens, more subjunctive verbs—in short, more "speculative thought": "thinking about what is going to happen as a result of what you see around you" ("Lectures," 72). "But for the revolution," James says in a passage written in 1938, retained and footnoted in the 1963 edition, and reread in his 1971 Atlanta lectures, "this extraordinary man and his band of gifted associates would have lived their lives as slaves, . . . standing barefooted and in rags to watch inflated little governors and mediocre officials from Europe pass by, as many a talented African stands in Africa today" (*BJ*, 265). Both the counterfactual verb "would have" and the comparative simile "as" preserve the "future in the past" as it was imagined, still in the conditional, an imperfect and uncompleted action, in 1938. Stressing the significance of that moment, not as fixed or frozen, finished in the past but rather in suspended animation, continuing on into the future, James underlines it three times in "How I Wrote *The Black Jacobins*," saying of the passage quoted: "I wrote that in 1938," "I was able to say that in 1938," "Written in 1938." African decolonization may have occurred, but that outcome does not change the urgency of futurity, the "bound-to-happen." In 1971, he reaffirms that the book, now revised with the appendix "From Columbus to Castro," "was written about Africa. It wasn't written about the Caribbean. . . . The book has something else in mind than Caribbean emancipation" ("Lectures," 73).

Simultaneously, James multiplies the comparative operations that help to produce the "something else." The history he has in mind is a series of conjunctures in multidimensional time and space, juxtaposing the original pairing of the Haitian-French revolutionary 1790s and the African 1930s with the Caribbean 1960s and '70s. It's no accident that the passage from *The Black Jacobins* that James chooses to quote twice in his 1971 close rereadings appears in the chapter titled "The Black Consul," nor that so much of the chapter concerns placing Toussaint comparatively in relation not only to Napoleon ("With the exception always of Bonaparte, no single figure in the whole period of the French Revolution traveled so fast and so far" [*BJ*, 256]) but also to Spartacus ("No wonder he came in the end to believe in himself as the black Spartacus, foretold by Reynal as predestined to achieve the emancipation of blacks" [*BJ*, 250]). The multiple times and the interrelations among them (the period of the French Revolution, in the end, foretold, predestined) are keyed to an analogous set of comparisons (Reynal's black Spartacus, Toussaint's Bonaparte), which together constitute what James calls (in the 1962 preface) "the history of our time." By this James means provisional history, driven by future planning, so that from his perspective in 1971 the important thing about *The Black Jacobins* is that it was written in 1938 and that he made very few changes, "about eight pages at most," for the 1963 edition ("Lectures," 90). "What I am thinking of is that anything that I write—that anybody writes—in 1971, must have in mind that by 1985, . . . people will be reading it and will know you see something that matters to them" ("Lectures," 90).

What does James have in mind not just with the book but with the whole text-network circulating by the time of the three 1971 lectures? As he works through "how I wrote" and "how I would rewrite" *The Black Jacobins*, there's a subtle shift in the nature of the textual timeline. The movement *from* 1938, the "first edition," *to* the "second edition revised" of the 1960s, from the original to final intention, doesn't quite disappear but gives way to thinking of the books relationally, as a simultaneity, contextualized through their "ages." One of James's favorite terms, the "ages" refers to the interrelations between the "different circumstances" in which the book was written (*BJ*, xi). Through both the book and the force it names, to use Blackburn's formula one last time, James thinks conditionally about "what I would have written if I were to write it today" ("Lectures," 71). The verb forms, conditional and subjunctive, enforce the "speculative thought," thinking about what is going to happen

("Lectures," 72). For James, this means that historiography must grapple with the way that the 1790s constituted an immediate historical context for the 1930s and '40s, neither simply an important precedent (though it is that) nor a tragically failed past future, foreclosed once and for all time, but an untimely futures past. "Untimely" refers to "practices of temporal refraction whereby people act 'as if'": as if they inhabit a different historical moment, as if the future were imminent in the past, as if alternative pasts that never materialized could be reanimated in the present.[33] James's term would be "the history of our time," of which his book and the (then) "coming emancipation of Africa" are a part; in 1938 "the history of our time" is produced only by James and associates, those who wrote and spoke "as if the African events of the last quarter of a century were imminent" (*BJ*, vii).

What Was Bound to Happen in the Future

Back to the future: James's appendix famously identifies the Cuban Revolution as both part of the historical conjuncture produced by the Haitian Revolution and part of "an original pattern, not European, not African, not a part of the American main, not native in any conceivable sense of that word, but West Indian, *sui generis*, with no parallel elsewhere" (*BJ*, 391–92). How can the West Indies be both historically unique and relational? For some, James's model of comparison *is* the problem, imposing the identity of Marx's proletariat on the slaves of new-world plantation societies, thus elevating Marxism and relegating to the footnotes the subaltern "history from below." In the process, according to this critique, James produces a teleology that minimizes Africa and maximizes France as "stages in the development of the West Indian quest for a national identity," and, finally, an articulation of class and racial struggles that translates the specific into the universal (*BJ*, 396). Better yet: mis- or even un-translates.

If we look back at the series of translations, both figurative and literal, that James works through, then a pattern of strategic refusal emerges: the persistence of incomplete, inconsistent, or imperfect translations, such as the misnomer "French San Domingo," that are only partially acknowledged *as* translations, or transparent translations, such as the many quotations from the sources, that are made silently. The extended passages, for example, that James takes from Pamphile de Lacroix's 1819 memoir of his service in the 1801 French military expedition, headed by Napoleon's brother-in-law Charles Leclerc, are James's own translations into English, only intermittently footnoted. Likewise, all of James's sources, documented in the footnotes and the bibliography, are predominantly written in French (the rest in English), with excerpts quoted in translations that are generally his own but only rarely noted. (Of the available Toussaint biographies, he comments in the bibliography that he read Anatoli Vinogradov's *The Black Consul* in a 1935 translation from the Russian.) Finally, in one more instance, also paratextual, this one from the 1963 appendix, James translates Aimé Césaire's poem *Cahier d'un retour au pays natal*, ending with the famous line, "and no race possesses the monopoly of beauty, of intelligence, of force, and there is a place for all at the rendezvous of victory" (*BJ*, 401). The translation is again James's own, and, notably, he translates Césaire's "*conquête*" as "victory" instead of "conquest," although Césaire does not use *victoire* here, and in the previous stanza James translates Césaire's verb "*conquérir*" as "conquer."[34] However we might read the significance of these anomalies, we can't miss what they all have in common: a will to open-ended and unfinished translation as yet another manifestation of the speculative history James is writing.

James himself thus emerges from within the "translator's invisibility." Reading the history of the Haitian Revolution written as a series of transparent comparisons, we can see his role along with the changing texts and contexts of two revolutions and then more, in response to different historical moments.[35] Throughout James has tried to show, he says in the bibliography, "the close parallels, hitherto unsuspected," between "two populations so widely separated and so diverse in origin and composition of its languages," but the parallels do not consistently align. Rather, James's parallelism allows for the possibility of incommensurability, lack of fit between the two histories. Who but Du Bois in *Black Reconstruction* was thinking in terms of the black worker in 1865, James says, just as he himself was looking for where "the Marxist analysis could fit" his account of the Haitian Revolution ("Lectures," 91). James gives us the text-network of *The Black Jacobins*, encompassing prior texts and future forms as well as the history of the text's multiple presents, all the biographical, socioeconomic, cultural, and political contexts in which the work is now and will be read. As translations without an original, they are constitutionally open-ended, set in motion like speculative thoughts.

Perhaps what we have here is a strategic failure to communicate. These moments of uncompleted communication are part of the complex act of translation that is foundational to *The Black Jacobins* as a network. Honoring its paratextual condition means keeping track of the different editions, prefatory and afterword material, and footnotes: a snapshot of a work in all its lives, from past literary and sociopolitical sources and influences, to contemporaneous texts and contexts of its own present, and finally to its afterlives, including those yet to come. Editions aren't just to be cited and done with, and by the same token, footnotes are more than just footnotes, an unofficial running commentary both buttressing and challenging the text, and possibly both creating and revealing a special relation between race and the paratextual condition. The pages themselves, particularly the concluding ones, are part of what James calls "the history of our time" (*BJ*, vii).

All the Wonderful Spartacuses

By way of a conclusion, I will end part 4 with an opening. James's Toussaint L'Ouverture, the surname, literally "the opening" (on the change from the slave name Bréda to L'Ouverture, see *BJ*, 126n8), is heralded as "the black Spartacus" two brief times in *The Black Jacobins*. Each time he is associated with an unfulfilled prophecy made by the French Enlightenment figure the Abbé Raynal: "No wonder in the end he came to believe in himself as the black Spartacus, foretold by Raynal as predestined to achieve the emancipation of the blacks" (*BJ*, 250), as "the black Spartacus, the Negro predicted by Raynal who would avenge the outrages done to his race" (*BJ*, 171). James here evokes Toussaint's reading of a famous passage in Raynal's *Philosophical and Political History of the Establishments and Commerce of the Europeans in the Two Indies*, a book in Toussaint's library, the title cited by James in English. While scholars debate whether Toussaint actually read Raynal, the idea is so important to James that his play *The Black Jacobins* (staged in London in 1936 and starring Paul Robeson as Toussaint) opens with a scene of Toussaint, seated, a copy of Raynal on his lap. But when James twice cites the key Raynal passage that his Toussaint reads—"over and over again Toussaint read this passage: 'A courageous chief only is wanted. Where is he?'" (*BJ*, 25); "Toussaint alone read his Reynal. 'A courageous chief only is wanted.'" (*BJ*, 82)—he leaves out Raynal's accompanying line, "Where is the new Spartacus who will not find a Crassus?" ("*Alors, où est-il ce Spartacus nouveau, qui ne trouvera point de Crassus?*").[36] With this rhetorical question Raynal speculates that Africans could free themselves with a rebel leader like Spartacus if colonial powers don't repeat the Roman response of 73–71 BC. But for James, imagining a Spartacus without the defeat historically inflicted by Crassus may be further from the conflict he wanted to foreground, so he jettisoned the *Spartacus nouveau* in favor of "the black Spartacus"—the specific, conflicted figure he summons forth in the book titled *The Black Jacobins*.

In making that direct speculation, James opens out his book, the whole text-network, to a series of far-flung Spartacuses that bring the classical Mediterranean, with all its baggage, into New World revolutionary thinking. The baggage can in part be summed up through the equation of the Mediterranean with Rome. Even Roberts, who imagines the Caribbean as a violent inversion of the Mediterranean, makes the Roman Empire a fulcrum when he comments, "It was as necessary for the Spaniards to keep the Caribbean their sea as it had been for the Romans to hold the Mediterranean" (*C*, 91). Similarly, Roberts takes the Jamesian route of strategic refusal in his constant negations of the Mediterranean metaphor, stressing what it is not, what it pushes back against. The Spartacus focus, too, works to offset the imperial balance of power, while maintaining the Mediterranean analogy—one reason, perhaps, why Spartacus proliferates in the American Mediterraneans. The multimedia Spartacus has been adapted in sculpture and on stage, page, and screen, ever since the late eighteenth century, when Toussaint is imagined by James as reading Raynal. That scene has been a flash point for many readers, who question both its accuracy and the ideological implications of centering revolution on the colonies in Enlightenment literature such as Raynal's.[37] The world history of that traveling figure has yet to be fully told, but some Spartacus clusters are well known. Most originate in Europe and travel elsewhere, translated into multiple languages.

The starting point is the Toussaint moment itself, with biographies in French, including Cousin d'Avallon's published in 1802, histories such as Captain Marcus Rainsford's 1805 *Historical Account of the Black Empire of Hayti*, and poetry, the most frequently cited, William Wordsworth's 1802 sonnet "To Toussaint L'Ouverture." The abolitionist 1830s–1850s were another Spartacus flash point. The long history of world abolition—deferred, slowed, unevenly achieved—was reaching different climaxes in the US and Cuba, when Denis Foyatier's 1830 statue *Spartacus Breaks His Chains*; Robert Montgomery Bird's melodrama, *The Gladiator*, first performed in 1831; Harriet Martineau's novel *The Hour and the Man* (1841); and Wendell Phillips's much republished 1861 lecture on Toussaint L'Ouverture, represented the Spartacuses of that conjuncture. World War I spearheaded a Spartacus movement, with the *Spartakusbund*, and its newspaper *The Spartacus Letters*, organized in Germany in 1916 by Rosa Luxemburg and others. Biographies of Toussaint published in the 1930s war decade (when Arthur Koestler's 1939 *The Gladiators* was published in English translation) are cited in James's bibliography (Percy Waxman's *The Black Napoleon* [1931]; Anatoli Vinogradov's *The Black Consul* [1935]). A series of Italian Spartacus films mark a different conjuncture, from the 1913 version of Ernesto Pasquali to a new Italian Spartacus in 1953, followed by two in the 1960s.[38]

But none of these references is as proximate to the network of *The Black Jacobins* as the era of Stanley Kubrick's *Spartacus* (1960), an era that ushered in a series of film adaptations, in Havana and Hollywood, of Spartacus, the Roman Empire, and other slave rebellions, both old- and new-world. This is the long 1960s in which the 1963 revised edition of *The Black Jacobins* begins the afterlife of the 1938 edition, continuing into and beyond 1971 with James's Atlanta lectures. It is also the time when Fernández Retamar wrote both his famous essay "Caliban" (1971) and the far less well-known "Sobre *Ramona*" (1973).

A surprising Spartacus constellation emerges from those essays and the hemispheric history of Martí's "*Nuestra América.*" In "Sobre *Ramona*" Fernández Retamar makes two paradigmatic texts of North American feminist reformism by Jackson and Stowe into avatars of a traveling tradition of revolution, that of "siempre los maravillosos Espartacos de todas las épocas y lugares" ("all the wonderful Spartacuses of all epochs and places"; 700). This is the history of struggle against capitalism, embedded, before its time, so to speak, in the history, both preceding and parallel, of protest against slavery. The untimely palimpsest, filled with various temporal terms, establishes another moment when the *translatio imperii* is turned upside down, reversed multiple times. "From the first moment" ("desde el primer momento"; 700) of protest by such "isolated voices" ("voces aisladas"; 700) as that of Bartolomé de Las Casas, Fernández Retamar says, it was apparent that the crimes committed against Africans and aborigines in "the lands that would be baptized 'América'" ("en las tierras que iban a bautizar 'América,'"; 700) were the "logical antecedent of contemporary fascism" ("el antecedente lógico del fascismo contemporáneo"; 700), and, further, that "our continent was yoked to the history of capitalism" ("nuestro continente fue uncido de la historia del capitalismo"; 700). Not only that wrinkle in time, where what would be precedes rather than follows, but one could look back still farther, to the ancient Greco-Roman world, and find traces of the future that Engels predicted. This view of the past requires yet another subjunctive to express the time in which slavery "would pass to the museum of antiquities" ("pasara al museo de antigüedades"; 700). For the fulfillment of this future, though, "something drastic had to happen . . . as all the wonderful Spartacuses of all epochs and places have always known" ("como han sabido siempre los maravillosos Espartacos de todas las épocas y lugares"; 700). The verb tenses "would be" and "had to" mark uncompleted actions, as yet unfulfilled prophecy, as well as the simultaneous coexistence of all those wonderful Spartacuses. This spacetime concept could not differ more radically from the one-dimensionality and unidirectionality of the *translatio imperii.*

Without naming the actual Spartacus, Fernández Retamar identifies "all these Spartacuses" with that specific, historical figure, the Thracian slave who led the largest uprising in Roman history. He brings the texts of his nineteenth-century, reform-minded feminists—"their paternalist vision, in this case, better maternalist" ("su vision paternalista—en su caso, más bien maternalista"; 701)—into what is, for Jackson and Stowe, an unrecognized context, the revolutionary orbit of slave rebellion against the Roman Empire. But this loose adaptation of Jackson and Stowe is possible only "*after* Du Bois, Ortiz, Langston Hughes, Nicolás Guillen, Richard Wright, Malcolm X, . . . and, above all, *after* the October Revolution, the Cuban Revolution" ("*después* de Du Bois, de Ortiz, de Langston Hughes, de Nicolás Guillen, de Richard Wright, de Malcolm X, . . . y, sobre todo, *después* de la Revolución de Octubre, de la Revolución Cubana"; 701; emphasis original). Looking farther back, beyond the nineteenth century of *Ramona* and other sister texts, to the partially recognized, ancient world of Spartacus, leads forward, to this star-studded cast of international, new-world, male revolutionaries.

The backward glance at those different pasts thus simultaneously looks further forward, pointing unexpectedly, again in ways not fully recognized within the 1973 essay, to the film *Spartacus*, released in 1960—as well as a host of other historical movies, also made during the long 1960s, in Havana as well as Hollywood. As with the actual Spartacus, the Kubrick film itself is never named, but instead Fernández Retamar locates his reference to "all the wonderful Spartacuses" in the larger context of Hollywood cinema during the postwar years. He specifically mentions Errol Flynn and Marlon Brando, both actors loosely associated with film genres that elsewhere—in the "Caliban" essay—are excoriated as "shameful" ("Caliban," 7). Recalling autobiographically, "by way of self-inflicted punishment, the forgettable pleasures of the Westerns and Tarzan films by which we were inoculated, unbeknownst to us, with the ideology that we verbally repudiated in the Nazis" ("Caliban," 22), the essay concludes broadly that what some applauded as a "healthy Sunday diversion in Westerns and Tarzans films," actually "proposed to the world . . . the monstrous racial criteria that have accompanied the United States from its beginnings to the genocide in Indochina" (24). "Sobre *Ramona*" broadens the "Caliban" critique even further. The pirate movies that made Flynn famous and the (sometimes anti-) westerns that starred Brando romanticize the history of exploitation under capital, in the same way that the "Yankee imperialists" would distort their "pillage of Indochina"—"if they had time for that, but they will not have the time" ("*si tuvieran tiempo . . . pero no tendrán ese tiempo*"; 702). Again, it takes a temporal distortion, a disjunctive temporality to pinpoint the spaces and times of the multiple imperialisms of the Americas.

Although Fernández Retamar doesn't say it, there are multiple racial and political ripples outward from this era when Kirk Douglas starred in the blockbuster *Spartacus*, directed by Stanley Kubrick, from a screenplay by the blacklisted writer Dalton Trumbo, and based on Howard Fast's novel, which had a significant readership in Communist circles. Blackness is introduced into the film with the African slave Draba, Spartacus's black buddy, who reappears in later black-white pairs in *Gladiator* (2000), directed by Ridley Scott, and other films. And the other major Hollywood films of Roman slavery, the sand-and-sandals epics of the time, *Quo Vadis* (1951) and *Ben-Hur* (1959), differed markedly from the *Spartacus'* political ethos in their focus on Christianity at the heart of anti-Roman imperialism. Further, by invoking the historical Spartacus and placing that history of slave rebellion in the contemporary context of Hollywood films that he denounces as imperialist, Fernández Retamar also brings into his orbit, again without naming it, the broad context of Cuban filmmaking, as a vibrant form of *cine rescate* (cinema of historical recovery, to use Michael Chanan's term) of the 1960s and '70s. During these years Humberto Solás, Tomás Gutiérrez Alea, Sergio Giral, and other Cuban directors produced their famous films recasting the history of slavery in Cuba and beyond—and so did the Italian Gillo Pontecorvo (*Queimada/Burn!* [1969], starring Marlon Brando).[39] This was also a period of homophobic politics in Cuba when, simultaneously, elsewhere, Spartacus, the "emblem of contemporary gay sexual liberation," was just on the verge of coming out.[40]

The circuit Fernández Retamar traces here, without fully recognizing it, from nineteenth-century history to twentieth-century film, from ancient slave revolt to modern revolution, from Old to New World, provides a means to bridge the divides between the different, incommensurable histories, the "incomparable" empires of the Americas.[41] Now is the time, Fernández Retamar concludes in "On *Ramona*," "after the revolutionary triumph," to take up again "the tradition of the last century" and, through that backward glance, to recognize the presence of a long, international and revolutionary history in the present, in the emerging literatures of the Americas." He has constructed a kind of palimpsestic temporality in which past traces are not only present in afterimages but also given to eruption, as Benjaminian flash points, at times of crisis.

Splendid Failures and Unfinished Revolutions II

Here is where James and the black Jacobins meet up with Fernández Retamar and Caliban. Both operate by maintaining strategic silences when invoking Spartacus as a revolutionary model, omitting elements from the history of the classical Spartacus, in part, perhaps, because of the limits of the

Mediterranean analogy. Roberts reaches one of those limits when he uses the Roman Mediterranean as comparator to the Spanish Caribbean. Beyond that, to make Roman slavery of the Mediterranean world a historical precursor of the Caribbean New World raises the problem that classicists are now addressing, how to talk about race in a nominally pre-race period.[42] Moreover, Spartacus was, after all, historically defeated, hence Raynal's counterfactual invocation in the form of the rhetorical question of whether there is "a new Spartacus who will not find a Crassus." The repeated question in James via Raynal, "Where is he?" underlines that as-yet unknown "great man," via Marx, who has not yet made the history that great men make. There are echoes here of the 1938 preface, the ambivalent line "great men make history, but only such history as it is possible for them to make" (*BJ*, x). Scholars, most prominently David Scott, have suggested that the 1963 edition revises the romanticism of the anticolonial redemptive narrative of 1938, showing how the "tragedy of colonial enlightenment" (the subtitle of Scott's *Conscripts of Modernity*) limited the options available to Toussaint.

Yet perhaps this is a harbinger of the other major move we've seen throughout part 4, to place front and center the splendid failures, the unfinished revolutions of the past as unrealized predictors of the future, waiting to be reactivated. Roberts and Street highlight the wars of independence in Cuba in their novels of Jamaican and Southern self-determination; Du Bois offers nineteenth-century black Reconstruction as a solution, a beacon for the twentieth-century problem of the color line; and above all the Haitian Revolution is a history of liberation that ends multiple times in a turn "back toward slavery," the title of the penultimate chapter of *Black Reconstruction*. Carpentier, writing *El reino* in the 1940s, skips almost entirely over Toussaint in the novel (he is named only once), barely includes the revolution itself, and concentrates instead on the brutal aftermath of Henri Christophe's tyrannical reign. James casts his history of the San Domingo revolution as Scott's "tragic dilemma," the leader Toussaint himself "a tragic hero," descending into betrayal of the ideals and people of the revolution, but that very end becomes an opening to and for the future.[43]

The unfulfilled freedom of the San Domingo slaves in the 1800s sets the conditions of possibility first, in 1938, for African decolonization in the 1950s–1960s and then, in 1963, for Cuba and all of the West Indies. In all these ways, James and company add an explicit revolutionary, speculative dimension to the Mediterranean thinking of this book. Together they suggest that possible futures as unrealized possibilities of the past are the best, and perhaps only, political alternatives we have. Their writings ask how to reanimate past but unrealized political projects, historical "openings" prematurely foreclosed, to anticipate possible futures by reconstructing historical narratives *as if* they had happened. The implications for the American Mediterraneans as a whole will come next in the epilogue, which will return us to Braudel's Mediterranean, both a world and worldview, different from the one that every Rome is said to need.

Ending with Braudel

In the speculative spirit that has inspired so much of this book, let me end with another opening, a thought experiment: how Braudel's Mediterranean world in the age of Philip II, might (accent on the possible) explain (confirm, challenge, deny, other) the American Mediterraneans of the New World. Is there a Braudel for any other ocean besides his particular Mediterranean in the age of Phillip II? How would a Braudel for the Mediterranean world of the Americas not only look different from the scholar we know but also sharpen the difference between that world and his own? And, reciprocally, how do the American Mediterraneans of this book appear anew from the Braudelian perspective as well as call for a different Braudel? This line of questioning, in the spirit of the multidirectional *translatio imperii* of the Mediterranean contact zone, aims to end with a renewed sense of what is distinctive about the Humboldtian tradition and the cultural work it does. Looking forward to Braudel's much earlier Mediterranean world in the age of Philip II should highlight new features of the three dimensions—space, time, and the languages of both—that have encompassed my American Mediterraneans in the age of Humboldt to the present.

First and foremost is the place itself. A series of three nested prefaces opens *The Mediterranean* with a layout of Braudel's thinking through the spatial dimension, in reverse chronological order, the 1972 preface to the English edition, the 1963 preface to the second edition, and the most famous of all, the 1949 preface to the first edition. The paratextual form is only the start of the connections, linkages, and departures to and from the American Mediterraneans. The three prefaces, written for the first French edition of 1949, the second revised work of 1972, and the English translation of that work, are still the gold standard, the most frequently cited evidence, verging on manifestos, for Braudel's intent.[1] His Mediterranean has consistently been a singular, physical space, famous for its "unity" and "coherence," as well as "greatness," "two major truths [that] have remained unchallenged," he declares in the 1972 preface to English edition (*MMW*, 14). This remains true, not despite but because, in another oft-quoted line from the preface to the first edition, "the Mediterranean is not even a *single* sea, it is a complex of seas" (*MMW*, 17). In this respect his Mediterranean corresponds to the strategic negation of the American Mediterraneans; "no simple biography," "no simple narrative" can be written of this sea (*MMW*, 17). Braudel repeatedly insists on the contradictory plural nature of the Mediterranean's singularity, whether he speaks, as he does in the opening of part 1, "The Role of the Environment," in terms of its "faces" ("The Mediterranean has at least two faces" [*MMW*, 23]) or, as in the preface to the English edition, its "voices" ("The Mediterranean speaks with many voices; it is a sum of individual histories" [*MMW*, 13]).

The keyword "sum" reappears later when Braudel adapts a Lucien Febvre line describing the Mediterranean as "the sum of its routes"—one of Braudel's chapter titles is "Land Routes and Sea Routes," in homage to Febvre—defining the "movement of boats, vehicles, pack animals and people themselves." Arithmetically speaking, the sum of these routes makes the Mediterranean a "unit" and gives it "a certain uniformity despite local resistance" (*MMW*, 277). The total is equal to, not greater than, the sum of its routes. "The whole Mediterranean consists of movement in space" (*MMW*, 277). This Braudel signature idea, the singularity of the plural Mediterranean, marks his "attempt to encompass the history of the Mediterranean in its complex totality" (*MMW*, 20). So sui generis is this idea that the most recent publication of the two-volume work by the University of California Press features a book description that emphasizes the Mediterranean multiplicity: Braudel "ranges back in history . . . and forward to our time, moving out from the Mediterranean area to the New World and the other destinations of traders."[2]

This sounds in principle like the Humboldtian tradition of a Mediterranean on the move. But the plural Mediterraneans of my title reflect a different approach to the "other Mediterraneans" from Braudel's trade/transport/shipping-based examples. While Braudel definitely invokes and names multiple Mediterraneans, including the Caribbean—"the Sahara, the second face of the Mediterranean" (*MMW*, 6), "Mediterraneans, of the North," "several Atlantics" (*MMW*, 224), "a *global* Mediterranean" (*MMW*, 168)—they are all linked physically to the classic Mediterranean through networks of trade routes. Tracing the lines along which "Mediterranean influence" was transmitted parallels the "great trade routes" of Europe (*MMW*, 223). The Sahara, which we know also falls under Humboldt's Mediterranean umbrella, counts for Braudel as another point on the trade route ("an abundant caravan traffic entered into contact with Mediterranean trade, . . . both essential to it . . . and dependent on it" [*MMW*, 171]). The emptiness of the desert, which is said to have produced Islam as a civilization, has a corollary in the emptiness of the sea, while neither is really a sufficient explanation (*MMW*, 187). In contrast, the empty space imagined by Humboldt, "that Mediterranean of moving sands," has its own independent existence as the translation of an oceanic metaphor adapted to the land.

This discrepancy between an ocean and land focus becomes the basis for the historian David Abulafia's challenge to Braudel in his revisionist work, *The Great Sea: A Human History of the Mediterranean* (2011).[3] Abulafia is best known for his insistence on centering the Mediterranean around the human agents Braudel subordinates. More important for my book is Abulafia's focus on Mediterraneans, plural, pointing out that the Mediterranean is a sea with many names, that most Mediterranean historians are concerned with the lands that border the sea, while his is a history of the Mediterranean as a sea, and that thinking this way shifts attention to other Mediterranean seas around the world, as far away as Japan and the Caribbean.

What this means is that for any of the American Mediterraneans to be more than merely a terminus on a trans-Mediterranean shipping route, Braudel would need to rethink the Mediterranean as a comparative concept. It would not necessarily need to be a metaphor, like mediterraneanity and Mediterraneanism and its cognates, the Mediterranean analogy or metaphor, we've seen from Humboldt to Ellen Churchill Semple to Kevin Starr and Mike Davis, but something more than a physical space. For Braudel the Mediterranean is exactly that, a geographical space with a definable "historical character" that he sets forth to "discover" in his book: "It will be no easy task to discover exactly what the historical character of the Mediterranean has been" (*MMW*, 17.) This is the burden and the opportunity of his geohistory, making connections between history and geographical space through the example of the Mediterranean. What Braudel does not have is a methodological concept of Mediterraneanizing, like Starr's term the "mediterraneanizing mind" or Davis's "deep Mediterraneaneity" or Arrault's "le concept de *méditerranée*." That approach, developing the mediterranean as a method or heuristic, would differentiate the shifting set of Mediterraneans Braudel lists, encompassing the Caribbean Sea, the Atlantic and Pacific Oceans, from the relatively stable unit that he defines as a concept: "the historical Mediterranean seems to be a concept capable of infinite extension. But how far in space are we justified in extending it?" (*MMW*, 167). Braudel's reluctance to pursue a "difficult and controversial question" that he says is "perhaps the fundamental question we should be asking" if we are seeking "to explain the history of the Mediterranean" (*MMW*, 167) stands in distinct opposition to the turn to multiple possible Mediterranean seas around the world that has been described as one of the recent rich outgrowths of new Mediterranean studies, post-Braudel.[4]

The current interest in an expanded set of middle ("mediterranean") seas also allows for a rethinking of time, extending Braudel's geohistory in ways that work well and differently for the Mediterraneans of the Americas. He himself uses the various prefaces to describe a "multidimensional" approach, more consonant with the strange career of the American Mediterranean as a whole, to how historians have managed "simultaneously" the fundamental contradiction between the time of "conspicuous history" and that of "submerged history" (*MMW*, 16), which is "almost timeless" (*MMW*, 21). From this perspective, all the mediterraneanizers in my book come together in a new Braudelian "unity" (*MMW*, 14), one of the two defining terms for his Mediterranean, a framework that accounts for the ephemeral networks of the American Mediterraneans, their pattern of appearing and disappearing, via a different spatiotemporal relation than we have yet seen. "History accepts and discovers multidimensional explanations," Braudel writes in the preface to the second edition, "reaching, as it were, vertically from one temporal plane to another. And on every plane there are also horizontal relationships and connections" (*MMW*, 16). If we take this image of temporal planes in concert with a line from the earliest first-edition preface, part 1, "The Role of the Environment" (the longest section of the three-part book, the one devoted to the *longue durée*), "the final effect then is to dissect history into various planes, or, to put it another way, to divide historical time into geographical time, social time, and individual time" (*MMW*, 21).

The planes here correspond to both physical (geographical) and human (social, individual) time, relating and entangling geography with history in theoretical ways that eluded Ellen Churchill Semple and Frederick Jackson Turner. Yet both Semple and Turner wanted, like Braudel, to bring their disciplines of geography and history into closer relation, though perhaps not on his terms. He speaks as a historian more than a geographer, balancing the known boundaries ("charted, classified, and labelled" [*MMW*, 17]) of the classic Mediterranean ("nothing could be clearer than the Mediterranean defined by oceanographer, geologist, or even geographer" [*MMW*, 17]) with its "historical character," still to be "discovered" ([*MMW*, 17]). In contrast, we know that the Semple-Turner alliance aimed for a marriage of equals between their two disciplines, which eluded them and remains an unfinished possibility, a splendid failure in Du Bois's words.

So it's not just the unit of space but also what Braudel calls, temporally, the Mediterranean "influence," for how the Mediterranean world works as a model civilization, precursor to other times and places, that fails to fully fit the American Mediterraneans. A term extending across time, "influence" goes strictly in one direction, east to west, like the *translatio imperii*. "The Mediterranean shaped the Atlantic," Braudel says in a chapter titled "Boundaries: The Greater Mediterranean" (*MMW*, 168), "and impressed its own image on the Spanish New World" (*MMW*, 226). From Humboldt on, this unidirectional view simply doesn't apply to the import-export exchange of transferable "Mediterranean" knowledges back and forth, across time short- and long-term, between New and Old Worlds. Humboldt not only gathered flora and fauna, raw materials and written data, to send back to Berlin, but also speculated on how the evidence of missing land bridges on the ocean floor might account for the history of language spread and change in Europe and Asia as well as in the Americas. Brother Wilhelm's research on ancient languages—Sanskrit, Persian, and Old Icelandic—appears in the footnotes of *Personal Narrative*, both as evidence documenting what Alexander observed of Indigenous languages in the Americas and as theories to be tested against the American data. In turn, the linguistic patterns observed in the Americas themselves become the basis for new hypotheses competing with those of the ancient historians Humboldt cites.

Thinking from the American Mediterraneans backward and forward to Braudel's Mediterranean world reveals his own moments, akin to these, of thinking against the grain of westward-goes-the-empire. Both efforts at counterdiscourse engage in, perhaps necessitate, what James calls the speculative thinking in *The Black Jacobins* that produces the Haiti/past-Cuba/future revolutionary effect. Toward the end of part 1, section 2, "The Heart of the Mediterranean: Seas and Coasts," Braudel mentions "an interesting hypothesis, hastily formulated" by a scholar of Malta, that "Mediterranean civilization may not have originated in the East, as has always been supposed" (*MMW*, 166). Even if "the suggested route" of this civilization, spreading from Spain and North Africa to Italy and the East—"then and only then would the movement have flowed back westwards"—is "not correct," he concludes, "it is pleasant to imagine this relay race . . . fanciful, perhaps, but . . . easy to imagine and even probable that the life of the sea, a vital force, would have taken control" (*MMW*, 166). This may be as far as Braudel goes in his speculative thinking, a momentary decentering of the Mediterranean that imagines other directions and other possible seas beyond the scope of the classic Mediterranean, 1550–1600.

Finally, when Braudel explains his method ("the insidious questions of method once more raise their heads, as they inevitably must in a book of this scale, which takes as subject the Mediterranean region . . . in the widest sense" [preface to second edition, *MMW*, 15]), the idea of mediterraneanism itself as a heuristic, as distinct from the geographical space of the Mediterranean, is simply not something he contemplates at all. The key role played by mediterraneanity, the mediterranean metaphor, Mediterraneanism, in producing the American Mediterraneans, in enabling their expansion from a space of comparison into a comparative concept, gets no purchase in his book. Partly, it's Braudel's care not to elevate method ("the historical narrative is not a method, or even the objective method *par excellence*, but quite simply a philosophy of history like any other" [*MMW*, 21]). Rather the accent falls, as we saw earlier, on Braudel's questioning the potentially infinite expansiveness of the concept, how far "in space we are justified in extending it" (*MMW*, 167). He will not or cannot go the distance to embrace the hypothetical in his moments of speculative Mediterranean thinking.

In another of those notable moments, this one at the opening of the opening chapter of part 1, "The Role of the Environment," titled "Mountains Come First," Braudel brings up the great mountain ranges that had once existed, formerly linking Spain and Morocco, Greece to Asia Minor, and with volcanic activity were covered by waters of the sea. Speaking somewhat dismissively of these lost Baetic and Adriatic ranges, he concludes, "There remain only a few islands and fragments scattered along the coast to mark the spot, that is, if geological hypotheses have some foundation in reality—for these are all hypotheses" (*MMW*, 26). Even a footnote on "the return to the apparently outdated theory of vanished continents and mountain ranges" in a recent, stimulating book states categorically that "this is not the place for a detailed discussion of this controversial issue" (*MMW*, 26n1). Humboldt, in contrast, embraced the fragments appearing on the sea floor as possible geological evidence of the disappearance of land masses—which in turn would, hypothetically, explain the data he observed and recorded on otherwise unaccountable continuities and divergences among languages and language speakers in the Americas. In all these ways, the lack of correspondence between Braudel's Mediterranean world and the one invented in the Americas points to the distinctiveness of the Humboldtian tradition—and perhaps to untapped possibilities, roads not yet taken in the Braudelian world.

Put another way, Braudel's Mediterranean bridges space and time in the form of "geohistory," which sets a different bar for spatiotemporal interrelations than the American Mediterraneans. The term in French, *géohistoire*, is sometimes translated as historical geography, but "geohistory," as Braudel preferred, captures the two fields as well as "the dialectic of space and time (geography and history), which was the original justification of the book" (*MMW*, 16). Making the connections between history and geographical space was, Braudel comments in the preface to the second edition (*MMW*, 16), "the basic approach around which the whole work is structured."[5] He uses the various editions of his book itself, much as James does in *The Black Jacobins*, to outline his philosophy of history. Contemplating the fifteen years since the first edition was published, Braudel insists, while it was impossible not to change even "the basic approach," nevertheless, "the problem confronting every historical undertaking," remains the same, "to convey simultaneously both that conspicuous history . . . [of] continual and dramatic changes—and that other, submerged history, almost silent, . . . virtually unsuspected either by its observers or its participants . . . , little touched by the obstinate erosion of time" (*MMW*, 16). This "fundamental contradiction" can be described, he says, as historians have tended to, "in terms of *structure* and *conjunction*," or "long-term" (the former) and "short-term" (the latter) realities (*MMW*, 16). Yet Braudel concludes at the end of this second-edition preface that he still prefers his own timeline with three levels, laid out in the first-edition preface, which expresses not only his "original intentions" but also his "feeling," "simply and unequivocally," and "explains the arrangement of the chapters of the book" (*MMW*, 16).

This is his famous schema of three scales of historical time. Summarized in the first-edition preface, these are: the shortest, *l'histoire événementielle*, concerned with the event; a time of intermediate duration, *l'histoire conjoncturelle*, associated with cycles, economic and demographic; and the most vast and slow moving, analogous to deep geological time, *la longue durée*, Braudel's signature term (*MMW*, 21).[6] Reflecting its status as the most important unit of analysis, the *longue durée* is the subject of the first and longest section of the book, titled "The Role of the Environment." Part 1 is dedicated to geography as a determining, not determinant, factor, variously defined as the "means to an end," "combined across time and space . . . to give us a history in slow motion," "to see the slow unfolding of structural realities," "to discover the almost imperceptible movement of history" (*MMW*, 23). The question of Braudel's own philosophy of history, the degree of his environmental determinism, is, we know, an issue that dogged him throughout his career in the discipline. Mediterranean-studies scholars commenting on that issue frequently cite as evidence one key line from the first-edition preface on the human history of events as mere "surface disturbances, crests of foam that the tides of history carry on their strong backs" (*MMW*, 21). It is also a question he himself is known for raising and trying to lay to rest. Part 1 of *The Mediterranean* originally ended with a section titled "Geohistory and Determinism," where Braudel took on the tendency to geographical determinism associated with the German school, especially Friedrich Ratzel—and by extension, we know, his student, Ellen Churchill Semple, the most prominent geo-determinist of the American mediterraneanizers. The title, along with the term "geohistory," was omitted in the second edition of 1966, where the whole section concluding Part 1 was also radically revised.[7] Thus, Braudel's concept of geohistory succeeded in marrying the two disciplines as Semple had wanted and failed to, while he muted its presence and toned down the discussion of environmental determinism in *The Mediterranean*.

Despite this pull away from explicit geohistory, the marriage of space-time as well as the two disciplines, Braudel's definition of the partnership creates an orderly hierarchy that the Humboldtian tradition belies. The spatiotemporal relations of Braudel's Mediterranean world adhere to a highly structured, schematic philosophy of history that contrasts with the more disorderly historical movement characteristic of the American Mediterraneans. The latter's strange career of appearing and disappearing across space, time, and language, from the late eighteenth century to the present, doesn't really correspond to any of Braudel's three timescales. Neither the unit of the event nor the cycle captures the movement of fleeting presence and partial absence that characterizes the American Mediterraneans as both an entity and a methodology, a physical space and a mode of knowledge. Most of all, the "almost timeless history" (*MMW*, 23) of the *longue durée* doesn't apply: "virtually unsuspected either by its observers or its participants . . . , little touched by the obstinate erosion of time" (*MMW*, 16), the American Mediterraneans are marked by the multiple times of its eruption. Rather than either a singular event or a cyclical pattern, the Mediterraneans, plural, leap erratically into view, recognized by mediterraneanizing participants and observers, often at moments of racial crisis. As ideas that erupt suddenly, they mark ruptures characteristic of their own history of discontinuities.[8] The differences from Braudel's time could hardly be more pronounced.

Yet the temporality of the Americas Mediterraneans, combining history with physical and human geography, does not so much reject outright as swerve from Braudel. While he looks to the geological past to document and explain the very slow, almost imperceptible historical change of the classic Mediterranean world, the American Mediterraneans discourse consistently takes a futurist outlook based on informed speculation. For Humboldt, the geohistory of his *Mediterranée de l'Amérique* lays out the unfinished past of slave revolt as repository for future reactivation in the islands of Haiti, Cuba, and, by extension,

all the slave societies of the new-world Mediterranean. Reading the revolutionary future of Cuba as a reiteration of Haiti as prophecy is the subject *tout court*
of James's *The Black Jacobins*. From this perspective, reading back west to east,
from the New to the Old World, from the Mediterraneans of the post-1800
American future in relation to the Mediterranean world of Phillip II, Braudel's
world lacks a future tense. Only one chapter, titled "Unfinished Revolutions,"
looks to the past as prophecy in the whole massive two-volume, six-hundred-
page *The Mediterranean*. Yet while it may be minimal, we could say, speculate,
that in this case the American Mediterraneans take a cue from Braudel's Mediterranean, taking what is only his part for its whole.

Reading Braudel from this counterfactual point of view, we could see him
as even more of an oceanographer, further going over to the sea than to the
land that borders it. "Its life is linked to the land, . . . and its history can no
more be separated from that of the lands surrounding it than the clay can be
separated from the hands of the potter that shapes it," he declares in the first-
edition preface (*MMW*, 17). Perhaps he would have started the book not with
"Mountains Come First" (part 1, section 1) but instead with "The Heart of
the Mediterranean: Seas and Coast," now section 2 of part 1. Or alternatively
he'd consider them together, integrating the geological formations undersea
and on land. Surely he'd devote more than the two short paragraphs he does
now in which he quickly considers and dispenses with the lost continents and
mountain ranges on the sea floor (*MMW*, 252–6). Most important, were he
less skeptical about the hypothetical, Braudel would take a Humboldtian cue
and follow through on the missing or lost land bridges of the ocean floor that
could account for language spread, change across time.

Specifically, were Braudel writing about the Mediterraneans of the Americas
as opposed to the Mediterranean world in the age of Philip II, he could have
developed a through line on the multilingual consciousness of the Mediterranean and mediterraneanism, both the place and the heuristic. The language
dimension would have a greater presence than it does in *The Mediterranean*.
There is definitely evidence of attention to questions of language scattered
throughout the two-volume work, but as a significant analytical dimension,
it is largely implicit, vestigial. Our imagined Braudel, for example, would
pay more attention to the "polyglottism" of the Ottoman Empire, as one
scholar revisiting Braudel characterizes the multireligious, multiethnic empire, which "from its emergence until its collapse, spoke in many languages,"[9]
Overall, Braudel has a systematic line neither on the "question of polyglottism
in its political contexts" nor on the broad role of languages in producing the
Mediterranean world, either its unity or something else (Pierce, "Polyglottism," 78).

Yet a cluster of tantalizing comments, starting with the prefaces, suggests the range of Braudel's linguistic interests—and possible new directions for them. Unsurprisingly, the preface to the English edition, "faced with the prospect of a translation" (*MMW*, 13), refers more explicitly to language than either of the others. Thanks go to those, Braudel writes, who have worked "to ensure it has a quality rare I believe in the realm of translation"; "it is no small task to adapt my not uncomplicated style to the vigorous rhythms of the English language" (*MMW*, 14). Aside from these lines, almost all references to translations, are relegated to scholarly sources in the footnotes. On the other end of the spectrum is one of Braudel's own characteristic, seemingly offhand uses of metaphoric language. "The Mediterranean speaks with many voices," he notes near the beginning of the preface to the English edition; "it is the sum of individual histories" (*MMW*, 13). His readers have noted how he draws similarly, without much self-reflection, on the ocean as a figurative resource for central concepts, notably in the oceanic language that describes each of the three timescales. His Mediterranean history consists in part of his own figures of speech that he occasionally incorporates. In so doing he leaves open the route to more explicit thinking about the "acts of language" that construct his history of the Mediterranean, his world and that of the Americas.

This counterfactual takes on more weight when we consider how the prefaces link the "historiographical problem" of the archive that Braudel brings up in the first-edition preface to the translation question in the 1972 preface to the English edition. There, "faced with the prospect of a translation," he makes brief suggestive comments on the limits and possibilities thereof: "Need I confess that I have not been able to examine all the documents available to me in the archives, no matter how hard I tried. This book is the result of a necessarily incomplete study" (*MMW*, 18). There, surely not coincidentally, he also speaks to "a major historiographical problem, a zone of formidable uncertainty: the Ottoman empire" (*MMW*, 13), with its "secrets [that] lie hidden in the vast archives in Istanbul," the difficult-to-access sources (*MMW*, 13).

A sampling of these comments suggests the varieties of historical uses Braudel finds for language in the role of the environment, intersecting with nation, race, migration, and assimilation. Tracing the spread of Latin and Italian across the geography of the sixteenth-century Mediterranean documents the uneven history of conquest and resistance, in relation to the environment. Latin didn't penetrate the mountains, he comments in part 1, in a section titled "Mountains, Civilizations, Religions," suggesting how human agency must be considered environmentally. "Mountains are as a rule a world apart from civilizations. . . . Their history is to have none. . . . Neither did Latin as a language take root in the hostile massifs of north Africa, Spain or elsewhere, and the Latin or Italic house type remained a house of the plains. In a few places it may have infiltrated locally, but on the whole the mountains resisted it" (*MMW*, 34). A footnote quotes two sources, a seventeenth-century translation of a Spanish text and an eighteenth-century text that provide evidence of the "separate religious geography" that seems to have emerged in these mountains: the inhabitants are Christian Moriscos "who have retained 'their old way of life, their costume and their particular language which is a monstrous mixture of Arabic and Spanish'" (*MMW*, 35n51). Braudel, who is not known for being drawn to literary and artistic forms as evidence (preferring data on population, money, and trade), comments that in the mountains of Asia Minor, an "aggressive form of nomadism" developed, possibly Braudel speculates linguistically, in broad response to the "Turkish words for coolness" (*MMW*, 97). "Perhaps it was because of 'what the term *yala*—summer stay—means in the Turkish language and culture, where the notions of coolness, icy running water, and luxuriant pastures combine to form an image of Paradise.' . . . A Turkish proverb, freely translated, says 'a *Yürük* [nomad walker] does not need to go anywhere but needs to be moving,' obeying traditional urges as much as, if not more than geographical necessities" (*MMW*, 97). Here Braudel's environmental determinism finds its own self-imposed limits, activated by the nature of the linguistic evidence. Taking the measure of seasonal migration by reading a Turkish proverb, Braudel makes the ambiguities of the Turkish language into a means of informed speculation on geohistory in the mountains of Asia Minor.

The clash between Latin and Italian offers another, even broader based linguistic measure of the geohistory of civilizations. The Adriatic gulf in the sixteenth century emerges as "the sphere of triumphant Italian culture," with "Italian" defined primarily linguistically: "This is not to suggest . . . 'Italian' in the sense that apologists for racial expansion would have understood it. . . . Italianism was a commodity: Italian was the commercial language of the entire Mediterranean. . . . It was considered desirable that the secretaries of the republic should be as fluent in Italian as Latin" (*MMW*, 131–32). Language leads to race, which enters the picture only to be dismissed as the kind of deterministic category associated with racial apologists—or environmental geographers like Semple and Ratzel. Braudel then explores, again linguistically, the conflict between the "invented Italian genealogies" and the spoken language of Slavonic: "the Italianized names betray their Slavonic origins, Slavonic was the spoken language, the familiar tongue of the women and the people, and even, after all, of the elite . . . the registers of Ragusa frequently record strict orders to speak only Italian at the assemblies of the Rectors;

if an order was necessary, clearly Slavonic was being spoken" (*MMW*, 132). The geohistory of Italian hegemony as regional Mediterranean power here emerges in the conflicts between the Italian language, written Latin, and spoken Slav.

Similarly, on the "unassimilable" Bulgarian in the Spanish Empire, language is a prerequisite for identity, both local and national. The island isolation and archaism of Sardinia are registered through language ("it was a self-contained world with its own language" [*MMW*, 150]) along with their opposite, Mediterranean connectivity: "some accidental change of ruler or fortune may bring to the island's shores an entirely different civilization and way of life, with its dress, customs, and language, which the island may receive and preserve intact over several centuries, bearing living witness to forgotten revolutions" (*MMW*, 150). Language takes pride of place as a key indicator of national consciousness: like "the spread of the Tuscan language" in Italy, "similarly the Castilian language spread over the whole Iberian peninsula in the sixteenth century, and became the language of literary expression used by Aragonese writers from the time of Charles V" (*MMW*, 163). Different geographies, similar histories: nations are both connected and separated by what I would call, after Braudel, their geo-linguistic locations. The French channel was not only a trade route of salt north and textiles south "but also the route taken by the victorious advance after the 1450s of the French language, . . . the language and civilization of the *Langue d'Oc*, down to the shores of the Mediterranean itself" (*MMW*, 222). This is perhaps the broadest statement of the entangled relations of space, time, and language that together produce Braudel's Mediterranean world.

Braudel could have made this cluster of comments into a third dimension parallel to "The Mediterranean as a Geographical Unit" and "The Mediterranean as a Human Unit," the titles of two sections. This chapter, "The Mediterranean as a Linguistic Unit," would extract language out from other observable data as an independent product of both geophysical and historical processes, a unique record of the geological past preserved in the changing forms of human communication. Put another way, the imagined Braudel of the American Mediterraneans could fill in the unfinished language work of the actual Braudel.

I am hardly the first to consider whether other oceans have their own Braudels. Barry Cunliffe's *Facing the Ocean: The Atlantic and Its Peoples* (2001) seeks to do for the Atlantic what Braudel had done for the Mediterranean. And Alison Games comments on the "delicious irony" of the José de Acosta epigraph with which Braudel started his book—and I mine—that while Europeans never found their own Mediterranean in the Americas, historians have since discovered the Atlantic as a unit of historical analysis. In light of this book, the irony may be even more delicious, but more meaningful is Games's ensuing critique of the attempts to write a Braudelian Atlantic history. It's a litany of nos and nots: "the Atlantic does not have the coherence that Acosta first identified for the Mediterranean, nor that Braudel proposed and delineated centuries later; nor, indeed, is it possible to speak with confidence of an Atlantic system."[10]

Perhaps Braudel's Mediterranean is an impossible act to repeat, encompassing a "totality," the world in an ocean—and perhaps this is the wrong question. The one better posed by my book is how would the double counterfactual of a Braudel for the plural American Mediterraneans imagine a different past as repository for possible futures? First, this is a subterranean history in the broad sense of its fugitive coming and going, appearing and disappearing from the surface of history and historiography. Second, in a specific sense, the Caribbean Mediterranean identified with Édouard Glissant as a theorist and poet of "subterranean convergences," a "submarine history" of the sea as a historical text representing different layers of historical memory, differs from both a Braudelian look inland to the lands that surround the sea, the place of cultivation and labor, and an Abulafian corrective: "My 'Mediterranean' is resolutely the surface of the sea," Abulafia declares.[11] And third, Glissant as a twentieth-century theorist of the Caribbean from the Caribbean would have to bring in an earlier, nineteenth-century polymath of Spanish America to produce a composite rather than singular mediterraneanizer, as yet unidentified, still to emerge in the future.

Possible candidates emerge from among the untapped, unsung sources Humboldt sometimes cites in footnotes and sometimes uses without acknowledgment. Some are primarily botanists and astronomers (the Spanish naturalist, mathematician, physician, and priest José Celestino Mutis), others geographers and cosmographers (Mutis's colleague on Spain's Royal Botanical Expedition, the head of Bogota's first observatory, and "patriot naturalist" Francisco José de Caldas), and still others, most speculatively, historiangeographers (e.g., the Mexican Manuel Orozco y Berra, president of the Mexican Society of Geography and Statistics, member of the Mexican Academy of Language, and author of *Geography of Languages and Ethnographic Letter of Mexico* [1864] and the four-volume *Ancient History of the Conquest of Mexico* [1880–81]).[12] The creators of "patriotic sciences," this particular nineteenth-century Spanish-American network has no Mediterranean—sea, concept, or method—association to speak of. Yet some of them are known for adapting a mode of hypothetical or "conjectural history" that resonates with Glissant's speculative philosophy of history—and more broadly with the historical consciousness of the American Mediterraneans.[13] Collectively they point to a possible composite Americas figure, not yet known, who will speak for oceanic histories within and beyond Braudel's horizon. Like his Acosta epigraph at the head of his book and mine, I close with a negative, "what they have not discovered," that leaves an opening, the possibility of other future mediterraneans and other mediterraneanizers of the Americas to be both discovered and invented.

Acknowledgments

This book is the product of a *longue durée* when Americanists were slowly rushing to adapt to a worldview that aimed to displace the nation as the field-definer. I can't think of a better way to acknowledge those who have been part of my book over these many years than to summon forth this disciplinary history. The concept of the "long" century took hold just as I was first encountering José Martí at conferences in the late 1990s, around the one hundredth anniversary of the Cuban-Spanish-American War, "'Our America' and the Gilded Age: José Martí's Chronicles of Imperial Critique" (Humanities Research Institute, University of California, Irvine, 1995) and "Bastards of US Imperialism" (Stanford University, 1998). From that start date, in various institutional locations, I kept thinking about Martí and different modes of literary adaptation in the Americas—at that point the Spanish acute accent (é) wasn't yet in use, but the name "America" was already under scrutiny.

Amy Kaplan, to whom this book is dedicated, was already a critical presence and sheer force in my life and work. By 2003, her American Studies Association presidential address, "Violent Belonging and the Question of Empire Today," brought new ways of talking politics around empire transnationally, and I took off on a series of collaborations that produced more possible subtitles for my work in progress. Intercampus conversations on "states of emergency" around 2005 between the University of California, Santa Cruz, and the University of Wisconsin, Madison (co-organized with Russ Castronovo), pushed me toward Walter Benjamin's ideas about translation. I returned to Martí as a translator in a 2008 conference at the University of Illinois celebrating twenty years of the journal *American Literary History* (edited by Gordon Hutner), and then a conference in 2009 called the "American Tropics" at the University of Essex (spearheaded by Peter Hulme), which gave me a way into

C. L. R. James's *The Black Jacobins*. Thereafter, two fellowship stints—at the Huntington Library, in San Marino, California (2009–10), and at the Schomburg Center for Research in Black Culture, at the New York Public Library (2018–19)—bookended the final phase of the "American Mediterranean," first singular, then plural. In the farthest past, my year at the Stanford Humanities Center (1993–94) helped to launch this book with work on American race melodramas that has inspired me ever since. I am deeply grateful for all of this personal and institutional support.

Amy Kaplan's presence in my life has been a boon beyond measure since we first met so long ago at yet another conference, in Cambridge, Massachusetts, in 1990, called "Nationalisms and Sexualities." Amy's continuous presence—the way we write and teach our students—in the present tense extends from her nineteenth century, my touchstone, to today. Her death in July 2020 has not changed that. I thanked her specially in *Blood Talk*, my earlier book published by the University of Chicago Press, for our long-term bonding over the work of Mark Twain and W. E. B. Du Bois, and here I am, now, eighteen years later, and over three decades since we met, thanking her once again. I intend to keep it up. Her passion and modesty, her voice, critical and intellectual, personal and political, her own wildness and domesticity, are an ongoing source of inspiration. I hope this book lives up to the openings she helps me see in the most unlikely of places and times. To Amy, beloved genius loci temporisque.

Thanks particularly for permission to republish modified versions of parts of the introduction and part 4:

"Humboldt's American Mediterranean," in "Las Américas Quarterly," special issue, *American Quarterly* 66, no. 3 (September 2014): 505–28. Reprinted with permission of Johns Hopkins University Press.

"Mediterraneans of the Americas: Going Anti-Imperial, Comparatively," in *A Question of Time: American Literature from Colonial Encounter to Contemporary Fiction*, ed. Cindy Weinstein (Cambridge: Cambridge University Press, 2018), 242–65. Reproduced with permission of Cambridge University Press through PLSclear.

"Black Jacobins and New World Mediterraneans," in *Surveying the American Tropics: A Literary Geography from New York to Rio*, ed. Peter Hulme et al. (Liverpool: Liverpool University Press, 2013), 159–82. Reproduced with permission of Liverpool University Press through PLSclear.

Abbreviations

A C D : Kevin Starr, *Americans and the California Dream, 1850–1915* (New York: Oxford University Press, 1973)

A H : Ellen Churchill Semple, *American History and Its Geographic Conditions* (Boston: Houghton, Mifflin, 1903)

A M : Stephen Bonsal, *The American Mediterranean* (New York: Moffat, Yard, 1912)

B J : C. L. R. James, *The Black Jacobins: Toussaint L'Ouverture and the San Domingo Revolution* (New York: Vintage, 1938; 2nd ed., rev. 1963).

B R : W. E. B. Du Bois, *Black Reconstruction in America, 1860–1880* (1935; rpt. with an introduction by David Levering Lewis, New York: Simon and Schuster, 1995)

C : W. Adolphe Roberts, *The Caribbean: The Story of Our Sea of Destiny* (Indianapolis: Bobbs-Merrill, 1940)

E F : Mike Davis, *Ecology of Fear: Los Angeles and the Imagination of Disaster* (New York: Metropolitan Books, 1998)

E I : Élisée Reclus, *The Earth and Its Inhabitants, North America,* ed. A. H. Keane, *vol. 2, Mexico, Central America, West Indies* (New York: D. Appleton, 1897)

I G : Ellen Churchill Semple, *Influences of Geographic Environment, on the Basis of Ratzel's System of Anthropo-geography* (New York: Henry Holt, 1911)

M D : James Street, *Mingo Dabney* (New York: Dial Press, 1950)

M M W : Fernand Braudel, *The Mediterranean and the Mediterranean World in the Age of Philip II*, trans. Siân Reynolds, 2 vols. (London: Collins, 1972–73)

M S : P. C. Remondino, *The Mediterranean Shores of America: Southern California; Its Climatic, Physical, and Meteorological Conditions* (Philadelphia: F. A. Davis, 1892)

N G : Élisée Reclus, *La nouvelle géographie universelle: La terre et les hommes*, 19 vols. (Paris: Hachette, 1876–94)

O I : Charles Dudley Warner, *Our Italy* (Hartford, CT: American Publishing, 1891)

O W I : Frederick Albion Ober, *Our West Indian Neighbors: The Islands of the Caribbean Sea, "America's Mediterranean"; Their Picturesque Features, Fascinating*

History, and Attractions for the Traveler, Nature-Lover, Settler and Pleasure-Seeker (New York: James Pott, 1904; rpt. 1916)

P N : Alexander von Humboldt, *Personal Narrative of Travels to the Equinoctial Regions of the New Continent, during the Years 1799–1804,* trans. Helen Maria Williams, 7 vols. (London: Longman, Hurst, Rees, Orme, and Brown, 1814–29)

R : Helen Hunt Jackson, *Ramona: A Story,* introduction by Michael Dorris (New York: Signet, 1988)

R H : *Alexander von Humboldt, Relation historique,* in *Voyage aux régions équinoxi-ales du nouveau continent, fait en 1799, 1800, 1801, 1802, 1803 et 1804,* vols. 1–13 (Paris: Librairie Grecque-Latine-Allemande, 1815–31)

S C : Carey McWilliams, *Southern California: An Island on the Land* (Salt Lake City, UT: Peregrine Smith, 1983)

S S : W. Adolphe Roberts, *The Single Star: A Novel of Cuba in the 90s* (Indianapolis: Bobbs-Merrill, 1949)

T M Y : W. Adolphe Roberts, *These Many Years: An Autobiography,* ed. with intro-duction by Peter Hulme (Kingston, Jamaica: University of West Indies Press and National Library of Jamaica, 2015)

T R : James Street, *Tap Roots* (New York: Sun Dial Press, 1942)

T W R : James Street, *Tomorrow We Reap,* with James Childers (New York: Dial Press, 1949)

Notes

Preface

1. If you google the term, see, for example: Mediterranean California, Landscope America, the Conservation Guide to America's Natural Places, a collaborative project of NatureServe and the National Geographic Society, 2021, http://www.landscope.org/explore/natural_geographies /divisions/mediterranean_california/; Mediterranean House Plans, Architectural Designs, 2021, https://www.architecturaldesigns.com/house-plans/styles/mediterranean; California Mediterranean Style Homes: Influences, Inspirations, and Resources for Designing Yours, lmb, Laura Martin Bovard Interiors, August 18, 2018, https://www.lmbinteriors.com/california-mediterranean /california-mediterranean-style-homes-influences-inspiration-and-resources-for-designing-yours/.

2. Edmundo O'Gorman, *The Invention of America, an Inquiry into the Historical Nature of the New World and the Meaning of Its History* (1958 Spanish ed.; Bloomington: Indiana University Press, 1961). On America as intellectually invented and the space of America as "the Indies," see Martin W. Lewis and Kären Wigen, *The Myth of Continents: A Critique of Metageography* (Berkeley: University of California Press, 1997), 25. O'Gorman resigned in 1969 from the *Academia Mexicana de la Lengua* (Mexican Academy of the Spanish Language) after disagreements over concepts such as the "discovery of America," "encounter between two worlds," and "cultural fusion" (or "natural mixing"). See Rodrigo Lazo, "The Invention of American Again: On the Impossibility of an Archive," in "History, Historicism, and Historiography," special issue, *American Literary History* 25, no. 4 (Winter 2013): 751–71.

3. Andrea Wulf, *The Invention of Nature: Alexander von Humboldt's New World* (New York: Knopf, 2015). For a compelling critique of Wulf, see Jorge Cañizares-Esguerra, "How Derivative Was Humboldt? Microcosmic Nature Narratives in Early Modern Spanish America and the (Other) Origins of Humboldt's Ecological Sensibilities," in *Colonial Botany: Science, Commerce, and Politics in the Early Modern World*, ed. Londa Schiebinger and Claudia Swan (Philadelphia: University of Pennsylvania Press, 2005), 148–65.

4. On the various terms for an Americas Mediterranean tradition, see the introduction; see also Eric Hobsbawm and Terence Ranger, eds., *The Invention of Tradition* (Cambridge: Cambridge University Press, 1982; rpt. 2000).

5. For "doubled vision" and "inverted telescope," see Benedict Anderson, *The Spectre of Comparisons: Nationalism, Southeast Asia, and the World* (London: Verso, 1998), 2; for "incomparable," see Gayle Rogers, *Incomparable Empires: Modernism and the Translation of American*

and Spanish Literatures (New York: Columbia University Press, 2016). Anderson makes Rizal a focal point at various key junctures in his work; see Benedict Anderson, *Imagined Communities: Reflections on the Origin and Spread of Nationalism* (London: Verso, 1983; rpt. 1991; 2006); Benedict Anderson, *Under Three Flags: Anarchism and the Anti-colonial Imagination* (London: Verso, 2005).

6. When capitalizing or using lowercase for the word Black, I generally adopt the usage from the historical figure I'm talking about. C. L. R. James, for example, uses lowercase when he refers to "black Spartacus" and even, most suggestively, to "black Jacobins," excepting only when it is used as a title. When I am using the term myself, I capitalize it, per current usage. For this historical reason, my overall use throughout the book cannot be reconciled.

7. I take the term "Humboldt current" from Aaron Sachs, *The Humboldt Current: Nineteenth-Century Exploration and the Roots of American Environmentalism* (New York: Viking, 2006). On "a comparative history that, along the way, turns into something else," see Rebecca Scott, *Degrees of Freedom: Louisiana and Cuba after Slavery* (Cambridge, MA: Harvard University Press, 2005), 4; on the multiple Mediterraneans, see William V. Harris, ed., *Rethinking the Mediterranean* (Oxford: Oxford University Press, 2005), especially W. V. Harris, "The Mediterranean and Ancient History": "For years now scholars have been discovering Mediterraneans" (8), "If we are going to engage in comparative history . . . , we should pay more attention to difficulties of translation and to linguistic nuances" (28); David Abulafia, "Mediterraneans," 64–93 (the "Classic Mediterranean" is his term for "the Mediterranean Sea," 66); and Michael Herzfeld, "Practical Mediterraneanism," 45–63.

Introduction

1. *Relation historique*, published as part of *Voyage aux régions équinoxiales du nouveau continent, fait en 1799, 1800, 1801, 1802, 1803 et 1804*, the multivolume narrative of Humboldt's American travels, 1799–1804, was published in French, 1814–1825, *brought out* in thirty volumes and numerous smaller abridged editions between 1805 and 1839, and translated in English as *Personal Narrative of Travels to the Equinoctial Regions of the New Continent, during the Years 1799–1804*, between 1818 and 1829, and again in 1852. I use Helen Maria Williams's seven-volume English translation of the travel account because the record of her correspondence and collaboration with Humboldt provides unusual contextual insight into the process of translation: Alexander von Humboldt, *Personal Narrative of Travels to the Equinoctial Regions of the New Continent, during the Years 1799–1804*, trans. Helen Maria Williams, 7 vols. (London: Longman, Hurst, Rees, Orme, and Brown, 1814–29); hereafter cited parenthetically in the text as *PN*. For French quotations, I use the original edition, titled *Relation historique*, in *Voyage aux régions équinoxiales du nouveau continent, fait en 1799, 1800, 1801, 1802, 1803 et 1804*, vols. 1–13 (Paris: Librairie Grecque-Latine-Allemande, 1815–31); hereafter cited as *RH*. On the multidirectional reinvention process of the "thirty-volume voyage," see Mary Louise Pratt, *Imperial Eyes: Travel Writing and Transculturation*, 2nd ed. (London: Routledge, 2008), 112, 115; on all those "new" place-names, see Benedict Anderson, "Memory and Forgetting," in *Imagined Communities: Reflections on the Origins and Spread of Nationalism* (London: Verso, 1991), 187–206.

2. Aaron Sachs, *The Humboldt Current: Nineteenth-Century Exploration and the Roots of American Environmentalism* (New York: Viking, 2006), 120; Alexander von Humboldt, *Cosmos: A Sketch of a Physical Description of the Universe*, trans. Elise C. Otté, 2 vols. (New York: Harper and Bros., 1850; rpt. 1858).

3. Fernand Braudel, *The Mediterranean and the Mediterranean World in the Age of Philip II*, trans. Siân Reynolds, 2 vols. (London: Collins, 1972–73), 1:17; hereafter abbreviated *MMW*, cited parenthetically in the text.

4. See Laura Dassow Walls, *The Passage to Cosmos and the Shaping of America* (Chicago: University of Chicago Press, 2009); Jorge Cañizares- Esguerra, "How Derivative Was Humboldt? Microcosmic Nature Narratives in Early Modern Spanish America and the (Other) Origins of Humboldt's Ecological Sensibilities," in *Colonial Botany: Science, Commerce, and Politics in the Early Modern World*, ed. Londa Schiebinger and Claudia Swan (Philadelphia: University of Pennsylvania Press, 2005), 148–65.

5. See W. V. Harris, ed., *Rethinking the Mediterranean* (London: Oxford University Press, 2005): on "a vast Mediterranean culture" as "disdainful cultural imperialism," see Michael Herzfeld, "Practical Mediterraneanism: Excuses for Everything, from Epistemology to Eating," 48, and on "a cousin of Orientalism," see W. V. Harris, "The Mediterranean and Ancient History," 2.; Braudel, *The Mediterranean*, 20.

6. See Anne Buttimer, "Bridging the Americas: Humboldtian Legacies," in "Humboldt in the Americas," special issue, *Geographical Review* 96, no. 3 (2006): vii; on translation, see Alison E. Martin, *Nature Translated: Alexander Von Humboldt's Works in Nineteenth-Century Britain* (Edinburgh: Edinburgh University Press, 2018), http://www.jstor.org/stable/10.3366/j.ctv7h0vkr.

7. Qtd. in Andrea Wulf, *The Invention of Nature: Alexander von Humboldt's New World* (New York: Knopf, 2015), 88. Humboldt's Chimborazo drawing, his so-called *Naturgmälde*, was published in *Essay on the Geography of Plants* (1807).

8. Humboldt, *Cosmos*, 1:119; hereafter cited parenthetically in the text as *Cosmos*. Another English translation by Elizabeth Sabine was published in London, 2 vols. (London: Longman, Brown, Green, and Longmans, 1849).

9. Hermann Klencke and Gustav Schlesier, *Lives of the Brothers Humboldt, Alexander and William*, trans. Juliette Bauer (New York: Harper, 1853), 190–91.

10. The French *bords* (as opposed to *frontières*) would usually be translated as shores or banks, as Helen Maria Williams does elsewhere (see above); perhaps her onetime use of "borders" here is symptomatic of the racial and national divisions highlighted in this political context.

11. See David Abulafia, "Mediterraneans," in Harris, *Rethinking the Mediterranean*, 64–65.

12. Élisée Reclus, *La nouvelle géographie universelle: La terre et les hommes*, 19 vols. (Paris: Hachette, 1876–94), 11; hereafter cited parenthetically as *NG* in the text; Élisée Reclus, *The Earth and Its Inhabitants, North America*, ed. A. H. Keane, vol. 2, *Mexico, Central America, West Indies* (New York: D. Appleton, 1897), 649; hereafter cited parenthetically as *EI* in the text.

13. W. Adolphe Roberts, *The Caribbean: The Story of Our Sea of Destiny* (Indianapolis: Bobbs-Merrill, 1940), 14, 176, 339; hereafter abbreviated *C*, cited parenthetically in the text.

14. See Reclus, *The Earth and Its Inhabitants*, chap. 6, "The American Mediterranean: Gulf of Mexico and Caribbean Sea," 338–53; Stephen Bonsal, *The American Mediterranean* (New York: Moffat, Yard, 1912); hereafter cited parenthetically as *AM* in the text.

15. Charles Dudley Warner, *Our Italy* (Hartford, CT: American Publishing, 1891), 18; hereafter abbreviated *OI*, cited parenthetically in the text; on California's "fantasy heritage," see Carey McWilliams, *North from Mexico: The Spanish-Speaking People of the United States* (1948; rpt. New York: Greenwood Press, 1968), 35–47; Édouard Glissant, *Poetics of Relation*, trans. Betsy Wing (Ann Arbor: University of Michigan Press, 1997), 33.

16. José de Acosta, *The Naturall and Morall Historie of the East and West Indies* (London, 1604), qtd. in Braudel, *The Mediterranean*, title page.

17. Roberto Fernández Retamar, *Caliban and Other Essays*, trans. Edward Baker (Minneapolis: University of Minnesota Press, 1989), 6.

18. Here I draw on Sachs, *The Humboldt Current*, which starts from the premise that despite all the places named for him in the US, including the eponymous Pacific Northwest current, the signal fact is that Humboldt's once-influential theories "now constitute barely a rivulet in American intellectual culture." See *The Humboldt Current*, 10.

19. See David Abulafia, "Mediterranean History as Global History," *History and Theory* 50, no. 2 (May 2011): 220–28. The "Mediterranean-like spaces" include dry open spaces such as the Sahara Desert (220), one of Humboldt's examples (see "the Sahara, that Mediterranean of moving sands," *Personal Narrative*, vol. 6, 64).

20. On "the dream of California as a Mediterranean littoral," and the "Mediterranean metaphor" or "analogy," see Kevin Starr, *Americans and the California Dream, 1850–1915* (New York: Oxford University Press, 1973; rpt. 1985), 1:408, 370–71, 376–77 and chap. 12, "An American Mediterranean," passim, 365–414; hereafter abbreviated *ACD* and cited parenthetically in the text. On "Deep Mediterraneaneity," see Mike Davis, *Ecology of Fear: Los Angeles and the Imagination of Disaster* (New York: Metropolitan Books, 1998), 9–20; hereafter abbreviated *EF* and cited parenthetically in the text;

21. See Bruce Cumings, *Dominion from Sea to Sea: Pacific Ascendancy and American Power* (New Haven, CT: Yale University Press, 2009); Edmund Burke III, "Toward a Comparative History of the Modern Mediterranean, 1750–1919," *Journal of World History* 23, no. 4 (2013): 907–39; on the "turn" to ocean studies in literature and history, see two recent journal issues, *AHR* Forum: "Oceans of History," *American Historical Review* 111, no. 3 (2006); and *PMLA* Theories and Methodologies: "Oceanic Studies," *PMLA* 125, no. 3 (2010): 657–736. On the "classic Mediterranean" and the need to better define its history and that of "other Mediterraneans," see Abulafia, "Mediterranean History as Global History," 220–21; and Iain Chambers, *Mediterranean Crossings: The Politics of an Interrupted Modernity* (Durham, NC: Duke University Press, 2008).

22. Jean-Baptiste Arrault, "A propos du concept de *méditerranée*: Expérience géographique du monde et mondialisation" [About the Mediterranean analogy: Geographical experience of the world and globalization], *Cybergeo: European Journal of Geography* [En ligne], Épistémologie, Histoire de la Géographie, Didactique, article 332, mis en ligne le 03 janvier 2006: "*À comprendre pourquoi, entre le milieu du XIXᵉ et le milieu du XXᵉsiècles, nombre d'auteurs, géographes en particulier, ont recours à cette analogie: ne cherchent-ils pas à traduire une expérience nouvelle du monde, celle de la mondialisation?*" ("To understand why, between the middle of the nineteenth to the middle of the twentieth century, many writers, geographers in particular, resorted to this analogy: aren't they trying to translate a new experience of the world, that of globalization"; translation mine). Arrault references a subgroup of French geographers linked to research on the invention of the Mediterranean (Bourguet, 1998; Deprest, 2002; Lacoste, 1993, p. 995; O. Dollfus, 1995, p. 196; R. Knafou 2003, p. 601), http://cybergeo.revues.org/13093.

23. See Desmond Gregory, *Brute New World: The Rediscovery of Latin America in the Early Nineteenth Century* (London: British Academic Press), 148.

24. Wulf, *The Invention of Nature*, 87–89; Pratt, *Imperial Eyes*, 125, 120–24; Aaron Sachs, "The Ultimate 'Other': Post-colonialism and Alexander von Humboldt's Ecological Relationship with Nature," *History and Theory* 42, no. 4 (2003): 111–35.

25. W. E. B. Du Bois, *Dusk of Dawn: Toward an Autobiography of a Race Concept* (New York: Harcourt, Brace, and World, 1940).

26. See Mathew Frye Jacobson, *Whiteness of a Different Color: European Immigrants and the Alchemy of Race* (Cambridge, MA: Harvard University Press, 1999); Matthew Pratt Guterl, *The Color of Race in America, 1900–1940* (Cambridge, MA: Harvard University Press, 2001).

27. To trace the histories of two post-emancipation societies, where the legacies of slavery play out differently and even the units of comparison, Louisiana and Cuba, state and island nation, are uneven, Rebecca Scott advocates alternating between panoramic and microhistorical views that do justice to the differences of "these two nearby possible worlds"; see Scott, *Degrees of Freedom: Louisiana and Cuba after Slavery* (Cambridge, MA: Harvard University Press, 2005), 7.

Part One

1. *Peregrine Horden and Nicolas Percell, The Corrupting Sea: A Study of Mediterranean History* (Oxford: Blackwell, 2000), chapter 5, "Connectivity," 123–72; see also Horden and Percell, *The Boundless Sea: Writing Mediterranean History* (London: Routledge, 2019).

2. On literary geography, see Peter Hulme, *Cuba's Wild East: A Literary Geography of Oriente* (Liverpool: Liverpool University Press, 2011), 4; on fugitivity and race, see Stephen Best and Saidiya Hartman, "Fugitive Justice," *Representations* 92, no. 1 (Fall 2005): 1–15; Stephen Best, *The Fugitive's Properties: Law and the Poetics of Possession* (Chicago: University of Chicago Press, 2004), especially chap. 3, "Counterfactuals, Causation, and the Tenses of 'Separate but Equal,'" 203–68.

3. See Aaron Sachs, *The Humboldt Current: Nineteenth-Century Exploration and the Roots of American Environmentalism* (New York: Viking, 2006).

4. See Tom Andersen, *This Fine Piece of Water: An Environmental History of Long Island Sound* (New Haven, CT: Yale UP, 2002): "It was Daniel Webster who first called Long Island Sound the 'American Mediterranean,'" an association based not on raw physical shape or geographic magnitude—"the Mediterranean Sea is many hundreds of times larger—but on how the sheer hospitality of the two bodies of water have shaped the destinies of the people who populate their shores. . . . Both are exemplars of classic maritime worlds" (2).

5. Qtd. in Matthew Guterl, *The American Mediterranean: Southern Slaveholders in the Age of Emancipation* (Cambridge, MA: Harvard University Press, 2008), 12; hereafter cited parenthetically in the text. Guterl names "Gulf of Mexico, 1854" as the source but I have been unable to locate it.

6. Matthew F. Maury, *The Physical Geography of the Sea* (New York: Harper and Bros., 1855); Charles L. Lewis, *Matthew Fontaine Maury: "The Pathfinder of the Sea"* (Annapolis, MD: US Naval Institute, 1927), 68. For recent critical work on Maury, see Steven J. Dick, *Sky and Ocean Joined: The U.S. Naval Observatory, 1830–2000* (Cambridge: Cambridge University Press, 2003); John Grady, *Matthew Fontaine Maury, Father of Oceanography: A Biography, 1806–1873* (Jefferson, NC: McFarland, 2015).

7. Frederick Jackson Turner, "The Significance of the Frontier in American History," *Annual Report of the American Historical Association for the Year 1893* (Washington, DC: Government Printing Office, 1894), 227.

8. Charles Dudley Warner, *Our Italy* (Hartford, CT: American Publishing, 1891), 18.

9. Warner, *Our Italy*, 18; P[eter] C[harles] Remondino, *The Mediterranean Shores of America: Southern California; Its Climatic, Physical, and Meteorological Conditions* (Philadelphia: F. A. Davis, 1892); W. C. Riley, *Puget Sound: The American Mediterranean and the Pacific Coast* (St. Paul, MN, 1892).

10. Frederick Albion Ober, *Our West Indian Neighbors: The Islands of the Caribbean Sea, "America's Mediterranean"; Their Picturesque Features, Fascinating History, and Attractions for the Traveler, Nature-Lover, Settler and Pleasure-Seeker* (New York: James Pott, 1904; rpt. 1916); see also Frederick Albion Ober, *In the Wake of Columbus: Adventures of the Special Commissioner Sent by the World's Columbian Exposition to the West Indies* (Boston: D. Lothrop, 1893); Stephen Bonsal, *The American Mediterranean* (New York: Moffat, Yard, 1912); Jacques Crokaert, *La Méditerranée américaine: L'Expansion des États-Unis dans la mer des Antilles, Préface de M. Henri Jaspar, 1er ministre et ministre des colonies de Belgique* (Paris: Payot, 1927).

11. See W. Adolphe Roberts, *These Many Years: An Autobiography*, ed. with introduction by Peter Hulme (Kingston, Jamaica: University of West Indies Press and National Library of Jamaica, 2015), 2; Alejo Carpentier, Prologue to *El reino de este mundo* (1949); a revised and expanded version of the prologue reappeared under the title "De lo real maravilloso americano" in a collection of Carpentier's essays, *Tientos y diferencias* (Montevideo: Arca, 1973), 96–112. This network also includes Édouard Glissant, who took up Carpentier's point that the Caribbean Sea is the Mediterranean of the New World, in an oceanic transference later refracted in the 1950s by the Haitian novelist Jacques Stéphen Alexis.

12. Laurence A. Breiner, "Caribbean Voices on the Air: Radio, Poetry, and Nationalism in the Anglophone Caribbean," in *Communities of the Air: Radio Century, Radio Culture*, ed. Susan Merrill Squier (Durham, NC: Duke University Press, 2003), 94.

13. See Ober, "Toussaint l'Ouverture Was Haiti's George Washington," in *Our West Indian Neighbors*, 169.

14. C. L. R. James, *The Black Jacobins: Toussaint L'Ouverture and the San Domingo Revolution*, 2nd ed., rev. (New York: Vintage, 1963), on the "black Spartacus," see 171, 250; W. E. B. Du Bois, *Black Reconstruction in America, 1860–1880* (1935; rpt. with an introduction by David Levering Lewis, New York: Simon and Schuster, 1995), on the "second slavery," see "Back toward Slavery," 670–710.

15. Lester Langley, *Struggle for the American Mediterranean: US-European Rivalry in the Gulf-Caribbean, 1776–1904* (Athens: University of Georgia Press, 1976); Jorge I. Domínguez, "The Pirates, the Powers and International Norms and Institutions in the American Mediterranean," in *From Pirates to Drug Lords: The Post-Cold War Caribbean Security Environment*, ed. Michael Charles Desch, Jorge I. Domínguez, and Andrés Serbín (Albany: SUNY Press, 1998); Tom Andersen, *This Fine Piece of Water: An Environmental History of Long Island Sound* (New Haven, CT: Yale University Press, 2002); Robert H. Gore, *The Gulf of Mexico: A Treasury of Resources in the American Mediterranean* (Sarasota, FL: Pineapple Press, 1992).

16. See back-cover image and text, Marilyn E. Weigold, *The American Mediterranean: An Environmental, Economic and Social History of Long Island Sound* (Port Washington, NY: Kennikat Press, 1974; rev. ed., *The Long Island Sound*, New York: New York University Press, 2004). See also *The EPA Blog*, "Long Island Sound: Comprehensive Conservation and Management Plan, 2015," October 22, 2015, https://blog.epa.gov/blog/2015/10/long-island-sound-comprehensive -conservation-and-management-plan-2015/; *Long Island Sound Study*, "Long Island Sound: Comprehensive Conservation and Management Plan, 2015, Public Summary," July 2015, https:// longislandsoundstudy.net/wp-content/uploads/2015/07/CCMP-Public-Summary-Brochure -with-correct-sequence-optimized.pdf. The opening line: "Called the 'American Mediterranean' by the statesman Daniel Webster, the Long Island Sound is a national treasure."

17. Kevin Starr, *Americans and the California Dream, 1850–1915* (New York: Oxford University Press, 1973; rpt. 1985), chap. 12, "An American Mediterranean" (365–414), appears in the 1973

Americans and the California Dream, devoted largely to Northern California, but there is no parallel chapter in the later companion volume on Southern California, *Inventing the Dream* (1985).

18. Gérard Genette and Marie Maclean, "Introduction to the Paratext," *New Literary History* 22, no. 2 (Spring 1991): 261, cited parenthetically hereafter.

19. See Gérard Genette, *Seuils* (Paris: Éditions du Seuil, 1987), translated by Jane E. Lewin as *Paratexts: Thresholds of Interpretation* (Cambridge: Cambridge University Press, 1997).

20. Brent Hayes Edwards, *The Practice of Diaspora: Literature, Translation, and the Rise of Black Internationalism* (Cambridge, MA: Harvard University Press, 2003), 39, 45, 44; Beth A, McCoy, "Race and the (Para)Textual Condition," *PMLA* 121, no. 1 (January 2006): 156–69.

21. Genette says of the paratext that it is "a zone of an influence on the public . . . that is at the service of a better reception for the text and a more pertinent reading of it" (Genette and Maclean, "Introduction to the Paratext," 261).

22. Bonsal refers to the 1897 English translation by Augustus Henry Keane and Ernest George Ravenstein of Reclus's *La nouvelle géographie universelle*; see Bonsal, *The American Mediterranean*.

Part Two

1. Varenius is best known for his *Geographia Generalis* (1650), a work of scientific and comparative geography that saw multiple editions and was translated into English, Italian, Dutch, Turkish, and French. Both Humboldt and Friedrich Ratzel acknowledged his importance as the first geographer to divide geography into "general or universal geography" and "special geography" or "chorography." Ratzel's two-volume *Anthropogeographie* (1882, 1891) was divided into three parts: absolute, relative, and comparative geography. See Margret Suchuchardt, ed., *Berhard Varenius (1622–1650)*, Brill Studies in Intellectual History 159 (Leiden: Brill, 2008).

2. Robert V. Rohli and Merrill L. Johnson, "The Legacy of Jedidiah Morse in Early American Geography Education: Forgotten and/or Forgettable Geographer?," *Geographical Review* 106, no. 3 (July 2016): 465–83; Donald C. Dahmann, *Geography in America's Schools, Libraries, and Homes*, Pathways in Geography Series 39 (Washington, DC: National Council for Geographic Education, 2010).

3. Kenneth Silverman *Lightning Man: The Accursed Life of Samuel F. B. Morse* (New York: Knopf, 2003), 112. See also Martin Brückner, *The Geographic Revolution in Early America: Maps, Literacy, and National Identity* (Chapel Hill: University of North Carolina Press, 2006) and *The Social Life of Maps in America, 1750–1860* (Chapel Hill: University of North Carolina Press, 2017); Laura Dassow Walls, *Passage to Cosmos* (Chicago: University of Chicago Press, 2009), 119; Kent Mathewson, "Alexander von Humboldt's Image and Influence in American Geography, 1804–2004," *Geographical Review* 96, no. 3 (2006): 416–38. The Humboldt-Morse network extends to Morse's son, Samuel Morse, inventor of the telegraph and the Morse code, who met Humboldt in Paris in 1831–32, where they bonded over both his painting and scientific thinking. See Rosaly Toma Kurth, *Susan Fenimore Cooper: New Perspectives on Her Works* (Bloomington, IN: iUniverse, 2016), 37–38.

4. Jedidiah Morse, *The American Universal Geography, or A View of the Present State of All the Kingdoms, States, and Colonies in the Known World*, 6th ed. (Boston: Thomas and Andrews, 1812). References cited parenthetically in the text.

5. Alexander von Humboldt, *Political Essay on the Kingdom of New Spain, vol. 1, A Critical Edition*, ed. with introduction by Vera M. Kutzinski and Ottmar Ette (Chicago: University of

Chicago Press, 2019), 515–18; hereafter cited parenthetically as *Political Essay*; see also in French, *RH*, 2:614–19; Sandra Rebok, *Humboldt and Jefferson: A Transatlantic Friendship of the Enlightenment* (Charlottesville: University of Virginia Press, 2014); Kent Mathewson, "Élisée Reclus' Latin Americanist Geography: Extensive Writings Bookended by Episodic Travels," *Terra Brasilis*, July 2016, https://doi.org/10.4000/terrabrasilis.1849; Mathewson quotes a different version of the comment: "The facility with which the banana can be cultivated has doubtless contributed to arrest the progress of improvement in tropical regions" (6–7).

6. Alexander von Humboldt, *Personal Narrative of Travels to the Equinoctial Regions of America, during the Years 1799–1804*, trans. and ed. Thomasina Ross (London: Henry G. Bohn, 1852–53), 1:206.

7. See John Soluri, *Banana Cultures: Agriculture, Consumption and Environmental Change in Honduras and the United States* (Austin: University of Texas Press, 2005), 33–34; on "biogeographic stratigraphy," see Margarita Serje, "The National Imagination in New Granada," in *Alexander von Humboldt: From the Americas to the Cosmos*, ed. Raymond Erickson, Mauricio A. Font, and Brian Schwartz (New York: Bildner Center for Western Hemisphere Studies, The Graduate Center, CUNY: 2005), 92.

8. Edward Everett, *An Oration Delivered at Plymouth* (Boston: Cumings, Hilliard, 1825), 41–42; William Robertson, *The History of America* (New York: printed for Samuel Campbell by Robert Wilson, 1798), 1:250; on Robertson as a practitioner of "conjectural history," see Jorge Cañizares-Esguerra, *How to Write the History of the New World: Histories, Epistemologies, and Identities in the Eighteenth-Century Atlantic World* (Stanford: Stanford University Press, 2001), 48, 54, 95–96, 171–80.

9. Élisée Reclus, *The Earth and Its Inhabitants, North America*, ed. A. H. Keane, vol. 2, *Mexico, Central America, West Indies* (New York: D. Appleton, 1897), 1, 338–53; see map, p. 342; *La nouvelle géographie universelle: La terre et les hommes*, vol. 17, *Indes occidentales: Mexique, Isthmes Américains, Antilles* (Paris: Librairie Hachette, 1891), 2.

10. Letter from A. H. Keane, January 28, 1902, cited in Hathi Trust bibliographic record 008723998; vols. 1–4 were edited and translated by E. G. Ravenstein, vol. 5 by E. G. Ravenstein and A. H. Keane, vols. 6–19 by A. H. Keane. See Robert E. Dickinson, *The Makers of Modern Geography* (New York: Praeger, 1969); Alfred R. Wallace, "The Origin of Human Races and the Antiquity of Man Deduced from the Theory of 'Natural Selection,'" *Journal of the Anthropological Society of London* 2 (1864), clviii–clxxxvii.

11. See Jean-Baptiste Arrault, "A propos du concept de *méditerranée*: Expérience géographique du monde et mondialisation" [About the Mediterranean analogy: Geographical experience of the world and globalization], *Cybergeo: European Journal of Geography* [En ligne], Epistémologie, Histoire de la Géographie, Didactique, article 332, mis en ligne le 03 janvier 2006, http://cybergeo.revues.org/13093; J. P. Clark and C. Martin, *Anarchy, Geography, Modernity: Selected Writings of Élisée Reclus* (Oakland, CA: PM Press, 2013); S. Springer, *The Anarchist Roots of Geography: Toward Spatial Emancipation* (Minneapolis: University of Minnesota Press, 2016).

12. See Élisée Reclus, "Fragment d'un voyage à la Nouvelle Orléans," *Le tour du monde* 1 (1855): 177–92; "Le Mississippi, Études et souvenirs," and "Le delta et la Nouvelle-Orléans, *La Revue des Deux Mondes* 22 (1859): 608–46; on "disguised slavery," his final book, published posthumously, Élisée Reclus, *L'homme et la terre* (Paris: Librairie Universelle, 1908), 6:107; on generalized miscegenation, see *L'homme et la terre*, 108–9. On Reclus, see Federico Ferretti, *Élisée Reclus, Pour une géographie nouvelle* (Paris: CTHS Edition, 2014); F. Ferretti, "Networking Print Cultures: Reclus' *Nouvelle Géographie Universelle* at the Hachette Publishing House," *Journal*

of Historical Geography 63 (January 2019), early view: https://www.sciencedirect.com/science/article/pii/S0305748817302670.

13. See John Sidney Thrasher's *The Island of Cuba* (New York: Derby and Jackson, 1856), an English translation (not of Humboldt's French original but of the 1827 Spanish translation, *Ensayo político sobre la Isla de Cuba*) that omitted an entire section on slavery and "systematically distorted the Spanish text to create the impression that Humboldt, like Thrasher himself, supported slavery." On this "systematically distorted Spanish text," a "fraudulent fabrication," and Humboldt's angry response to it, see Vera M. Kutzinski and Ottmar Ette, eds., *Political Essay on the Island of Cuba* (Chicago: University of Chicago Press, 2011), introduction, xxii–xxiii. For further materials on Thrasher, see Alexander von Humboldt in English, a series edited by Vera M. Kutzinski and Ottmar Ette, University of Chicago Press, https://www.turabian.com/books/humboldt/1_7_thrasher.html.

14. See Reclus on the fate of the original inhabitants of the American Mediterranean: "*On sait qu'en un petit nombre d'années les îles que baigne la méditerranée américaine furent complètement dépeuplées de leurs habi tants aborigènes les insulaires haïtiens et cubains, qui accue1]lirent avec amitié les premiers marins d'europe, il y a quatre cents ans, ont complète ment péri," Nouvelle géographie universelle,* 17:12.

15. Ellen Churchill Semple, *American History and Its Geographic Conditions* (Boston: Houghton, Mifflin, 1903), chap. 18, 397–419; hereafter abbreviated *AH*, cited parenthetically in the text.

16. "[The Indian Ocean] has linked together the history of Asia and Africa: and by the Red Sea and Persian Gulf, it has drawn Europe and the Mediterranean into its sphere of influence. At the western corner of the Indian Ocean, a Semitic people, the Arabs of Oman and Yemen, here first developed brilliant maritime activity, like their Phoenician kinsmen of the Lebanon seaboard. . . . From the dawn of history the northern Indian Ocean was a thoroughfare. Alexander the Great's rediscovery of the old sea route to the Orient sounds like a modern event in relation to the gray ages behind it. Along this thoroughfare Indian colonists, traders, and priests carried the elements of Indian civilization to the easternmost Sunda Isles; and oriental wares, science and religion moved westward to the margin of Europe and Africa. The Indian Ocean produced a civilization of its own, with which it colored a vast semi-circle of land reaching from Java to Abyssinia." Ellen Churchill Semple, *Influences of Geographic Environment, on the Basis of Ratzel's System of Anthropo-geography* (New York: Henry Holt, 1911), 309; hereafter abbreviated *IG*, cited parenthetically in the text.

17. Ellen Churchill Semple, "The Anglo-Saxons of the Kentucky Mountains: A Study in Anthropogeography," *Geographical Journal* 17 (1901): 588–623; Ellen Churchill Semple, *The Geography of the Mediterranean Region* (New York: Henry Holt, 1931). On the label "modern apostle of determinism," see Innes M. Keighren, *Bringing Geography to Book: Ellen Semple and the Reception of Geographical Knowledge* (London: I. B. Taurus, 2010), 530.

18. No full-length biography of Semple has yet been written; see Charles C. Colby, "Ellen Churchill Semple," *Annals of the Association of American Geographers* 23, no. 4 (December 1933): 229–40; Keighren's chapter, titled "Anthropogeography: A Biography," has substantial biographical detail on Semple (see *Bringing Geography to Book*, 9–45).

19. Albert Bushnell Hart, Review, *American Historical Review* 9, no. 3 (April 1904): 571–72.

20. See Innes M. Keighren, "Bringing Geography to the Book: Charting the Reception of *Influences of Geographic Environment," Transactions of the Institute of British Geographers* (2006): 525–40.

21. Frederick Jackson Turner, "Geographical Interpretations of American History," *Journal of Geography* 4 (1905): 37.

22. On Turner's frontier thesis and geographers, see Robert H. Block, "Frederick Jackson Turner and American Geography," *Annals of the Association of American Geographers* 70, no. 1 (March 1980): 31–42; William A. Koelsch, "Miss Semple Meets the Historians: The Failed AHA 1907 Conference on Geography and History and What Happened Afterwards," *Journal of Historical Geography* 45 (2014): 50–58; see also Alan R. H. Baker, *Geography and History: Bridging the Divide* (Cambridge: Cambridge University Press, 2003).

23. See Frederick Jackson Turner, "Report of the Conference on the Relation of Geography and History," in *Annual Report of the American Historical Association for 1907* (1908), 46–47; Ellen Churchill Semple, "Geographical Location as a Factor in History," *Bulletin of the American Geographical Society* 40 (1908): 65–81; see the opening line, "The location of a country or people is always the supreme geographical fact in its history" (65).

24. Keighren, "Bringing Geography to the Book," 535–36.

25. On the "luckless," see H. Meller, *Patrick Geddes: Social Evolutionist and City Planner* (1993), qtd.in Keighren, "Bringing Geography to the Book," 534; on the "alleged" and "third and final book," see Koelsch, "Miss Semple Meets the Historians," 57, 56.

26. See Wilford A. *Bladen* and Pradyumna P. *Karan, The Evolution of Geographic Thought in America: A Kentucky Root* (Dubuque, IA: Kendall/Hunt Publishing, 1983); Tim Cresswell, *Geographic Thought: A Critical Introduction* (Malden, MA: Wiley-Blackwell, 2013), 50; see also Miles Ogborn and Charles W. J. Withers, eds., *Geographies of the Book* (New York: Routledge, 2016).

27. It took until the early twenty-first century for the historian Bruce Cumings's book to comprehensively document and establish the "Pacifist" perspective in US studies; see Bruce Cumings, *Dominion from Sea to Sea: Pacific Ascendancy and American Power* (New Haven, CT: Yale University Press, 2009).

Part Three

1. Charles Dudley Warner, *Our Italy* (Hartford, CT: American Publishing, 1891), 18.

2. See Carey McWilliams, *North from Mexico: The Spanish-Speaking People of the United States* (1948; rpt. New York: Greenwood Press, 1968), 35–47.

3. Carey McWilliams, *Southern California: An Island on the Land* (Salt Lake City, UT: Peregrine Smith, 1983), 7; hereafter abbreviated *SC*, cited parenthetically in the text.

4. Jackson first used the line in an 1883 *Century Magazine* piece, republished with other California essays in Helen Hunt Jackson, *Glimpses of California and the Missions*, illustrated by Henry Sandham (Boston: Little, Brown, 1907), 214. See the Glen McLaughlin Collection, Stanford University, Branner Earth Sciences Library. Perhaps it's just what the Spanish wanted, suggested Rebecca Solnit, who was a Stanford Library fellow, with a project on the McLaughlin collection when it was first donated to the university in 2012. "I've been told that Spain knew it wasn't an island, but it was politically expedient for others to think it was," qtd. in Cynthia Haven, "Largest Private Map Collection of 'California as Island' Comes to Stanford," *Stanford Report*, August 30, 2012, https://news.stanford.edu/news/2012/august/california-island-maps-083012.html. See also Dora Beale Polk, *The Island of California: A History of the Myth* (Lincoln: University of Nebraska Press, 1991); Michael Blanding, *The Map Thief: The Gripping Story of an Esteemed Map-Dealer Who Made Millions Stealing Priceless Maps* (New York: Gotham Books, 2014); Andrew Rolle and Arthur C. Verge, *California: A History*, 8th ed. (New York: Wiley Blackwell, 2015), chap. 3, 21–32.

5. See Kevin Starr, *The Dream Endures: California Enters the 1940s* (New York: Oxford University Press, 1997), 98; P. C. Remondino, *The Mediterranean Shores of America: Southern California; Its Climatic, Physical, and Meteorological Conditions* (Philadelphia: F. A. Davis, 1892); hereafter abbreviated *MS*, cited parenthetically in the text.

6. Charles Nordhoff, *California: For Health, Pleasure, and Residence; A Book for Travellers and Settlers* (New York: Harper and Brothers, 1873), 11.

7. Thomas Huxley, "On the Geographical Distribution of the Chief Modifications of Mankind," *Journal of the Ethnological Society of London* 2, no. 4 (January 1, 1870): 404–12. On whiteness and Italians as an immigrant group in the US context, see James R. Barrett and David R. Roediger, "Inbetween Peoples: Race, Nationality, and the 'New Immigrant' Working Class," *Journal of American Ethnic History* 16, no. 3 (1997): 3–44; Jennifer Guglielmo and Salvatore Salerno, eds., *Are Italians White? How Race Is Made in America* (New York: Routledge, 2003); Thomas A. Guglielmo, *White on Arrival: Italians, Race, Color, and Power in Chicago, 1890–1945* (New York: Oxford University Press, 2003); David R. Roediger, *Working toward Whiteness: How America's Immigrants Became White* (New York: Basic Books, 2005); Stefano Luconi, "Whiteness and Ethnicity in Italian American Historiography," in *The Status of Interpretation in Italian American Studies*, ed. Jerome Krase (Stony Brook, NY: Forum Italicum Publishing, 2011), 146–63; Peter G. Vellon, *A Great Conspiracy against Our Race: Italian Immigrant Newspapers and the Construction of Whiteness in Early 20th Century* (New York: New York University Press, 2015).

8. McWilliams quotes this unidentified writer (*Southern California*, 103); see also William Deverell and Douglas Flamming, "Race, Rhetoric, and Regional Identity: Boosting Los Angeles, 1880–1930," in *Power and Place in the North American West, ed.* Richard White and John M. Findlay (Seattle: University of Washington Press, 1999), 119.

9. Frederick Albion Ober, *Our West Indian Neighbors: The Islands of the Caribbean Sea, "America's Mediterranean"; Their Picturesque Features, Fascinating History, and Attractions for the Traveler, Nature-Lover, Settler and Pleasure-Seeker* (New York, James Pott, 1904; 1916); hereafter abbreviated *OWI*, cited parenthetically in the text; on Ober as a travel writer and novelist, see Peter Hulme, *Cuba's Wild East: A Literary Geography of Oriente* (Liverpool: Liverpool University Press, 2011), 147–48, and "In the Wake of Columbus: Frederick Ober's Ambulant Gloss," *Literature and History* 6, no. 2 (1997): 18–36.

10. Lawrence Venuti, *The Translator's Invisibility: A History of Translation* (New York: Routledge, 2008).

11. *Report on the Conditions and Needs of the Mission Indians, Made by Special Agents Helen Jackson and Abbot Kinney to the Commissioner of Indians Affairs* (Washington, DC: GPO, 1883); Helen Hunt Jackson, *Ramona: A Story*, introduction by Michael Dorris (New York: Signet, 1988): "pure Indian" (30), "a Mexican gentleman" (9); hereafter abbreviated *R*, cited parenthetically in the text. On the conflict between nostalgia and social protest in *Ramona*, see also Starr, *Americans and the California Dream, 1850–1915* (New York: Oxford University Press, 1973; rpt. 1985), 396–97. For a summary of the scholarship on Jackson's romanticization of *Californio* life, see Karen Ramirez, *Reading Helen Hunt Jackson's Ramona* (Boise, ID: Boise State University, 2006), 19–23.

12. *The Ramona Pageant* includes a 1959 performance with eighteen-year-old Raquel Welch, née Tejada, playing the title role; the four US films include the surviving Griffith and King adaptations as well as the 1916 version directed by Donald Crisp and Edwin Carewe's Dolores del Rio vehicle of 1928; one Spanish-language film is the 1946 Mexican production by Victor Urruchua, starring Esther Fernandez. This film and other Spanish-language stage and screen adaptations

address broad issues of textual and performative circulation and possible links to translingual communities within and beyond the US. See also Vincent Brook, *Land of Smoke and Mirrors: A Cultural History of Los Angeles* (New Brunswick, NJ: Rutgers University Press, 2013).

13. Jackson to Amelia Stone Quinton, president of the Women's National Indian Association (April 2, 1884) in *The Indian Reform Letters of Helen Hunt Jackson, 1879–1885*, ed. Valerie Sherer Mathes (Norman: University of Oklahoma Press, 1998), 319; James Baldwin, "Everybody's Protest Novel," in *Notes of a Native Son* (Boston: Beacon Press, 1957; rpt. 1984), 14–15; Helen Hunt Jackson, *Ramona: A Story*, introduction by Denise Chavez (New York: Modern Library, 2005).

14. On "Indian matters," see Phil Brigandi and Valerie Sherer Mathes, eds., *A Call for Reform: The Southern California Indian Writings of Helen Hunt Jackson* (Norman: University of Oklahoma Press, 2015); Evelyn Banning, "Helen Hunt Jackson in San Diego," *San Diego Historical Society Quarterly* 24, no. 4 (Fall 1978): 457–67; Kate Phillips, *Helen Hunt Jackson, A Literary Life* (Berkeley: University of California Press, 2003), 239, 247; for a comparison of *Ramona* and the Jackson-Kinney *Report*, see John R. Byers, "The Indian Matter of Helen Hunt Jackson's *Ramona*: From Fact to Fiction," *American Indian Quarterly* 2 (Winter 1975–76): 331–46.

15. Jackson so deeply associated Kinney with her Indian crusade that later she wrote a children's book, *The Hunter Cats of Connorloa*, based on Kinney at his home at Kinneloa (where he had seventeen cats trained to trap gophers); see Jackson to Kinney, September 18, 1884, in Mathes, *The Indian Reform Letters*, 328.

16. Among the works Jackson studied in California libraries and later cited were several written in Spanish by early Franciscan missionaries, including *La vida de Junipero Serra* (Mexico, 1787). On Jackson's Spanish and her use of interpreters, see Phillips, *Helen Hunt Jackson*, 244, 247.

17. On "fanciest promotion," see McWilliams, *Southern California*, 130. On Venice, see Historic Places LA/Los Angeles Historic Resources Inventory, Venice Arcades, Historic Resource Report, Survey LA, Los Angeles Historic Resources Survey, 2017, http://www.historicplacesla .org/reports/0f858295–172c-46e6-a541-c1146dc4eeff; on Edward Biberman's 1941 mural, *Abbot Kinney and the Story of Venice*, see "Biberman Mural Comes to LACMA," LACMA, May 19, 2014, https://www.lacma.org/art/exhibition/edward-biberman-abbot-kinney-and-story-venice; "LACMA Exhibits Recently Conserved Mural, 'Abbot Kinney and the Story of Venice,'" *Art-Daily*, August 1, 2014, https://artdaily.cc/news/71634/LACMA-exhibits-recently-conserved -mural—Abbot-Kinney-and-the-Story-of-Venice-#.XupPyRd7lo4. On Abbott Kinney Boulevard, see also "About the Boulevard," Abbott Kinney Boulevard 90291, Venice, California, 2016–20, https://www.abbotkinneyblvd.com/about-abbot-kinney.

18. See "Italian Architectural Evocations in Los Angeles," *Italian Los Angeles*, October 26, 2016, http://www.italianlosangeles.org/italian-architectural-evocations/: "*Ramona* (1884) was born of Helen Hunt Jackson's collaboration with Abbot Kinney to ascertain the sorry state of the Franciscan Missions and their Native American converts. A kindred New England transplant, Charles Lummis, Los Angeles' librarian, launched the *Landmark Club* to save, most conspicuously, the Missions (*circa* 1895)."

19. Robert Stam, "Beyond Fidelity: The Dialogics of Adaptation," in *Film Adaptation*, ed. James Naremore (New Brunswick, NJ: Rutgers University Press, 2000), 54, 64, 68. See also Robert Stam, "Introduction: The Theory and Practice of Adaptation," in *Literature and Film*, ed. Robert Stam and Alessandra Raengo (Malden, MA: Blackwell Publishing, 2005), 1–52.

20. See Jackson to Coronels, November 8, 1883, in Mathes, *The Indian Reform Letters*, 297–99.

21. See Helen Hunt Jackson, *Ramona: A Story*, with appendix, "Ramona's Home: A Visit to the Camulos Ranch and to the Scenes Described by 'H.H.,'" by Edward Roberts (Boston: Roberts Brothers, 1887); later editions of *Century of Dishonor* also expanded paratextually to include the *Report*: see Helen Hunt Jackson (H.H.), *A Century of Dishonor: A Sketch of the United States Government's Dealings with Some of the Indian Tribes*, new ed., enlarged., by the addition of the report of the needs of the mission Indians of California (Boston: Roberts Bros., 1885). See Dydia DeLyser, *Ramona Memories: Tourism and the Shaping of Southern California* (Minneapolis: University of Minnesota Press, 2005), 70; Phoebe S. Kropp, *California Vieja: Culture and Memory in a Modern American Place* (Berkeley: University of California Press, 2006), 39; A. C. Vroman and T. F. Barnes, *The Genesis of the Story of Ramona: Why the Book Was Written, Explanatory Text of Points of Interest Mentioned in the Story* (Los Angeles: Kingsley-Barnes and Neuner, 1899).

22. Qtd. in Mathes, *The Indian Reform Letters*, 330.

23. For the two letters, dated January 1, and February 5, 1884, see Mathes, *The Indian Reform Letters*, 313–14.

24. See William Deverell, *Whitewashed Adobe: The Rise of Los Angeles and the Remaking of Its Mexican Past* (Berkeley: University of California Press, 2004), 8.

25. For example, a June 1888 article, "The Doom of the California Aborigines" (*Overland Monthly and Out West Magazine*), 613, on the treatment of Indians by Spaniards, Mexicans, and Americans in California as well as "the typical baptismal and family names of the Spanish Californians," excoriates "Mrs. Jackson [who] knew so little that she blundered in every direction"; see Phillips, *Helen Hunt Jackson*, on the naming of Alessandro, 322n91.

26. Helen Hunt Jackson, "Echoes in the City of Angels," *Century Magazine* 27 (December 1883): 205, qtd. in DeLyser, *Ramona Memories*, 41; Jackson to Kinney, qtd. in Wallace E. Smith, *This Land Was Ours: The Del Valles and Camulos* (Ventura, CA: Ventura County Historical Society, 1977), 179; see also Kropp, *California Vieja*, 33.

27. See Kropp, *California Vieja* on ghostwriters, 45; on Vallejo and Bancroft, see Genaro M. Padilla, *My History Not Yours: The Formation of Mexican American Autobiography* (Madison: University of Wisconsin Press,1993), 54–55, 85, 105–6, 253n4, and on Sra. De la Guerra, 148–52.

28. On translation by a Coronel niece, see Jackson to Henry Dawes, August 27, 1884, in Mathes, *The Indian Reform Letters*, 324; on Mariana as translator, see Jackson, "Echoes in the City of the Angels," 194–209.

29. On Griffith, see Chon Noriega, "Social Protest, Tourism, and D. W. Griffith's Ramona," in *The Birth of Whiteness: Race and the Emergence of U.S. Cinema, ed.* Daniel Bernardi (New Brunswick, NJ: Rutgers University Press, 1996), 203–26; DeLyser, *Ramona Memories*, 165–66; Kemp R. Niver and Bebe Bergsten, eds., *D. W. Griffith, His Biograph Films in Perspective* (Los Angeles: John D. Roche, 1974); on nonpersons, see Deverell, *Whitewashed Adobe*, 41.

30. José Martí, Prólogo to *Ramona: Novela americana*, by Helen Hunt Jackson, trans. José Martí, in *Obras completas*, by José Martí (Havana: Editorial Nacional de Cuba, 1965), 199; 199–205; hereafter cited parenthetically in the text.

31. On "the New England mind Mediterraneanizing," see Kevin Starr, *Inventing the Dream: California through the Progressive Era* (New York: Oxford University Press, 1985), 61, and on "dishonest architecture," see *Americans and the California Dream*, 47, 396; on memory places as "sites of cultural production and venues for struggles over public space, racial politics, and citizenship in America," see Kropp, *California Vieja*, 15.

32. Deverell, *Whitewashed Adobe*, 15.

33. Deverell, *Whitewashed Adobe*, 8, 15, 41–42.

34. George R. Stewart, *Names on the Land: A Historical Account of Place-Naming in the United States* (1945); rev. ed. with introduction by Matt Weiland (New York: New York Review of Books, 2008); Deverell, *Whitewashed Adobe*, vii.

35. Erwin C. Gudde, *1000 California Place Names: Their Origin and Meaning*, based on Gudde, *California Place Names: A Geographic Dictionary* (Berkeley: University of California Press, 1947); William Bright, *1500 California Place Names: Their Origin and Meaning* (Berkeley: University of California Press, 1998), a revised version of Gudde, *1000 California Place Names*, 3rd ed., hereafter cited parenthetically. The Gudde guides most likely originated with the WPA California Writers' program; see Paul C. Johnson, *California Folklore Quarterly* 1, no. 2 (April 1942): "The California Writers' program of the WPA has been compiling a book on California Place Names, to be published by the University of California Press" (201). Johnson was assistant state supervisor of the Northern California Writers' Program.

36. Web page for *1500 California Place Names: Their Origin and Meaning, a Revised Version of 1000 California Places Names* by Erwin C. Gudde, Third edition, University of California Press website, Regents of the University of California, 2021, https://www.ucpress.edu /book/9780520212718/1500-california-place-names.

37. See Robert Rennick, Review of *California Place Names, The Origin and Etymology of Current Geographical Names/1500 California Place Names: Their Origin and Meaning, Journal of American Folklore* 114 (Summer 2001): 385–87.

38. Erwin G. Gudde, *California Place Names: The Origin and Etymology of Current Geographical Names*, 4th ed., revised by William Bright (Berkeley: University of California Press, 2004), 122.

39. Charles F. Lummis, "The Making of Los Angeles," *Out West* 30, no. 4 (April 1909): "a matter of race," 241, "glamour of California," "glamour made by histories," 240.

40. See Nellie Sanchez, *Spanish and Indian Place Names of California* (San Francisco: A. M. Robertson, 1914), 244–45, 309. See Charles F. Lummis, "Los Angeles: Metropolis of the Southwest," *Land of Sunshine* 3, no. 1 (June 1895): 18; "Learning Spanish," *Land of Sunshine* 3 (1895): 281; "In the Lion's Den," *Land of Sunshine* 4 (1896): 288; "Borrowed from the Enemy," *Land of Sunshine* 4 (1896): 26–30; Phil Townsend Hanna, compiler, *The Dictionary of California Land Names*, rev. and enlarged (Los Angeles: Automobile Club of Southern California, 1946, rpt. 1951); on Lummis, see also Mark Thompson, *American Character: The Curious Life of Charles Fletcher Lummis and the Rediscovery of the Southwest* (New York: Arcade, 2001).

41. Bright, *1500 California Place Names*, 122; George Wharton James, *Through Ramona's Country* (Boston: Little, Brown, 1909), 75; *Moreno's Dictionary of Spanish-Named California Cities and Towns* (Los Angeles: Holmes Book Company, 1916), 22; *A Pronouncing Dictionary of California Names in English and Spanish* (San Francisco: Press of H.J. Carle and Son, 1925), 30.

42. See DeLyser, *Ramona Memories*, on how Ramona accepts the name only in a "hispanicized version," Majella, "to make it feminine" (200–201n77); William Bright, *Native American Placenames of the Southwest: A Handbook for Travelers* (Norman: University of Oklahoma Press, 2004, rpt. 2013).

43. Sanchez is decried by the historian Leonard Pitt, for defending pastoral labor in her *Spanish Arcadia* (Los Angeles: Powell Publishing, 1929), a symptom of what he calls the "schizoid heritage"; on how Sanchez contemplates "the benefits of paternalism, the joys of the caballeros, the piety of the Indians," see Leonard Pitt, *The Decline of the Californios: A Social History of the Spanish-Speaking Californians, 1846–1890* (Berkeley: University of California Press, 1966), 289. On imperial nostalgia, see Renato Rosaldo, *Culture and Truth: The Remaking of Social Analysis* (Boston: Beacon Press, 1989, rpt. 1993).

44. Gertrude Mott, *A Handbook for Californiacs: A Key to the Meaning and Pronunciation of Spanish and Indian Place Names* (San Francisco: Harr Wagner Publishing, 1926).

45. Hanna, *The Dictionary of California Land Names*, xiii.

46. See Barbara Marinacci and Rudy Marinacci, *California's Spanish Place Names: What They Mean and the History They Reveal* (Santa Monica, CA: Angel City Press, 2005), 128–29, 131.

47. Laura Lomas notes that Mexicans and Argentines were the principal intended audience for the translation, because both countries supplied Martí with the support needed for his publishing ventures; see Laura Lomas, *Translating Empire: José Martí, Migrant Latino Subjects, and American Modernities* (Durham, NC: Duke University Press, 2008), 264.

48. On "traducir es *transpensar*," see José Martí, Prólogo, *Mis hijos* de Victor Hugo, in *Obras completas*, by José Martí (Havana: Editorial Nacional de Cuba, 1965), 24:16; Prólogo, *Ramona: Novela americana*, by Helen Hunt Jackson, trans. José Martí, in *Obras completas*, by José Martí (Havana: Editorial Nacional de Cuba, 1965), 24:199–205; hereafter cited parenthetically in the text; translations here are mine unless otherwise noted. See also English translation by Esther Allen, "Introduction to the 1888 Spanish edition of Helen Hunt Jackson's *Ramona*, translated and published by José Martí," in *Ramona: A Story*, by Helen Hunt Jackson (New York: Modern Library, 2005), appendix, 355–60.

49. Fernández Retamar, "Sobre *Ramona* de Helen Hunt Jackson y José Martí," in *Mélanges à la Mémoire d'André Joucla-Ruau* (Provence: Editions de l'Université de Provence, 1978), 2:699–705, 700; hereafter cited parenthetically in the text. For the translations of this essay, I am indebted to my then graduate research assistant David Luis-Brown, to whom I am immeasurably grateful.

50. Fernando Ortiz, *Contrapunteo Cubano: Del tabaco y el azúcar*, ed. Jesús Montero (Havana: Heraldo Christiano, 1940), translated by Harriet de Onís as *Cuban Counterpoint: Tobacco and Sugar* (New York: Knopf, 1947). The second chapter is entitled "The Ethnography and Transculturation of Havana Tobacco and the Beginnings of Sugar in America."

51. Fernando Ortiz y Fernández, "Cuba, Martí and the Race Problem," *Phylon* 3, no. 3 (1942): 253–76.

52. See Rafael Pérez-Torres, *Mestizaje: Critical Uses of Race in Chicano Culture* (Minneapolis: University of Minnesota Press, 2006), xiii; Maria Josefina Saldana-Portillo, *The Revolutionary Imagination in the Americas and the Age of Development* (Durham, NC: Duke University Press, 2003), 12, 220–26.

53. Roberto Fernández Retamar, "Caliban," in *Todo Caliban* (San Juan, PR: Ediciones Callejón, 2003), 43; the essay was originally published in Spanish in *Casa de las Américas* 68 (September–October 1971); *Caliban and Other Essays*, trans. Edward Baker (Minneapolis: University of Minnesota Press, 1989), 14 (for "What is our history, what is our culture . . . ?"); hereafter cited parenthetically in the text; on the "school of Caliban," see José David Saldívar, *The Dialectics of Our America: Genealogy, Cultural Critique, and Literary History* (Durham, NC: Duke University Press, 1991), 123–48; on "the Age of Caliban," see Harold Bloom, ed., *Caliban*, Bloom's Major Literary Characters (New York: Chelsea House Publishers, 1992), 1.

54. José Martí, *José Martí: Selected Writings*, trans. Esther Allen (New York: Penguin, 2002), 295; hereafter cited parenthetically in the text.

55. See *Essai politique sur l'île de Cuba par Alexandre de Humboldt: Avec une carte et un supplément que renferme des considérations sur la population, la richesse territoriale et le commerce de l'archipel des Antilles et de Colombia* (Paris, 1826), a text that was banned in Cuba because of its antislavery sentiments.

Part Four

1. See David A. Lupher, *Romans in a New World: Classical Models in Sixteenth-Century Spanish America* (Ann Arbor: University of Michigan Press, 2006).

2. On this extranational, regional conception of the Caribbean, see Peter Hulme, "Expanding the Caribbean," in *Perspectives on the "Other America": Comparative Approaches to Caribbean and Latin American Culture*, ed. Michael Niblett and Kerstin Oloff (Amsterdam: Rodopi, 2009), 29, and Silvio Torres-Saillant, *An Intellectual History of the Caribbean* (New York: Palgrave Macmillan, 2006), 21; on literary geography, see Maria Cristina Fumagalli et al., *Surveying the American Tropics: Towards A Literary Geography from New York to Rio* (Liverpool: Liverpool University Press, 2013). The "American Tropics," according to a description of the book on the Liverpool University Press website, "refers to a kind of extended Caribbean, an area which includes the Southern USA, the Atlantic littoral of Central America, the Caribbean islands, and northern South America" (accessed July 2, 2021, https://www.liverpooluniversitypress.co.uk/series/series-12354/).

3. Fernand Braudel, "*Histoire et sciences sociales: La longue durée*," in *Annales: Histoire, Sciences Sociales* 13, no. 4 (October–December 1958): 725–53; Fernand Braudel, *The Mediterranean and the Mediterranean World in the Age of Philip II*, trans. Siân Reynolds, 2 vols. (London: Collins, 1972–73).

4. On reading the Caribbean as "a geographical area fraught with cultural divides that are primarily 'linguistic' in character," see Grant Farred, "The Ellisonian Injunction: Discourse on a Lower Frequency" (review), *Small Axe* 8, no. 2 (September 2004): 205–13.

5. On the question of James's oceanic consciousness, see Laurent Dubois: "Though he didn't use the term to describe what he did, James helped lay the foundation in his work for the field now known as 'Atlantic history.' . . . His book transformed the historiography produced about the Caribbean and Atlantic slavery more broadly during the past decades." Laurent Dubois, "Reading 'The Black Jacobins,' Seven Decades Later," February 25, 2009, https://nacla.org/article/reading-%E2%80%98-black-jacobins%E2%80%99-seven-decades-later.

6. W. Adolphe Roberts, *These Many Years: An Autobiography*, ed. with introduction by Peter Hulme (Kingston, Jamaica: University of West Indies Press and National Library of Jamaica, 2015), introduction, xv; hereafter abbreviated *TMY*, cited parenthetically in the text.

7. On the topographical analogy, see Laurence A. Breiner, "Caribbean Voices on the Air: Radio, Poetry, and Nationalism in the Anglophone Caribbean," in *Communities of the Air: Radio Century, Radio Culture*, ed. Susan Merrill Squier (Durham, NC: Duke University Press, 2003), 94.

8. C. L. R. James, *The Black Jacobins: Toussaint L'Ouverture and the San Domingo Revolution* (New York: Vintage, 1938; 2nd ed., rev. 1963); hereafter abbreviated *BJ*, cited parenthetically in the text.

9. C. L. R. James, "Lectures on *The Black Jacobins*," Summer Research Symposium, Institute of the Black World, Atlanta, *Small Axe* 8 (September 2000): 65–112; lecture 2, "How I Would Rewrite *The Black Jacobins*," 73.

10. See Eric Williams, *From Columbus to Castro: The History of the Caribbean, 1492–1969* (Washington, DC: Brassey's, 1997, rpt. 2002).

11. Rolf Petri, "The Mediterranean Metaphor in Early Geopolitical Writings," *History: The Journal of the Historical Association* 101, no. 348, 671–91, *Wiley Online Library*, first published December 31, 2016, https://onlinelibrary.wiley.com/doi/full/10.1111/1468-229X.12326.

12. James Street, *Tap Roots* (New York: Sun Dial Press, 1942), foreword, n.p.; hereafter abbreviated *TR*, cited parenthetically in the text; James Street, *Mingo Dabney* (New York: Dial Press, 1950); hereafter abbreviated *MD*, cited parenthetically in the text.

13. W. Adolphe Roberts, *The Single Star: A Novel of Cuba in the 90s* (Indianapolis, IN: Bobbs-Merrill, 1949); hereafter abbreviated *SS*, cited parenthetically in the text.

14. Eric Foner, *Reconstruction: America's Unfinished Revolution, 1863–1877* (New York: Harper Collins, 1988; updated edition, 2014).

15. Rebecca Scott, *Degrees of Freedom: Louisiana and Cuba after Slavery* (Cambridge, MA: Harvard University Press, 2005), 4.

16. Talal Asad, "The Concept of Cultural Translation in British Social Anthropology," in *Writing Culture: The Poetics and Politics of Ethnography,* ed. James Clifford and George E. Marcus (Berkeley: University of California Press, 1986), 156.

17. On "Creole romance," see Faith Smith, "Between Stephen Lloyd and Esteban Yo-eed: Locating Jamaica through Cuba," *Journal of French and Francophone Philosophy / Revue de la philosophie française et de la langue française* 20, no. 1 (2012): 25.

18. James Street and James Childers, *Tomorrow We Reap* (New York: Dial Press, 1949), 105; hereafter cited parenthetically as *TWR* in the text.

19. On "linguistic flexibility," see Smith, "Between Stephen Lloyd and Esteban Yo-eed," 34.

20. See Fernando Coronil, introduction to *Cuban Counterpoint: Tobacco and Sugar,* trans. Harriet de Onís (Durham, NC: Duke University Press, 1995), xxxv. De Onís translated the work in 1947.

21. Virginia Lee Warren, "Cuba Libre," *New York Times,* November 27, 1949.

22. James Street, *Look Away! A Dixie Notebook* (New York: Viking Press, 1936); James Street, Jr., ed., *James Street's South* (Garden City, NY: Doubleday, 1955), 41–45, 279–82. With the success of *Look Away!* Street retired to Old Lyme, Connecticut, and after the war moved to Chapel Hill, North Carolina, where he died in 1954. He was working at the time on an article for the Democratic Central Committee of New York on the Bill of Rights.

23. Samuel Farber, "Cuba before the Revolution," *Jacobin Magazine,* September 6, 2015, https://www.jacobinmag.com/2015/09/cuban-revolution-fidel-castro-casinos-batista; see also Rosalie Schwartz, *Pleasure Island: Tourism and Temptation in Cuba* (Lincoln: University of Nebraska Press, 1997); Kristine Skwiot, *The Purposes of Paradise: U.S. Tourism and Empire in Cuba and Hawai'i* (Philadelphia: University of Pennsylvania Press, 2010); Robin D. Moore, *Music and Revolution: Cultural Change in Socialist Cuba* (Berkeley: University of California Press, 2006), chap. 1 "Revelry and Revolution: The Paradox of the 1950s," 26–55.

24. W. E. B. Du Bois, *Black Reconstruction in America, 1860–1880,* introduction by David Levering Lewis (New York: Simon and Schuster, 1962), 708; hereafter abbreviated *BR*, cited parenthetically in the text.

25. Inmaculada López Calahorro, *Alejo Carpentier, poética del Mediterráneo Caribe* (Madrid: Dykinson, 2010).

26. See Alejo Carpentier, "On the Marvelous Real in America," in *Magical Realism: Theory, History, Community,* ed. Lois Zamora and Wendy Faris (Durham, NC: Duke University Press, 1995), 83.

27. Alejo Carpentier, *"De lo real maravilloso americano,"* in *Tientos y diferencias* (Montevideo: Arca, 1967; rpt. Buenos Aires: Calicanto Editorial, 1976), 83–99. See the English translation of that essay, "On the Marvelous Real in America," in Zamora and Faris, *Magical Realism,* hereafter cited parenthetically in the text.

28. Walter Benjamin, "The Translator's Task," trans. Steven Rendall, in *The Translation Studies Reader,* 3rd ed., ed. Lawrence Venuti (London: Routledge, 2003), 75–83.

29. Robin Blackburn, "The Black Jacobins and New World Slavery," in *C. L. R. James: His Intellectual Legacies,* ed. Selwyn R. Cudjoe and William E. Cain (Amherst: University of

Massachusetts Press, 1995), 83; C. L. R. James, *The Future in the Present: Selected Writings* (London: Allison and Busby, 1977).

30. David Scott, *Conscripts of Modernity: The Tragedy of Colonial Enlightenment* (Durham, NC: Duke University Press, 2004). See Shalini Puri, who reviews Scott's *Conscripts of Modernity* as a "suggestive 'translation'" of *The Black Jacobins*, Review of *Conscripts of Modernity* in *New West Indian Guide / Nieuwe West-Indische Gids* 81, nos. 3 and 4 (2007): 11–14; on James's book and translation, see also Kara M. Rabitt, "C. L. R. James's Figuring of Toussaint Louverture: A Reassessment of C. L. R. James's Interpretation," in *C. L. R. James: His Intellectual Legacies, ed.* Selwyn R. Cudjoe and William E. Cain (Amherst: University of Massachusetts Press, 1995), 118–35.

31. David P. Geggus, preface to *The Impact of the Haitian Revolution in the Atlantic World, ed. David P. Geggus* (Columbia: University of South Carolina, 2001), xi.

32. This is Benedict Anderson's term for the future shock of José Rizal's proleptic novel *El filibusterismo* (1891); see *Benedict Anderson, Under Three Flags: Anarchism and the Anti-colonial Imagination* (London: Verso, 2005), 121–2.

33. See Gary Wilder, "Untimely Vision: Aimé Césaire, Decolonization, Utopia," *Public Culture* 21, no. 1 (2009): 101–40; see 106 for the "as if" comment; Gary Wilder, *Freedom Time: Negritude, Decolonization and the Future of the World* (Durham, NC: Duke University Press, 2015); for another view of James's proleptic thinking, see Kenneth Surin, "'The Future Anterior': C. L. R. James and Going *Beyond a Boundary*," in *Rethinking C. L. R. James,* ed. Grant Farred (Cambridge, MA: Blackwell, 1996), 187–204.

34. On this passage, see Brett St. Louis, *Rethinking Race, Politics, and Poetics: C. L. R. James' Critique of Modernity* (New York: Routledge, 2007), 64.

35. Lawrence Venuti, *The Translator's Invisibility: A History of Translation* (London: Routledge, 1995).

36. Guillaume Thomas Raynal, *Histoire philosophique et politique du commerce et des établissements des Européens dans les Deux Indes* (Genève: 1774), Livre XI, 227; translation mine.

37. See Laurent Du Bois, *Avengers of the New World: The Story of the Haitian Revolution* (Cambridge, MA: Harvard University Press, 2004); Srinivas Aravamudan, *Tropicopolitans: Colonialism and Agency, 1688–1804* (Durham, NC: Duke University Press, 1999), 23, 299; Louis Sala-Molins, *Les misères des lumières: Sous la raison, l'outrage* (Paris: Robert Laffont, 1992), 158–60.

38. See Margaret Malamud, *African Americans and the Classics: Antiquity, Abolition and Activism* (New York: I. B. Tauris, 2016), 58–59; Lydia Langerwerf, "Universal Slave Revolts: C. L. R. James' Use of Classical Literature in *The Black Jacobins*," in *Ancient Slavery and Abolition: From Hobbes to Hollywood*, ed. Richard Alston, Edith Hall and Justine McConnell, Classical Presences (New York: Oxford University Press 2011), 353–84; Aldo Schiavone, *Spartacus*, trans. Jeremy Carden (Cambridge, MA: Harvard University Press, 2013); Martin M. Winkler, ed., *Spartacus: Film and History* (New York: Blackwell, 2007); Natalie Zemon Davis, *Slaves on Screen: Film and Historical Vision* (Cambridge, MA: Harvard University Press, 2000), 17–40; Joanna Paul, *Film and the Classical Epic Tradition* (New York: Oxford University Press, 2013); Sudhir Hazareesingh, *Black Spartacus: The Epic Life of Toussaint Louverture* (New York: Farrar, Straus, and Giroux, 2020); B. Goff, ed., *Classics and Colonialism* (London: Duckworth, 2005).

39. Beginning in 1968, the anniversary of the start of the Cuban Wars of Independence, the film theorist Michael Chanan says, a series of films about slavery produced by the Cuban Institute of Cinematographic Art and Industry (*Instituto Cubano de Arte e Industria Cinematográficos—*ICAIC) constituted an "extended essay in *cine rescate,* the recovery of history." See Michael Chanan, *Cuban Cinema*, 2nd ed. (Minneapolis: University of Minnesota Press, 1985; rpt. 2004), 273.

40. On the shift from Spartacus as a nineteenth-century sentimental narrative of freedom, yoking discourses of Christian redemption with abolitionism and bourgeois family values, to the twentieth-century Spartacus as a queer figure associated with the struggle for sexual freedom (in the 1960 film and the *Spartacus International Gay Guide*, see Catherine Gunther Kodat, "I'm Spartacus!," in *A Companion to Narrative Theory*, ed. James Phelan and Peter J. Rabinowitz (New Malden, MA: Blackwell, 2005), 486.

41. See Gayle Rogers, *Incomparable Empires: Modernism and the Translation of American and Spanish Literatures* (New York: Columbia University Press, 2016).

42. See Steven A. Epstein, *Speaking of Slavery: Color, Ethnicity, and Human Bondage in Italy* (Ithaca, NY: Cornell University Press, 2001); Stephen A. Epstein, *Purity Lost: Transgressing Boundaries in the Eastern Mediterranean, 1000–1400* (Baltimore: Johns Hopkins University Press, 2007); Benjamin Isaac, *The Invention of Racism in Classical Antiquity* (Princeton, NJ: Princeton University Press, 2004).

43. Scott, *Conscripts of Modernity*, chap. 4, 134–69, 171–72; see also Scott, "The Tragic Vision in Postcolonial Time," *PMLA* 129, no. 4 (October 2014): 799–808.

Epilogue

1. Fernand Braudel, *La Méditerranée et le monde méditerranéen à l'époque de Philippe II* (1st ed., Paris, 1949; 2nd ed., 2 vols., Paris, 1966); translated by Siân Reynolds as *The Mediterranean and the Mediterranean World in the Age of Philip II*, 2 vols. (London: Collins, 1972–73).

2. Webpage for *The Mediterranean and the Mediterranean World in the Age of Philip II*, by Fernand Braudel, University of California Press website, Regents of the University of California, 2021, https://www.ucpress.edu/book/9780520203082/the-mediterranean-and-the-mediterranean -world-in-the-age-of-philip-ii.

3. David Abulafia, *The Great Sea: A Human History of the Mediterranean* (London: Oxford University Press, 2011).

4. John A. Marino, "Mediterranean Studies and the Remaking of Pre-modern Europe," *Journal of Early Modern History* 15 (2011): 385–412.

5. On translating Braudel, see Immanuel Wallerstein, "Braudel on the *Longue Durée*: Problems of Conceptual Translation," in "Commemorating the Longue Durée," special issue of *Review* (Fernand Braudel Center) 32, no. 2 (2009): 155–70.

6. See also Fernand Braudel, "History and the Social Sciences," in *On History*, trans. Sarah Matthews (Chicago: Chicago University Press, 1982), 27.

7. On "geohistory": Braudel developed the concept in "Géohistoire: la société, l'espace et le temps," written in his prison notebooks while a German prisoner of war during World War II, and he elaborated it in the first edition of *La Méditerranée* but later cut most of these key phrases from the second edition. Scholars speculate that he sought to distance himself from possible links between geohistory and determinism. See Samuel Kinser, "Annaliste Paradigm? The Geo-historical Structuralism of Fernand Braudel," *American Historical Review* 86, no. 1 (February 1981): 63–105; John A. Marino, "Braudel's Mediterranean and Italy," *California Italian Studies* 1, no. 1 (2010): 1–20; Guilherme Ribeiro, "The Origin of Geohistory in the Works of Fernand Braudel: A Chapter in the History of Geographical Thought," *Annales de géographie* 686, no. 4 (2012): 329–46.

8. On Michel Foucault's critique of the Braudelian conception of history, see *Les mots et les choses: Une archéologie des sciences humaines* (Paris: Éditions Gallimard, 1966), translated

by Alan Sheridan as *The Order of Things: An Archeology of the Human Sciences* (New York: Pantheon, 1970); *L'archéologie du savoir* (Paris: Éditions Gallimard, 1969), translated by A. M. Sheridan Smith as *The Archeology of Knowledge* (London: Routledge, 2002); see also Fernand Braudel, *Memory and the Mediterranean*, ed. Roselyne de Ayala and Paule Braudel, trans. Siân Reynolds (New York: Knopf, 2001), xvii.

9. Leslie Pierce, "Polyglottism in the Ottoman Empire: A Reconsideration," in *Braudel Revisited: The Mediterranean World, 1600–1800*, ed. Gabriel Piterberg, Teofilo F. Ruiz, and Geoffrey Symcox (Toronto: University of Toronto Press, in association with UCLA Center for Seventeenth- and Eighteenth-Century Studies and Clark Memorial Library, 2010), 76.

10. Barry Cunliffe, *Facing the Ocean: The Atlantic and Its Peoples, 8000 BC–AD 1500* (Oxford: Oxford University Press, 2001); Alison Games, "Atlantic History: Definitions, Challenges, Opportunities," *American Historical Review* 111, no. 3 (June 2006): 741.

11. Glissant's "submarine history" comes from a meditation on Kamau Braithwaite. See Édouard Glissant, "History-Histories-Stories," in *Caribbean Discourse*, trans. J. Michael Dash (Charlottesville: University Press of Virginia, 1989), 66–67; for Glissant's attention to language, see his comments on the relationship between Creole and French, the spoken and the written, in the French Lesser Antilles (120–34, 188–94); Abulafia, *The Great Sea*, preface, xvii.

12. See *History of Science in Latin America and the Caribbean* (*HOSLAC*), https://mypages .unh.edu/hoslac/home; Juan José Saldana, ed., *Science in Latin America: A History*, trans. Bernabe Madrigal (Austin: University of Texas Press, 2006); Jorge Cañizares-Esguerra, *Nature, Empire, and Nation: Explorations of the History of Science in the Iberian World* (Stanford: Stanford University Press, 2006); Jorge Cañizares-Esguerra, *How to Write the History of the New World: Histories, Epistemologies, and Identities in the Eighteenth-Century Atlantic World* (Stanford: Stanford University Press, 2001).

13. On "patriotic" sciences, see Cañizares-Esguerra, *Nature, Empire, and Nation*, 7–13, 64–95; on "conjectural history," see Cañizares-Esguerra, *How to Write the History of the New World*, 47, 95–97, 130, 202.

Index